CONTENTS

The captains of the clouds about to take off for Switzerland.

PROLOGUE

00

A few years ago, I was invited to write and direct a documentary about a 1948 Canadian hockey team. I played hockey as a kid. And like just about every other kid on our street in North Toronto, I had aspirations of hockey greatness and idolized the legends of my era—Bobby Clarke, Bobby Orr, Darryl Sittler, Raymond Bourque, Wayne Gretzky. But the RCAF Flyers hockey team? I had never heard of them. I had no idea who they were or what they had accomplished.

There were three surviving members of the team who were able to speak with me when I first dove into the research. Defenceman André Laperrière was in a palliative care unit in Montreal, his once hulking six-foot-two frame now withered by the ravages of bone cancer. Goalie Murray Dowey was doing well, living on his own in a tidy high-rise apartment in the west end of Toronto, and defenceman Roy Forbes was still firing on all cylinders in a trailer about a hundred feet from where his son Gary and his daughter-in-law Julie lived just outside Kelowna. All the other men once involved with the team were now gone, or in such a state that it was not possible for me to meet with them.

When Gary Forbes ushered me into his father's small trailer that first winter day, Roy was in his favourite lounge chair watching curling. His oxygen tank was at his side; his mackinaw shirt, a bit too large for him now, was hanging loosely on his wiry frame. Still sporting a good head of silvery hair, Roy had on a pair of booties to fend off an icy chill and keep his feet warm. At ninety-four he insisted on getting up to shake my hand before inviting me to sit in a lounger beside him. Although he was a little stiff in the hips, he could reach down and scratch the back of the stray cat that had just made its way into the house. Roy had cut into his screen window so the stray could come and go at will. It visited often, seeking warmth, a free meal, and a cozy spot at Roy's feet.

With some help from his son Gary, Roy started telling me about his time in the war as a bomb aimer, about being shot out of his "flaming buggy" at a thousand feet, living on the run in France, his love of hockey, his trip to the Olympics, and his early days in Rorketon, Manitoba, as his parents desperately tried to scratch out an existence in the midst of the Depression. At times, Roy would drift off, at a loss for words or just plain fatigued—frustrated that his body and mind, once so strong and acute, were now failing him. I was transfixed by his story and that of the sixteen teammates who came together to form a team of warriors that handily took down the world's best on the ice at St. Moritz, Switzerland.

I had no idea that Canada's 1948 Olympic hockey team was made up of men who had jumped from burning bombers over the skies of Germany during World War II, or who had lived off the land as escaped prisoners of war, hiding in the hills of the Carpathian Mountains. Nor had I known that a member of that crew had joined forces with the Polish resistance and liquidated Gestapo agents. I was amazed to learn that many of the men had grown up playing shinny using frozen balls of horse manure for pucks on windblown, frozen ponds. As I listened to the stories, spoke to family members of those who had already passed, and scoured old newspapers and diaries, I learned that these men—cut from a different cloth, raised in the Depression era, and fused in the fires of World War II—had achieved something most thought was impossible by capturing hockey gold.

Hailed by the media and the nation as champions, they were promptly forgotten not long after their return home to Canada. Roy's gold medal now sits safely in its original box, a few feet from his lounger on the mantelpiece beside photos of his family and himself in younger days. Murray's gold medal is proudly mounted and displayed in a glass case on the wall alongside framed hockey jerseys and baseball awards that his sons have prepared for him as gifts. André's medal is in a wooden box he crafted himself and in the care of his sister, Renée. The adventures of these unlikely and unsung heroes astounded and inspired me. I hope you will find their stories and lives just as fascinating as I do.

The Flyers returning to their hotel in a blizzard.

PART ONE
Operation Olympics

Selection Coach Buck Boucher on familiar ground with his son, Coach Frank Boucher.

OTTAWA

01

On Monday, October 20, 1947, the midday temperature in downtown Ottawa rose to a balmy seventy-three degrees Fahrenheit, or twenty-three degrees Celsius. It was a beautiful fall day, with clear skies and light winds.

At the corner of Argyle and O'Connor Streets, the Ottawa Auditorium was getting even hotter as dozens of hockey players raced along the ice in the midst of a rapid-fire tryout session. Built in the early 1920s, the auditorium was state of the art for its time. Traditionally home to the Ottawa Senators of the Quebec Senior Hockey League, it also sported a massive stage that could be assembled at one end of the arena, facing the length of the ice, for concerts, performances, and assemblies. With seventy-five hundred seats, it had a total capacity of ten thousand spectators including standing room. But today, the men who were careening around the impressive arena were skating for the eyes of just three men: NHL hockey legend George "Buck" Boucher; his son, Royal Canadian Air Force sergeant Frank Boucher; and the chief medical officer of the RCAF, Dr. Alexander "Sandy" Watson.

The men in this ragtag group being put through a series of drills and exercises under the watchful gaze of the Bouchers and Dr. Watson had never played together before. They came from all corners of the country, and none of them had ever been paid a nickel to play hockey in their lives. Most were in their late twenties to early thirties. They all had two key things in common: every one of them was an amateur, and every one of them was an active member in the Royal Canadian Air Force.

Sporting his trademark fedora and overcoat, Buck glided among the men on the ice and began running lines, pitting man against man. As selection coach, his mission was to separate the wheat from the chaff of the air force personnel who had been called in from service stations across Canada to compete for a spot on an all–air force hockey team. The Bouchers and Watson were facing a daunting task: in less than three months, the men chosen for the team would be lacing up in St. Moritz, Switzerland, to represent Canada at the first Winter Olympics in twelve years.

Ottawa Citizen sports editor Tommy Shields expressed concern over the soundness of sending these airmen as representatives of Canada's international hockey prowess. In his hockey column Round and About, he wrote: "Time will tell just how good this

RCAF team will be.... A first class team should go, or none at all."
Jack Koffman joined the chorus of sportswriters questioning the
rationale of this last-minute quest, fearing that a team made up of
only air force men would be a national embarrassment, doomed
to failure. On October 16, 1947, in his column Along Sport Row,
Koffman wrote: "Whether the Air Force can collect a team formidable enough to trim some of the highly-regarded European
Olympic representatives is another question."

No one would argue that these men were the best hockey players Canada had to offer. Our talent pool of exceptional hockey
players had always run deep. But the men trying out for the squad
that day shared a common bond and a shared experience born in
the fires of battle. Some had been shot down in flames over enemy
territory, and some had stared death in the face while escaping
from prisoner of war (POW) camps and fighting with the various
underground forces—all had beaten nearly impossible odds of
making it through World War II. United, they were infused with
a conviction that if given the chance they could prove themselves
on the world stage again, only this time on the ice.

For this "band of brothers," the unlikely quest for Olympic
gold would come to symbolize everything Canada had endured
during the war and everything the country was poised to become.
There were still weeks of tryouts and exhibition games to cull the
hundreds of men being invited to see if they had what it took
to gain a coveted spot on the team. Even if the public and the
media were not behind them, one thing was certain: come hell or
high water, a squad of players from the Royal Canadian Air Force

would be representing Canada on the ice in St. Moritz when the Olympics started in January.

But just a few weeks earlier, there had seemed no hope of sending any Canadian hockey team to the Olympics. In the summer of 1947, the International Olympic Committee dropped a bombshell, imposing strict new guidelines on what was considered suitable "amateur" status for Olympic competition. Under the new IOC rules, any player who had ever received any material benefit, either directly or indirectly, from pursuit of the sport would be deemed ineligible to compete. Normally, the top men's senior hockey team that claimed the Allan Cup the year before the Olympics would get the invitation from the Canadian Amateur Hockey Association to represent Canada at the upcoming Games. From 1920 on, this was how Canada had selected its Olympic hockey representatives. This new definition of what constituted an "amateur player," however, ruled out the customary Allan Cup–winning teams as competitors.

The players on the senior teams were not professionals. They held down day jobs to support themselves, but many of the men also received a stipend from their teams for playing. Under the new definition, amateurs on those teams could not in good conscience sign the new Olympic declaration vowing that they had never received gratuities in any form while playing hockey. The impact of the new "amateur" ruling on a potential Canadian hockey entry at the upcoming Olympics churned up a maelstrom of reaction across the country.

"Preposterous, fiction, not possible, a farce" were the thoughts rattling through the minds and off the pens of many in the press and from within Canada's hockey elite. Frank Selke, general manager of the Montreal Canadiens and the Allan Cup–winning Montreal Royals, commented: "Olympic hockey is now a fiasco as a result of phony amateurism which has spotted the harmful hypocrisy [that] has made it impossible for Canada to send a top notch hockey team to the Olympics." *Ottawa Citizen* sportswriter Jack Koffman added: "To get a civilian team capable of meeting Olympic standards, you would probably have to dig into the juvenile or midget ranks."

So late that summer, faced with the new IOC rules, the Canadian Amateur Hockey Association folded its arms and announced that Canada would not be sending an Olympic hockey team to the upcoming Winter Games in St. Moritz. The barrage of newspaper articles announcing the CAHA's landmark decision caused outrage in towns and cities across the country. The decision not to field a team also incensed many in the upper echelons of the Canadian government as well as Canadian Olympic Association brass. Even the Prime Minister's Office was flooded with letters from citizens outraged at the thought of not having Canadian players on the ice at the Olympics. Hockey was considered as much a part of our essence and national fibre as the maple leaf. It was seen as an intrinsic part of our national identity, a cornerstone of our heritage, and a great source of our national pride. Heck, many think we basically invented the sport.

Not only was hockey a popular symbol of who we were as a nation, but Canada had just proven itself soundly on the world stage in World War II. For many Canadians, shying away from the international spotlight at the Olympics seemed like a preposterous move and a missed opportunity to again showcase our global dominance in the sport we helped introduce to the world.

Canada had emerged from World War II economically invigorated and brimming with a great sense of confidence, self-assurance, pride, and optimism. Although we lost forty-three thousand men and women to the war effort and quadrupled our national debt, what we achieved between 1939 and 1945 was astounding. With a population of just twelve million, Canada had made a massive contribution of people and resources to the Allied war effort. We were now seen as a military superpower, home to the third-largest navy and the fourth-largest air force, and one of the few countries that had emerged from the war with a sizeable, functioning economy. We had been spared the physical destruction of war, our economy at home had been expertly managed, and we had moved to another level in the eyes of the world.

In these heady times, Canadians developed a fierce sense of nationalism. Up until 1947, "Canadians" were considered British subjects living in Canada, and for many, this lack of national recognition and actual citizenship stung.

After visiting a cemetery at Dieppe and seeing all the fallen Canadian soldiers listed as "British subjects," Liberal cabinet minister Paul Martin Sr. had dreamt up the Canadian Citizenship Act, giving the country the power to grant Canadian rather than British citizenship.

Introducing the bill in the House, Martin said, "For the national unity of Canada and for the future greatness of this country it is felt to be of utmost importance that all of us, new Canadians or old, have a consciousness of a common purpose and common interests as Canadians; that all of us are able to say with pride and say with meaning: 'I am a Canadian citizen.'" On January 1, 1947, the Canadian Citizenship Act came into effect, and Canada became the first Commonwealth country to create its own citizenship separate from Great Britain.

We were now being seen as an emerging world leader in the midst of throwing off the shackles of Britain. Yet here we were in the fall of 1947, at the first Winter Olympics since before the war, about to shy away from competing in the game we pioneered.

It was in this environment, on September 8, 1947, that one man decided to take it upon himself to strike up the charge and find a team for the nation.

Twenty-nine-year-old Dr. Alexander "Sandy" Watson was sitting in his office in a war-era temporary wooden building when he grabbed his copy of the *Ottawa Journal* and nearly hit the roof. There in front of him in black and white he spotted the CP news headline: "Olympic Hockey without Canada?" The story went on to report that "Canada, traditionally the world's greatest producer of hockey talent, appears destined for a spectator role when the Olympic hockey championships are held at St. Moritz next February."

Sandy was so offended by what he read that morning that he immediately dreamt up a plan to pull together an amateur team to represent Canada on the ice. But he had to move fast. The Olympic entry deadline was in just two days.

Fortunately, as chief medical officer of the air force, he was perfectly positioned to do something about it. With an active roster of sixteen thousand men still strong in the air force and thousands more in the reserves, Watson was convinced there were enough amateur hockey players to ice a good team. But first he had to fly his idea past the Canadian Amateur Hockey Association to see if they'd OK an RCAF team. Next, he had to get it approved by his air force supervisors. Then he had to pull it all together somehow.

AT SIX FOOT TWO, SANDY WATSON was a big man with a weakness for jujubes and sophisticated chocolate. Some said he'd never turn down a jujube no matter how stale it was. Born in Scotland and raised by Lake Erie in Port Dover, Ontario, Sandy wasn't a gifted hockey player as a child, despite his size. But what he lacked in terms of raw talent on the ice, he more than made up for with his steely will, rabid determination, and absolute passion for the sport.

Watson joined the RCAF in December 1944 as a flight lieutenant and a general duty medical officer. While serving overseas at the RCAF headquarters' medical branch in London, he seized upon an opportunity to be the doctor of the RCAF's hockey team. The team played against army teams and local English teams while men were waiting to be repatriated after the war. It was this experience that revealed to him that his skill set suited him far better as a manager than a player.

For most, pulling together an Olympic-caliber hockey team from scratch in a matter of months would seem like a Herculean task, but Watson was a real go-getter. He wasn't exactly a power-house on skates, but he could wield a phone and a pen like nobody else. What's more, Watson rarely took no for an answer. Persistent and confident, he was seen by those who worked with him as a force who ruled with an iron fist. He didn't suffer fools, and he could be authoritarian when he needed to be.

Simply put, if Sandy Watson was going to do something, he was going to do it well. And just as important, he was a proud Canadian: Sandy had the flag written all over him.

Sandy immediately got on the horn with George Dudley, secretary-manager of the CAHA. He told him about his plan and got Dudley's blessing that an air force squad would meet the IOC's new amateur status rule and would be a welcome submission to represent Canada. Next, Dr. Watson rallied his immediate superior, Air Commodore Dave MacKell, to get behind the plan. As a former elite athlete and lover of hockey, MacKell was an easy sell. Together, they took the proposal to Air Marshal Wilf Curtis, chief of the air staff.

Lady luck had nothing to do with it all coming together so smoothly and so rapidly. As the air marshal's personal physician, Dr. Watson already knew that Wilf Curtis was a hockey fanatic and a patriot, so it was little surprise that Watson soon found himself with MacKell and Curtis in the office of Defence Minister Brooke Claxton looking for the final seal of approval. Again, a love of hockey and a love of country made it an easy sell. Claxton was a rabid hockey fan and supporter of the Montreal Canadiens.

All told, it took Watson less than a day to get the green light to use air force resources to find the men to make up a team worthy of going to Switzerland that winter. But building a world-class team was a massive undertaking. The Olympics were just over three months away, and Watson was racing against the clock.

Not everyone outside the air force agreed with the concept. Questions circulated in the media and among other branches of the military about making the team an "all-military affair," or perhaps bringing in some players from the university teams. Sure the RCAF had a number of great hockey players, but why not include amateur players from the army or navy? Why not make the Olympic squad a tri-services team? The *Ottawa Evening Citizen* headline on October 18, 1947, boldly threw it out there: "All Three Services May Form Olympic Ice Team. Would Improve Chances."

But Defence Minister Brooke Claxton stuck to his guns. Although he was a staunch supporter of tri-services activities and agreed that the other branches of the military also possessed a number of fine hockey players, he chose to stay the course. "We have considered the formation of a tri-services team and have come to the conclusion that the original invitation to the RCAF to provide a team will stand. . . . We are going to let them go on ahead on their own." Truth is, it was the RCAF that had come forward with a plan to ease the headache that had been troubling the CAHA and the Canadian Olympic Association for months. They had the plan and the initiative, and if things went sideways, the makeup of the team could always be reanalyzed.

The team representing Canada in the Olympics would be called the RCAF Flyers.

The decision delighted the air force, but it infuriated the army.

THE MEN SANDY WOULD ULTIMATELY BE drawing from were accustomed to staring down heavy odds. Those who fought with the RCAF were part of an extraordinary bid by the Allies to cripple the Germans in a massive air war. Canada's contribution in the air had comprised three main parts, two of which were at home, with the third component being overseas.

In Canada, the RCAF ran the vital British Commonwealth Air Training Plan, which was created to train air crews from Australia, New Zealand, Canada, and Britain. Nearly half of the pilots, navigators, bomb aimers, air gunners, wireless operators, and flight engineers employed in all the Commonwealth air forces during the war—a force totalling more than 130,000—were trained in Canada under the BCATP. The plan was highly successful and regarded as an exceptionally important Canadian contribution to the war. But it was not without its challenges and dangers.

The second component of the RCAF's contribution to the Allied air effort was the Home War Establishment, designed for the protection of home turf. By the time the war was over, the HWE had thirty-seven squadrons stretching from coast to coast, to the far reaches of the North.

The third component was the Overseas War Establishment. Headquartered in London, it comprised forty-eight squadrons serving in western Europe, the Mediterranean, and the Far East.

The magnitude of the RCAF's contribution to the war effort was staggering. From its modest beginnings with a meagre pre-war strength of just over three thousand personnel, the RCAF grew and expanded to become the fourth-largest Allied air force by war's end. Its men and women played major roles in countless battles and operations, among them the Battle of the Atlantic, the high-intensity operations over northwest Europe, the Normandy invasion, the liberation of Europe, and operations in North America and the Mediterranean, as well as maritime patrols and operations in Southeast Asia, North America, Iceland, and the Aleutian Islands.

Signing up for a war fought in the clouds meant staring down a plethora of dangers and heavy odds. Thirteen thousand RCAF airmen were killed in operations, and another four thousand died in training. For those serving with Bomber Command, survival rates were shockingly low. Those who took to the skies in our bombers had a one-in-four chance of surviving their first tour of duty, and a one-in-ten chance of surviving their second. Fifty-five percent of the men who climbed into the lumbering metal beasts that flew night after night in Bomber Command would never come home. But for those who survived—like the men trying out for the RCAF Flyers—a bond was created that could never be broken.

It was little surprise on October 19, 1947, when Air Commodore Dave MacKell formally announced that Squadron Leader Alexander "Sandy" Watson, senior medical officer at air force HQ in Ottawa, would be the RCAF Flyers' team manager. It was time for the RCAF machine to kick it into high gear. Rumours and speculation flew off the pages of sports columns about who would get the nod to coach the squad. Would the RCAF get a big name like Mervyn "Red" Dutton to helm the bench? As the former president of the National Hockey League, Dutton certainly had the ability to put together a fine team. He had also lost both of his sons while they were serving in the RCAF, and there were no rules against having a professional on the bench.

Another name being bandied about by reporters was Frank Fredrickson. An illustrious RCAF flying ace and hero from World War I, Fredrickson had been a phenomenal hockey player in his youth. As captain of the Winnipeg Falcons in 1920, Fredrickson led his team to the Allan Cup championship and to the gold medal at the Olympics that year in Antwerp.

Although Red Dutton and Frank Fredrickson might have looked like odds-on favourites for the posting, Watson and MacKell had their eyes set on another man for team coach, RCAF corporal Frank Boucher.

Sandy and Frank had become friends during the war while they were both stationed in London. But it wasn't just this closeness and personal connection that made Frank Boucher Sandy's first choice. Frank was also a tremendous defenceman who had shown incredible prowess as a player and as a playing coach with a number of RCAF hockey squads at home and overseas during the war.

While serving at RCAF HQ in London, Boucher and Watson had worked together organizing, arranging, and coaching hockey games for Canadian armed forces personnel stationed at various bases waiting to be repatriated to Canada. Together they were part of an organization that strived to keep the boys who were killing time before heading home active and busy, playing hockey against the army, navy, and local players from the English league.

In 1946, Watson and Boucher took a team made up of RCAF and army men to Zurich and Basel to play the Swiss national team. They beat them. Later that same year, their squad defeated a Czech team at Wembley Arena in London. Next, they defeated the Canadian army team to win the inter-service championship. The pairing of Boucher as a playing coach with Watson as a team manager was smooth and natural, each man complementing the other's qualities.

Known for his calm, soft-spoken yet direct style, Boucher never raised his voice, never swore, and never spoke unkindly of anyone. He was the quiet in any storm. As a coach he was regarded as a kind man who earned heaps of respect from his players. He had an encyclopedic knowledge of hockey and treated all players with respect as long as they toed the line. If anyone got out of turn, Frank was not the kind of coach who would ever embarrass a player; rather, if he had a terse word to deliver, he would pull the bloke aside, set him straight, and then get back to business.

As the only son of legendary NHL player and coach George "Buck" Boucher, Frank Boucher came into the world in 1918 with hockey embedded in his DNA. Frank was born into a powerhouse of hockey royalty. His father was a tough defenceman who throttled opponents over thirteen seasons with the Ottawa Senators, three seasons with the Montreal Maroons, and one season with the Chicago Black Hawks. When Buck tapped out of playing professionally he took to coaching for the Maroons, the Senators, and the Boston Bruins in the NHL.

Frank's uncle Billy and uncle Bobby both played for Montreal in the NHL, and his uncle Frank, also known as "Raffles" for his ability to deftly steal the puck from opponents, was a trail-blazer with the New York Rangers over twelve seasons as a player and five as a coach. Raffles was also instrumental in instituting game-changing rules to NHL hockey, such as the introduction of the red line. Known for his sportsmanlike conduct, Raffles won the Lady Byng Trophy seven times in eight years. After his seventh win they gave Raffles the original trophy and commissioned a copy. Even young Frank's grandfather had been a professional athlete, playing rugby football in the late 1890s. It seemed everybody in the Boucher family was involved in professional sports, especially hockey.

For young Frank, hockey was the fuel that made him fly. Countless hours of his Ottawa childhood were spent walking miles in the wintertime with his skates slung over his shoulders to play on outdoor rinks or bumpy frozen ponds. In his later years he'd say how spoiled and soft kids of today were for playing on indoor heated rinks.

Frank shared a passion with his father, Buck. Both of them loved playing defence. Frank grew to be a gifted player with a hockey mind that was as sharp as his blades slicing along the ice. At just thirteen he was on the Ottawa team that won the city midget title. By his mid-teens he was rising in the hockey ranks playing in the Eastern Hockey League for the Bronx Tigers and then the New York Rovers, a farm team for the NHL's New York Rangers that was coached by his uncle Frank. By the age of twenty-two, Frank had moved up to the American Hockey League and was on the highest-scoring line in the league. In his prime, and poised for a jump to the big leagues, Frank's NHL career halted in its tracks once war broke out and he enlisted in 1940.

When Sandy Watson first got it in his bonnet to put together a team, Frank was his number-one choice for coach and one of the first people he bounced the idea off. With Sandy running the team as manager and Frank running the operations on the ice as head coach, they could make for a powerful combination. As a bonus, and in order to appease those who wanted a big name behind the bench, they could see if Frank's father, Buck, would be willing to lend his expertise to help with the initial selection process and whittling down of the recruits.

It all came together perfectly and a plan was set in motion. Although Buck was coaching for the Ottawa Senators in the Quebec Senior Hockey League, he agreed to offer his services free of compensation and was given carte blanche in the selection of players. Buck would build the machine, his son Frank would take over the reins and coach it overseas, and Sandy would manage the entire operation.

There was one dark cloud for Frank Boucher—it was killing him not to be able to lace up as a player for Canada's Olympic hockey team. He was certainly young enough, talented enough, and strong enough to take to the ice for the entry. But as a previously paid professional player, he was ineligible under the IOC rules to qualify as an amateur. Nonetheless he saw it as a great privilege to be a part of the team as its coach, representing his country from the bench. Now they just had to roll up their sleeves and pull it off.

Flying Officer Hubert Brooks when he joined the Missing Research and Enquiry Service.

THE GAMES

02

When the ball got rolling that mid-October, Air Marshal Wilf
Curtis assured team manager Sandy Watson that he would have
the full support of the force. Every resource the force possessed
would be at his disposal. That is, every resource except for money.
It was one thing to take up the torch to represent the country on
the world stage and win. But if the Flyers were to bomb out and
perform miserably in St. Moritz, the RCAF brass and the defence
minister had no interest in facing a torrent of questions from the
media and the public about squandering taxpayers' money on a
hockey team.

So with cap in hand, Sandy and Frank went knocking on
doors, scrounging for donations of gear and supplies to outfit

the RCAF Flyers hockey team. When Sandy called upon Conn Smythe, owner of the Toronto Maple Leafs, to give a hand with some equipment, Smythe turned him down. Some sources say the Leafs laughed him out of the room. Undeterred, Sandy, the consummate optimist, and Frank forged ahead, hitting up every supplier, manufacturer, and outfitter they could think of in their efforts to gear up for the Olympics.

Canadian supplier Northland pitched in with a donation of three hundred hockey sticks. CCM chipped in with new top-of-the-line Tackaberry skates for every player. At sixty-nine dollars a pair it was a generous donation. The Tackaberries didn't come with sewn-in tendon guards. Knowledge of the European players' predilection for slashing inspired Watson and Boucher to have tendon guards sewn into the skates for an added layer of protection. Sandy convinced Hackett's Shoe Repair in Ottawa to do it free of charge.

American sporting giant Spalding coughed up the vast majority of the rest of the equipment, kitting out the players with shin pads, elbow pads, jocks, cups, garter belts, braces, shoulder pads, pants, gloves, sweaters, and socks.

Traditionally Canada's hockey entry at the Olympics would sport a red maple leaf on a white background as the official team jersey. But this being an all–air force team, Air Marshal Wilf Curtis was interested in seeing if the Flyers could feature the distinctive RCAF roundel on a jersey that showcased the powder-blue colours of the air force. Watson mocked up a jersey and took it to a meeting of the Canadian Olympic Association. COA president Sidney Dawes came from a background in construction and was tough as nails. When Sandy presented the prospective jersey to the table of representatives of the sixteen sports Canada would be fielding at St. Moritz, it was resoundingly rejected. Nobody at the table was interested in the RCAF showcasing their logo and colours on the Olympic stage. But Sidney Dawes was a fan of the Flyers from the get-go. He stunned the room by accepting the jersey and decreeing it the official team sweater sanctioned by the Canadian Olympic Association. The deal was done. The Flyers would be wearing a pale-blue jersey with the RCAF roundel and a red maple leaf in the centre and the word *Canada* underneath.

In the ensuing weeks, Dawes went one further for the Flyers. He called Sydney Dobson, president of the Royal Bank of Canada, and asked if the bank could open up its purse strings to help pay for the team's tickets to Europe. Dobson agreed, and the Flyers became the first team of Canadian athletes to kick off the Royal Bank of Canada's commitment to supporting Olympians in their hunt for medal gold.

With ten weeks to go before the Olympics, time was ticking down for the trio of Sandy, Frank, and Buck to pull together a worthy team to represent Canada in Switzerland.

MEANWHILE, ALMOST FOUR THOUSAND MILES east of Ottawa, preparations were well under way in St. Moritz to accept the world in peace at the V Olympic Winter Games. The impact of World War II was still front and centre. These Winter Games were designated "the Games of Renewal" in hopes that this joining together of athletes in competition would serve as a symbol of a new beginning for the participants and for sport at large. It had been twelve long years since the last Winter Olympics, held at Garmisch-Partenkirchen, in Germany, in 1936. Both the 1940 and 1944 Games had been cancelled as the world was thrust into hell when war raged across the globe, and amateur sport and goodwill were put on the back burner.

At the upcoming Games of Renewal in St. Moritz, athletes from twenty-eight nations would be joining together in peace to showcase their best over a period of ten days between January 30 and February 8, 1948. Japan and Germany were ostracized for their involvement in the war and would not be attending. Interestingly, Italy was invited to attend. Chile, Denmark, Iceland, Korea, and Lebanon would all be making their Winter Olympic debut. The Stalinist Soviet Union had chosen not to participate but was sending ten delegates to observe the performance of other countries' athletes.

The Games would involve twenty-two events in nine disciplines: bobsleigh, skeleton, ice hockey, figure skating, speed skating, alpine skiing, cross-country skiing, Nordic combined, and ski jumping. Military patrol, now known as the biathlon, would be a demonstration sport that year. Fully 669 athletes would be attending—two hundred more than the last time the Winter Olympics had been held in St. Moritz, in 1928, but a far cry from the 2,780 athletes who would compete at Sochi in Russia in 2014.

For many European countries the impacts of World War II were still very present in 1948. Merely putting a team together was a daunting challenge because of a lack of athletic training during the war, a loss of athletes through injury and death, post-war food shortages, and a lack of resources. All of this was clearly evidenced in the once-dominant Norwegian Nordic ski team. It had lost many of its best athletes to the war, and those Norwegian skiers who did make it to St. Moritz had to borrow equipment from the Americans in order to compete.

In 1948, news from the Games would be broadcast to the world predominantly through newspaper wire services, theatre newsreels, and limited radio broadcasts. Over five hundred journalists from thirty-two countries would be coming to the Swiss Alps to document the pinnacle of amateur sport.

Coming out of the war, St. Moritz was an obvious choice as host for the Games. Switzerland had remained neutral during the war, and it had the physical means to mount the Games. The city had hosted the Winter Olympics in 1928, and most of the athletic venues were already in existence and in good condition, untouched by the ravages of battle. All the venues were outdoors, which meant the Games would be heavily dependent on favourable weather conditions.

For the RCAF Flyers, this meant all their matches would be played on outdoor ice, on rinks that were subject to blazing sun, frigid temperatures, and swirling snowstorms. Boards for the Olympic ice surfaces were also much shorter than those the boys were accustomed to at home. But different ice surfaces and varied outdoor conditions had never stopped Canadians from excelling on Olympic ice before. Canadian hockey teams had claimed gold at the Winter Olympics in 1920, 1924, 1928, and 1932.

But in 1936 at Garmisch-Partenkirchen, Canada's unbeaten streak in ice hockey came to a striking halt when Britain snatched the gold, beating the Canadians 2–1. Funny thing, though: the team from England secured its gold medal using almost exclusively Canadian players. Only one member of the British squad was 100 percent British. Nine of the other players on the team were born in the United Kingdom but had grown up in Canada and perfected their skills while playing hockey on Canadian ponds, rivers, rinks, and teams from childhood right on up. One of the British players was actually born in Canada and had served in the Canadian army. When it was time to don jerseys for the Olympics in 1936, those boys had either been called by the British Ice Hockey Association or felt the pull to "come home" and lace up for the Brits. Although using Canadian-raised men to bolster the English hockey squad may have been acceptable before the war and before Canada gained its independence from Mother England in 1947, this time things would be different.

Despite the Flyers' short timeline, critical press, and naysayers, Buck Boucher, Frank Boucher, and Sandy Watson knew they had something very special on their side—a group of airmen who had been forged in the fires of war.

There was no shortage of Canadian hockey players with wings. The challenge was time and creating that golden recipe of men who could read each other's minds and play together as a cohesive unit with just weeks of practice. Mere days after starting, Buck told reporters: "We're going to try and get the strongest possible team. It's going to give me a lot of extra work but it's also going

Milt Schmidt, Bobby Bauer, and Woody Dumart, also known as the "Kraut Line."

to be some extra pleasure. This is an honour and I'm going to do the best I possibly can."

The Bouchers and Watson knew there were a lot of great air force boys who were fantastic players. Milt Schmidt, Bobby Bauer, and Woody Dumart, also known as "the Kraut Line," had all played for the RCAF but were also unfortunately NHL veterans with the Boston Bruins. There were legions of outstanding RCAF players with experience in the American Hockey League, the senior hockey leagues, and the NHL farm teams. But like Frank Boucher, they were paid players, making them ineligible to join the team under the IOC rules.

With painstaking precision, the two Bouchers and Watson scoured the land for the best players the RCAF had to offer. They set off watching games on bases as well as local league matches in search for diamonds to pluck for their team. Calls were sent out to the sports officers at all air force stations across the country to send over their best players. Anyone with a Junior A or higher hockey history was invited to jump on an RCAF plane and get to Ottawa to try out for the team. Hopefuls like forward Andy Gilpin and goalie Ross King came flying in from as far away as the Yukon.

As the clock ticked down to departure day for St. Moritz, Buck, Frank, and Sandy continued to sift through hundreds of airmen. The proving grounds for the tryouts would be Tommy Gorman's Ottawa Auditorium. Conveniently located right next door to the RCAF Beaver Barracks, where the boys would be housed, it was a stand-out facility for testing the mettle of the future Olympic squad.

A former Olympic athlete and avid hockey lover, Gorman was a prominent local businessman who happened to own the auditorium as well as the rink's home team, the Ottawa Senators of the Quebec Senior Hockey League. As a man who had been to the Olympics before, with Canada's lacrosse team in 1908, Gorman had a passion for all sport as well as the means to help the Flyers. Like Buck, he also knew a thing or two about hockey, having coached or managed seven Stanley Cup champion teams. Gorman offered his rink to the Flyers free of charge to use all day, every day, in their race to get ready for Switzerland. He also offered to help out with a bit of perspective or a friendly ear if they so desired.

Day after day, through late October into November, RCAF pilots, gunners, navigators, radio operators, office clerks, and men working in all other reaches of the service were flown into Ottawa and put through a grinding session of twice-daily workouts. Nine men flew in one day, ten the next, and five or six the following day as new crops of potential players swarmed into the Ottawa Auditorium vying for a coveted spot on the team.

Buck's mantra was to work the boys hard, giving them an opportunity to get into sound hockey shape and show their wares before facing elimination from the team. Practice sessions designed to cull the talent pool and whip the chosen few into shape began at 5:00 a.m. each day, with some marathon sessions continuing late into the evening. Those who continued to shine on the ice during the test matches and practices would receive three square meals a day, a private room to sleep in at the barracks, and military pay according to their rank for a day's work.

Buck ran four full lines in the morning and four full lines in the afternoon. When Buck and Frank felt it necessary, a few of the boys were forced to sweat it up in back-to-back sessions. Black eyes, bruised noses, and battered limbs were part and parcel of the gruelling sessions. For a few of the unlucky guys, dislocated shoulders cut short their attempts to gain a place on the roster. Some men lasted a day, others a few days; a select core stayed on, rising to the top of the list as "possibles."

ONE OF THE MEN BEING PUT through the paces from day one of the tryouts was Flying Officer Hubert Brooks. "Brooksie" or "Hub," as he was referred to by his war buddies, struck a commanding presence with his shock of black hair, steely blue eyes, chiselled jaw, and movie star good looks. During the war Brooks was a navigator/bomb aimer in a Wellington bomber, part of 419 (Moose) Squadron. The 419 Squadron's motto was "Beware of the Moose."

Brooks was the real deal, a full-on war hero. He was one of only five RCAF officers to be awarded the Military Cross for his deeds of heroism during the war. He also received a Mention in Dispatches citation and the 1939–1945 Star, the Air Crew Europe Star, the Defence Medal, the Polish Cross of Valour, and the Polish Silver Cross of Merit with Swords. His Military Cross citation was the longest of anyone in the Royal Canadian Air Force during World War II.

Brooks was the embodiment of true grit. He not only survived bailing out from his bomber when its engines caught fire on a nighttime bombing run for Hamburg, but after hitting the dirt and being captured by the Germans, Brooks plotted and then engineered his own escape from German POW camps on three separate occasions.

When the war was over, Brooks didn't come home. Instead he volunteered for the Missing Research and Enquiry Service, or MRES. The MRES was set up by the Royal, Dominion, and Allied air forces at the end of World War II. Its mandate was to locate Commonwealth air force personnel who had gone down or had died in missions over enemy-held territory.

Around the globe, 41,881 airmen and -women had simply disappeared on operations or routine flights and were listed as missing, presumed dead. The bulk of them, some 37,000, were believed killed in Europe. Tens of thousands of Commonwealth air force personnel still lay in their aircraft, or were buried in poorly marked graves, or were simply lost in the blackness of war. As an MRES search officer, Brooks undertook the greatest detective job in the world. From war's end until the summer of 1947, he was part of an extraordinary group of men who scoured millions of square miles of battlefields, oceans, landscapes, and mass graves in an attempt to identify, account individually for, and bury their thousands of missing men and women. It was a monumental task involving the use of intelligence reports, official and unofficial sources, investigative sleuthing, various scraps of information, and forensic and semi-forensic work throughout Europe, the Middle East, and the Far East. Identifying the lost souls was of paramount importance. Every case solved laid a ghost to rest for a family back home.

Brooks's MRES work searching for downed airmen and aircraft took him through Denmark and Norway and into the American occupation zone of Europe. It was a gruelling and gruesome task that required a steel will, a high degree of knowledge and experience, and exceptional tact in potentially unorthodox situations with hostile or unfriendly locals. In July and August 1946, Brooks made MRES history as part of a two-man mission dubbed Operation Polesearch. With fellow search officer Eric "Chick" Rideal, Brooks scaled mountains, scoured fjords, and sailed a fishing smack around the most northerly part of mainland Europe, Cape Nordkinn in the Arctic Circle, in the search for downed airmen.

For Brooks and his colleagues in the MRES, it was simply unacceptable that any airmen heroes should remain in an unmarked grave in some nameless corner of a foreign field, or left exposed at a crash site on some windblown mountaintop. Every little clue needed to be examined and recorded carefully in the search for identification. The first and last thing Brooks and his colleagues would do on approaching or leaving a gravesite was to salute it. One can only imagine the mental fortitude and internal strength required to crawl into a mass grave to study remains in situ and conduct an examination. But it had to be done, and Brooks possessed the inner fire to do this for his fellow warriors. For Brooks the work was fraught with challenges and difficulties, but it was also deeply rewarding and satisfying.

In the quest for sanity and a little normalcy, the MRES encouraged its men overseas to engage in sports whenever possible. While in Copenhagen, Brooks leapt at the opportunity to play a little hockey with the local Kobenhavns Hold hockey team. Danish newspapers championed his impressive skills. "Canadians are the world's finest ice hockey players and Pilot Officer Brooks is no exception. Brooks will star with the Kobenhavns Hold against Oslo and Stockholm the 3rd and 10th February when the weather becomes cold again."

In February 1947, while he was stationed in the American occupation zone of Germany and in need of another break, Brooks got the chance to lace up and play with the U.S. Army All-Stars at Garmisch-Partenkirchen. Hockey was just the thing he needed to help his spirits soar. A few months later, Canada started calling its search officers home, and Brooks reluctantly closed down his activities and was repatriated to Ottawa in July.

The Hubert Brooks who returned to Ottawa in the summer of 1947 was a different man from the boy who had sailed to England on the *Mauritania* back in September 1941, sleeping in hammocks crammed in four-deep with eight inches between each man. Since then, Brooks had not only escaped death dozens of times but he had been through hell and back in captivity. He had seen unspeakable horrors in the aftermath of war, and he now spoke seven languages, most of them fluently: English, French, Polish, Russian, German, Czechoslovakian, and Ukrainian.

When his superiors at RCAF HQ in Ottawa tapped him on the shoulder to try out for the Flyers, Brooks was honoured to give it a shot. At twenty-six, his legs weren't quite as limber as they were in his late teens, but he had a great head for the game and he was still sharp on his skates.

His journey to the ice at the Ottawa Auditorium began decades earlier in the wide-open expanses of northern Alberta. Born on a crisp winter morning on December 29, 1921, Brooks was a product of the prairies. His father, Alfred, and mother, Laura, lived a pioneering life, homesteading on a plot of land some twelve miles south of the hamlet of Bluesky, Alberta. There was no plumbing or electricity in the eighteen-by-twenty-foot log cabin Alfred had built with his bare hands. The only source of heat to tame the biting winter temperatures, which could dip to sixty below zero, came from the woodstove fire.

Hubert's father was a resourceful, hard-working man. In those early years outside Bluesky, Alfred provided for his young family by farming, hunting, and trading furs at the local trading post in the Peace River district of northwestern Alberta. In the summer months the sun would shine until 10:00 p.m. The skies were predominantly clear and crystal blue, which allowed for long, back-breaking days of work.

Winter work was long and hard in a different way. Typically in this stretch near the Peace River, snow fell early in October and stayed until late March. With his brother Aimé, Alfred would set out and spend a week at a time on their trap line in the brush. At eighteen miles long and three miles wide, the line provided the brothers with upwards of five hundred pelts over a winter, including fox, coyote, lynx, weasel, muskrat, wolf, and squirrel. They would sell the pelts in the spring.

Using teams of horses, brute strength, and sheer determination, the homesteaders cleared the land to make room for crops and gardens to help provide the sustenance of life. Trees had to be extracted, rocks removed from the soil, stumps blasted with dynamite, ground broken by horses pulling a single bottom-breaking plow. To make the earth ready for a garden or crops, the final clearing was done using elbow grease with an axe, a grub hoe, and a plow.

Alfred kept a cow and some chickens on his homestead. To provide meat for his family, he would hunt moose, fox, and muskrat, as well as take advantage of the abundance of wild game, such as partridges and rabbits. In the winter, he built an ice house to preserve the perishables, using giant, sawdust-covered blocks of ice from the river. In the summer, after the ice had melted in the ice house, meat, cheese, and milk would be sent down the well to keep from spoiling in the baking summer months.

Roads in the area had been built by local farmers, and in the spring and early summer they were nearly impassable because of the ruts of soft, wet mud. High-wheeled wagons pulled by a team of horses were the only mode of transport.

For Hubert's mother, Laura, the loneliness and homesickness, especially in the winter months, could seem soul-crushing. Her family was thousands of miles away in Ottawa. And unlike Alfred, she had come from the city and was more accustomed to living somewhere less isolated that provided for the niceties of life.

With very little money, everyone in the community, for miles around, was in the same situation. Clothes were patched; flour and sugar sacks were used to make curtains. It was a hard life but not without its pleasures and beauty. There was a bond between neighbours, people were friendly, and homesteaders depended on one another as they squeaked out a humble existence. In the winter, there were house parties, dance parties, card parties. And in summer, there were picnics, ball games between communities, and plenty of things for kids to occupy themselves with down by the river. Young Hubert's world expanded on August 24, 1923, when his parents welcomed his baby sister, Doris, into the world. Hubert now had a new playmate.

For Alfred, finding a way to make a living off the land was a way of life. He tried his hand at prospecting and taking his boat out to pan for gold. But the shiny metal bonanza eluded him. Alfred, Laura, Hubert, and Doris soldiered on at the homestead outside Bluesky until 1925. Then the dream and idyllic country life collapsed. Subject to the whims of nature, the prairies were hit hard by drought—wheat wasn't growing, cattle were dying. Alfred had tried almost everything to provide for his growing family. Times had simply become too tough. Disillusioned with the homesteading dream and faced with a potentially grim future, Alfred and Laura sold the family farm and moved to Ottawa with hopes for a brighter future.

In Ottawa Laura could find solace and support from her family. The Brookses could also make a new beginning. Laura had been a seamstress of some note before leaving to marry Alfred in Alberta. Now that they were back in Ottawa, she resumed this work while Alfred chased the golden lure of prospecting opportunities in the wilds of northern Ontario and Quebec.

The Brooks family stayed in Ottawa for five years. Unfortunately Alfred's quest to strike it rich in the eastern gold fields never bore fruit. So in 1930, the family upped stakes once again, this time searching for greener pastures in Montreal.

Hubert was eight when the family put down new roots in Notre-Dame-de-Grâce, which was one of the poorer areas of the city. Once more they were hopeful that times would be better for them in their new home. But making ends meet did not come easy. Laura managed to get work as a seamstress, and Alfred initially continued his quest for mineral wealth. Young Hubert would take up caddying at a local golf course to help supplement the family coffers while his father was away prospecting up north.

Ultimately Alfred abandoned his dreams of mineral riches and landed steady work with a fire equipment company. Although times were tough and money was tight, Hubert and Doris were well loved by their hard-working parents, and the kids were able to maintain an active youth. Hubert had a natural passion for all athletics; he played golf and softball, rode bicycles, and started playing lots and lots of ice and street hockey.

Fortunately for Hubert, the streets in his poor section of Montreal were a veritable proving ground for future hockey greatness. Shinny games were a near daily occurrence around Notre-Dame-de-Grâce and nearby Bordeaux, and several future National Hockey League legends were growing up in the neighbourhood. One of Brooks's regular street hockey buddies was none other than Maurice "the Rocket" Richard. Young Hubert could not have asked for a better partner with whom to hone his stickhandling skills. Brooks and Richard were the same age, and they would while away the hours playing street hockey, setting up rocks to stand in for goalposts on the pavement. They also made up games like "hog," where one player would try to see if he could hog the puck or tennis ball as long as possible from the other guy. It was a great way for them to perfect their technique and have a blast.

While attending Plateau High School in Montreal, Hubert threw himself into his studies and displayed a keen interest in mathematics. His French now completely fluent, he also continued to excel in hockey while playing for his high school team. He loved playing left wing, and as a southpaw, that was the position he ended up landing on most teams.

Maybe it was the country air and challenging early years on the farm, maybe it was witnessing his father's dogged determination for a better life for his family, or maybe it was just innately within him—whatever it was, as a young man in Montreal with war raging overseas, Hubert possessed a fierce determination to carve out his own path.

Like the majority of young men of that era, Brooks felt it was his patriotic duty to volunteer for the war effort. When he tried to apply for the air force, he was only seventeen. The admissions officer deemed him too young, and he was rejected. Undeterred, he applied again in 1940. On his application, under "Skills of relevance to the RCAF," he listed "Building model airplanes." Under a question about sports he was engaged in, Hubert wrote: "Hockey extensively, golf extensively, rugby extensively, racing moderately, bicycle riding extensively." When asked whether he was interested in ground duties or flying duties, Brooks answered that he was keen to take to the sky as either a pilot or an observer. And with that, on August 14, 1940, he was accepted into the RCAF special reserve.

Although the war had halted Brooks's hockey development in its tracks, he was pleasantly surprised to be given the nod to audition for the RCAF Flyers hockey team in the fall of 1947. The last time he had played hockey was with the U.S. Army All-Stars in Europe about eight months earlier. Now back in Ottawa, Brooks was holding his own on the ice against the legions of air force boys jockeying for a spot. It was like a revolving door, with guys coming and going. At the end of each practice session, Buck Boucher would call out names. If he called your name, you were gone. As long as you didn't hear your name called, you were another day closer to wearing the official jersey in St. Moritz.

Outside the Beaver Barracks in Ottawa.

THE BOYS IN BLUE

03

As the fall leaves drifted off the trees along Elgin Street and morning frost settled on the windows of the Ottawa Auditorium, Sandy and Frank forged ahead in their quest to find the best among the RCAF's sixteen thousand men. With the full might of the air force supporting them, RCAF transport planes hummed through the skies, ferrying dozens of players from across the country into Ottawa for tryouts. Sandy, Buck, and Frank also continued testing out their "team in the making" by pitting the prospects against local clubs and other existing military teams. On October 21, they played the army team in the Ottawa City League and won 8–2. Though it gave the coaches a chance to eyeball their prospects, the win was largely thanks to Frank Boucher's impressive handiwork on the ice. Acting as a playing coach during the game, he was instrumental in scoring goals and setting up many of the team's successful plays.

On October 28, the team in the making squared off against the New Edinburgh Burghs. The Burghs were leaders in the Ottawa City League. This time the airmen lost 5–3. Hubert Brooks picked up the final goal in the game. On November 8, the Flyers beat the Hull Volants 4–1. Again, however, the Olympic-ineligible Frank Boucher was on the ice and pivotal in the win. Day after day, new candidates were flown in, and those who failed to perform or impress were sent back home.

WHILE MANY OF THE PLAYERS BEING assessed by the Bouchers had flown in from various places across the country, a number of local air force boys had received tryout invitations as well. One was Corporal Irving Taylor. Born in 1919, Taylor grew up playing hockey on frozen ponds, lakes, and rivers around the Ottawa area before he joined the air force in 1938, serving on Canadian bases in the supplies and services department. Another was Ottawa boy Patsy Guzzo. At thirty-two years of age, Guzzo was one of the elder statesmen still holding his own against the onslaught of newcomers vying for a coveted spot on the Olympic team. And like Hubert Brooks, he had been called in and invited to try out from day one. But unlike most of the men coming through the revolving door at Tommy Gorman's Ottawa Auditorium, Patsy was a well-known hockey commodity to Coach Frank Boucher. Nicknamed "Black Magic" by his teammates, Patsy had played with Frank when they were both stationed in Ottawa during the war as members of the 1942–1943 Ottawa RCAF Flyers hockey team. Together, they came close to winning the Memorial Cup that year, with Patsy as a left-winger and Frank playing centre.

At five foot seven and 145 pounds, Patsy was a nimble, speedy player, known for his finesse and playmaking ability. He was just as proficient at setting up goals as he was at rifling pucks into the net. He was also a strong backchecker and an excellent defensive player, often robbing wingers from opposing squads of scoring opportunities. While in high school, Patsy played on the team that won the Ontario championship. In doing so he set a scoring record after pocketing nine goals over two games. He played in the senior league with Ottawa LaSalle and then with the Hull Volants. But when the St. Louis Flyers of the American Hockey League came calling in 1940, he turned down an offer to play in the pros. Patsy wasn't interested in a life on the road; instead, he signed up for the air force.

Born in east Ottawa in 1917, Patsy grew up in a large but very poor Italian family. As a young boy he exhibited a passion for sports and showed a natural aptitude for all athletics. In the summer he played baseball and softball with his brothers and cousins in a field across from their house. Little Patsy was a natural and could always play with the bigger boys. Although he was colour-blind, that didn't stop him from developing into one of Ottawa's outstanding amateur athletes in multiple sports. Some say he was one of the best amateur pitchers in Canada. He was also mean at bat. Over a two-thousand-game career, he won 80 percent of his softball games and maintained a batting average that was customarily above .400.

When Patsy signed up for the war in 1941, he had to wait nine months before he was activated and took a position as a clerk. His colour-blindness prevented him from pursuing a career in the air. Almost immediately after entering the service, Patsy was on the ice playing for the local RCAF hockey team in the winter. As soon as summer rolled around, he was on the mound pitching for the RCAF baseball team. Friends described him as a jock with brains who possessed a sweet, kind, gentle disposition and a passion for quoting Shakespeare and poetry. He was also a deeply religious man with an infinite devotion to family. In the fall of 1947, Patsy and his wife, Mary, had a little girl at home, with another on the way.

When Orval Gravelle showed up for work as a bellhop at the Château Laurier on November 13, he could never have imagined he'd end up sleeping at the Beaver Barracks that night. The nineteen-year-old was a scrappy little fireball with a shocking mane of red hair. Nicknamed "Red" for both his temperament and his hair, Gravelle played Junior B hockey with the Aylmer Saints in the Ottawa and District League. Raising their family in Aylmer, Orval's parents didn't have a lot of money. His first pair of skates were hand-me-downs from their neighbours. The problem, however, was that they were men's skates. Young Orval didn't care. He just put on his shoes and then slipped into the huge skates. They may have looked like clown shoes, but those big old blades fit like a glove. He was ecstatic. As he progressed in hockey, the little dynamo supplemented his exercise and training by running up and down hills with a log over his shoulders.

Short, solid, and 150 pounds dripping wet, he was a tough forward with wheels who liked to grind it out and play a physical game on the ice. His coach at Aylmer was Bill Boucher, Buck's brother and Frank's uncle. Noticing the weakness up front in the current Olympic hopefuls, Bill suggested that Frank, Sandy, and Buck consider bringing in young Orval to bolster their roster.

Orval was not in the RCAF and was completely in the dark that his coach had suggested the Flyers' brain trust come take a look at him for their team. A recommendation from Billy Boucher was a ringing endorsement. In their search for raw talent, Sandy and Frank paid Orval a visit and took him out for a drive around Aylmer. While driving through neighbourhoods, they asked him to leave his job as a bellhop and join the air force so he could try out for the team. Orval leapt at the opportunity. He joined up as a machinist, impressed the pants off the selection coaches, and landed a spot as another "possible" coming through the revolving door at the auditorium.

The next day Frank and Sandy took the team to Trenton for an exhibition game against the local RCAF team on the base. Patsy Guzzo banged in a couple of beautiful back-to-back goals within the first three minutes of the game. Hubert Brooks and Red Gravelle joined in the scoring parade with a goal apiece as the Flyers beat the Trenton squad 7–4. During the exhibition match, Boucher and Watson also took notice of a player dressed for the opposing Trenton team. The defenceman was brimming with potential. His name was Roy Forbes.

LIKE HUBERT BROOKS, ROY FORBES WAS a decorated flying officer in the war. "Forbesie," as his war buddies called him, served as a bomb aimer in Bomber Command and also with the all-Canadian 419 Moose Squadron. Unlike Brooks, Forbes started out in Halifaxes and Wellingtons but ended up in the nose of the mighty Lancaster bomber. He flew mission after mission, being buffeted around in the bomb aimer's bay. Tense hours were spent prone, peering through his Plexiglas window, scanning the world as it raced past below him. As the mighty Lanc's four massive engines hummed towards their target, Forbes lay there with his hand on the trigger, ready to unleash thousands of tonnes of ordinance upon enemy train yards, radar stations, and munitions depots.

On his twelfth mission, Forbes and his crew of seven were shot down over German-occupied France. Forbes survived a low-level jump and spent five months on the run before making it home. At the end of the war he was awarded the Distinguished Flying Cross for his bravery and efforts in avoiding capture.

Tough as nails, Forbes was just as rough on the ice as he was in battle. At five foot six and 155 pounds, Roy was on the smaller side, but he more than made up for his bantam size with his huge heart and his scrappy, determined play. Forbes played a fast, tough game. He was a wiry defenceman who liked to hit, who never backed down from a fight, and who charged around like a Jack Russell terrier on the ice.

A prairie boy to the core, Roy Forbes was born on April 6, 1922, on a small patch of dirt in northern Manitoba. A poster child of the Depression, Roy was one of six siblings in the Forbes clan. His two sisters were the first born, with Roy the oldest of the four boys.

The plot of land the government had handed to the Forbeses to cultivate in tiny Rorketon, Manitoba, did not make for an easy existence. Roy's parents, Cecil and Elsie, worked themselves to the bone in an attempt to squeeze out a living on their patch of scrub brush, gravel, and dirt sandwiched between Lake Dauphin and Lake Winnipeg. It was a hard, hard life on the farm, and Cecil and Elsie struggled to keep their kids clothed and fed.

Although times were tough in the depths of the Depression, Roy's parents were resourceful and determined to do anything for their kids. Cecil had a knack for carpentry and ventured up north to work in prospecting camps for four or five months every year. Every dollar he made he sent back home. Elsie guarded the fort, tended to the garden and crops, kept the livestock going, and looked after the kids. Throughout it all Roy was his mom's little helper, glued to her side.

For young Roy the formative years on the farm outside Rorketon did little to inspire dreams of greatness or any inklings of the world beyond the farm. Isolated and alone, he wasn't exposed to very much. There were no other boys playing hockey, football, or baseball. He didn't even know those sports existed. His younger brothers were just babies, and little man Roy developed an uncanny ability to stir up trouble.

When he was three years old he took it upon himself to help out with one of his father's projects involving the family work-horses. Cecil's team of four horses had developed some nasty growths around their ankle areas, and his dad had procured a bucket of toxic goop in town to remove them. With the horses tied up in the barn and ready for the application, Roy's dad went into the house for a quick chat with his wife. Little Roy decided he would help out and surprise his father by taking care of the horses. He picked up a broom and was merrily slathering the goop onto the horses' ankles when Cecil returned to the barn. Grinning happily, Roy turned to look at his father and acciden-tally slopped the goop onto his own little ankle. The searing pain was immediate and intense. The toxic goop nearly burnt Roy's foot clean off!

With no doctor nearby, Roy's father raced around the country-side searching for a travelling doctor or a savvy farmer to help them deal with the serious injury. Cecil and Elsie's greatest fear was that Roy would lose his foot. One can only imagine their shock when the doctor Cecil found told them amputation was their best option and he could perform the surgery. But Elsie was having none of that. Taking her son's foot was absolutely out of the question. Over the course of the next year, there was a lot of limping, a lot of pain, a lot of hobbling around, and in Roy's words, "a lot of dirty months there." In the end his doting mother nursed him back to health, and his foot slowly healed.

Not long thereafter, when Roy was about five, his parents had had enough of Rorketon. Life on the farm was grinding the

Roy Forbes.

Forbes family into the earth. They packed up their few worldly possessions and moved down south to the booming metropolis of Portage la Prairie.

For young Roy, Portage la Prairie opened up a brand-new world of dreams and desires. He went from living in isolation in the sticks to living in a town of four thousand people. It was in Portage that Roy first saw young lovers skating on frozen ponds and gangs of kids playing hockey using sticks and pucks on homemade patches of backyard ice. Portage was an epiphany for him, and the idea and dream of one day playing hockey enveloped his soul.

Even at that tender young age, Roy knew he would have to wait to attain his dream. When your parents don't have a lot of money, you tend not to think too much about getting your own pair of brand-new skates or a sharp-looking hockey stick. Fortunately for Roy, he didn't have to wait very long. His uncle from Winnipeg came visiting that first winter in Portage, and he brought Roy a pair of four-bladed skates. They were funny-looking things, but they worked and Roy was ecstatic. The four blades helped provide additional support for his weak ankle. With his little foot burning in pain as he slid it into the boot, he persevered through the agony and developed a passion for skating on the lake. Hundreds of families in Portage were in the same boat as the Forbeses. Money was tight and unemployment was hovering above 50 percent, but the kids still managed to have a blast chasing each other around the frozen lake for hours on end, using balls of frozen horse dung as pucks.

In time Cecil was able to pick up some part-time work at the local airport. He also did odd jobs around the house for a doctor in town and continued to use his carpentry skills up north in the prospecting camps for four or five months of the year. As always, as soon as he got a cheque, he sent it home to Elsie and she would save most of it.

A ray of sunshine presented itself to the Forbes clan when a friend who worked for the city alerted Roy's dad to a derelict house the city was putting up for sale. Cecil snatched up the run-down shack for the princely sum of twenty dollars. With a hammer, nails, blood, and sweat, the entire Forbes clan threw their backs into the renovation project. It turned out Elsie wasn't just a talented gardener but a fine carpenter as well. The family converted that dilapidated house into a warm, loving home.

By the time Roy was around nine, the Forbeses were getting by and life now presented them with glimmers of hope. When Cecil and Elsie were able to cobble together a few extra dollars, they bought Roy a pair of hand-me-down skates, and he practically lived in them. As for sticks, well, that was something young Roy and his buddies had to carve out and fashion on their own.

The home in town became an anchor of stability for the Forbes family. While Cecil was up north hammering nails in prospecting camps all summer, young Roy acted as his mother's assistant gardener. He happily wielded the rake and did whatever he could to help cultivate the land, patting down the earth and getting the vegetable patch ready for planting. One of his favourite jobs was digging giant holes around the side of the house in late summer. All the vegetables and potatoes left over from the summer crop could then be stored in Roy's holes, which were dug below the frost line and then filled back in. In the dark days of winter Roy would go out, chip through the snow and dirt, and bring in fresh potatoes and root vegetables for his mom to cook up a feast for the family in the barren chill of January.

Roy's all-time favourite job with the vegetable patch was transforming it into the skating garden. Every fall he and his dad levelled off the garden and built up some nice dirt borders along the sides. It seemed nearly everyone in town turned their gardens into backyard rinks in Portage. Those with wells would get to work laying down the ice, bucket by bucket. The Forbeses had a well too, but they were also on town water, so Roy's ice required a little less elbow grease. It came in nice and smooth quite quickly, courtesy of a good old rubber hose. Every winter he relished the idea of playing hockey on top of his garden and then seeing the green shoots of vegetables sprout up in the late spring, heralding the approach of summer.

Roy remembers his father, Cecil, as a hard worker and a tough, resilient man who instilled in him the value of perseverance and determination. But he credits his mother, Elsie, with showing him the value of being tough. She was the tough one in the family.

For the kids in Portage, hockey was everything. Aside from practising on their homemade backyard rinks, Roy and his childhood buddies also spent countless hours blazing around the lake when they needed a larger surface for a proper game of shinny. Playing in the freezing prairie winters until their feet turned blue, they staved off the cold and prolonged their matches by lighting up a fire in an old oil drum, getting out of the wind, and warming up inside an abandoned railway boxcar that was nestled in the snowbanks beside the lake. Eventually, parents and kids got together and built a proper outdoor rink with boards. Then, luxury of all luxuries, the town built an indoor rink with lights.

As the boy grew into a young man, Roy learned quickly that

skill alone wasn't going to get him to the NHL. In the physical sport of hockey, he had to show his scrappiness or the bigger guys would plow him down. At thirteen, Roy was only about five feet tall and 130 pounds. His defence partner in junior hockey, "Jack Rabbit," was a Winnipeger who topped six feet and tipped the scales at more than 180 pounds. After one game where Roy was on the losing end of a scrap, Jack took him aside and set him straight. He told Roy: "Everybody likes to pick on the little guy. You gotta learn how to fight or you're going to get your head knocked off. You gotta hit 'em hard first, grab 'em, pull 'em in close. Hit 'em square in the nose and draw the blood. You need to make an impression. They won't want to try and take you on anymore. Just make sure the ref isn't looking."

Jack and Roy shared the blue line as defence partners for the next five years. They played beside each other through the juvenile leagues, midget, and all the way up to Junior A, when they won the Memorial Cup with the Portage la Prairie Terriers. Roy never let his partner down, and he never backed away from a fight. In hockey and in life Roy learned the value of taking care of yourself and your teammates.

At seventeen, Roy was too young to go to war when it broke out. But like so many of the boys across the nation, he was itching to do his bit and get into the action. He had been "playing soldier" in the army reserves, doing weekly drills for a couple of years, but when it was time to get into the tough stuff, the real stuff, Roy knew he didn't want to be a feet-on-the-ground soldier. He wanted to be a pilot.

Once they were all of age, he and three hockey buddies headed down to the recruitment office in Winnipeg to sign up. His friends were looking for jobs on the ground, but the army already had a lot of guys, and they weren't taking anyone just then. The desk sergeant suggested they all take a look at the air force, but his hockey pals were imbued with a deep desire to keep their feet solidly planted on terra firma. They left Roy to sign up solo with the air force, while they headed back to their dairy farms.

Noticing Roy's high school diploma and high aptitude for math, the recruiters earmarked him as a navigator, but he pushed hard to be considered for pilot training. Roy excelled in his studies at the British Commonwealth Air Training Plan and made it three-quarters of the way through Elementary Flying Training School until one snowy day just outside Regina. In the room where the boys hung their flight gear was a sign that read, in heavy block letters, "There are old pilots and bold pilots. There are no old bold pilots." Roy didn't know who penned that sentiment but whoever it was, he was a very wise man.

It wasn't snowing as Roy raced down the runway on his final solo test flight piloting the DeHavilland 82C Tiger Moth. The night before, mother nature had dumped a few feet of fresh white powder, blanketing the countryside. But as Roy eased on the stick throttle and rudder pedals and climbed into the crisp morning sky of the prairies, there was nothing but clouds. The Tiger Moth was a rather graceful and delicate little biplane with a plastic coupe top that covered the two tandem seats: one for a flight instructor, the other for the pilot.

About a hundred miles or so into his flight it started to snow, and boy did it snow. As inch after inch piled onto the canopy and wings of the tiny yellow biplane, Roy started thinking he had better find a spot to put her down and go grab a coffee. There was no way he was going to make it back to base in this snowstorm. By the time he pinpointed his spot and circled in for a landing, the unrelenting snow had covered the ground like a giant white mattress. With visibility next to nil, Roy put his buggy down hard, destroying one of the Tiger Moth's wheels and part of its under-carriage in the process. The scrappy little terrier from Portage la Prairie walked away without a scratch.

And with that, Roy's dreams of becoming a pilot were over. The next day the head instructor drove down to pick him up and clipped his wings. He told Roy point-blank, "You're not gonna make it as a pilot. You're better suited as a navigator. That's where we need you up there."

If he were to become a navigator, as Hubert Brooks had done, Roy was looking at many more months in the classroom. But Roy possessed all the math skills, the marks, and some of the training needed for a bomb aimer. With just a little more schooling, he could graduate as a pilot officer in no time. He would still get his commission and be riding in a bigger bus with a gun up front—and a huge responsibility to deliver the payload to the enemy.

Forbes was finished with schooling and courses. He wanted in on the fight. He looked the head instructor square in the eye and said, "No, thanks. I'd rather be a bomb aimer quick as I can get.

I want to get out there in the air in England. I want to get into action next month."

The dangers of a life in the air weren't lost on Roy. But the glory and the glamour of sporting the RCAF blue were intoxicating. He and his crewmates were fully aware that they could go down and go down heavy at any time. In order to suit up and climb into the flying metal beasts night after night, they could not allow themselves to think that it might be them going down next. To do their jobs and to do them well, they needed to think they were going to live forever. With fear as a constant companion, they were young, confident, full of bravado, and willing to stare down the odds and risk it all in a nasty war. Although he was shot down over France, Roy was one of the lucky ones in Bomber Command who beat the numbers and made it home. He continued flying on operational duties right up to October 1945.

When Forbes got back from the war, he considered picking up his hockey career and giving it a go. He still loved the game, and he still had the wheels to attract offers to play on senior hockey teams and make a few bucks. But with a young family and mouths to feed, Roy opted for the security of a military life, and he set his sights on building on his career in the RCAF by studying meteorology. He continued to play hockey for the local team on the base, but that was just for fun.

On the evening of November 14, 1947, Roy stepped onto the ice in Trenton for a friendly match against another RCAF team. In his mind this game was no different from any of the others he'd played on the base. He was totally oblivious to the drama circling around the world of hockey and politics. His head was focused on his career path and finishing up his courses. He had no idea who Sandy Watson and Frank Boucher were, or that they were watching him play hockey that night. All he knew was that he was playing centre for a change, just to mix things up a little. He played a decent game, but they lost to the guys who had come in from Ottawa.

The next morning Roy was called in for a meeting with his commanding officer. Standing at attention, he was told, "You're going to Ottawa in an air force plane tomorrow morning." Roy answered, "Why? What am I going to do?" His boss replied, "You're going to try out for the Olympic hockey team." Caught off guard, Roy laughed and said, "No, I don't want to do that. I want to stay here and finish my course."

But Roy's bosses were having none of that. They impressed upon him the significance of this team to the highest echelons of the RCAF brass. The chief of the air staff, the air marshal, and the defence minister were all behind this endeavour. If they wanted him to take a break from his courses to go play hockey, he had better get his butt down there and play. Refusing to go would be just plain stupid. For a guy interested in building a career in the air force, bowing out from this invitation to try out for the RCAF Flyers was career suicide.

That night Roy's military buddies on the base decided to throw him a big send-off party. Like Roy, a healthy number of the men at Trenton had been in the air force overseas during the war, and they knew how to fire up a good party. The alcohol was flowing until the wee hours of the morning, and Roy allowed himself to get stinking drunk. With barely a wink of sleep he grabbed his pre-dawn transport flight and showed up just in time for the 5:00 a.m. skate still reeking of booze. He performed miserably and was certain they would be shipping him back to Trenton that afternoon with his tail between his legs. He had blown his chance.

As Roy skated off the ice past Buck Boucher, Buck pulled him aside and said he wanted to have a word. Buck told him he was giving Roy a second chance. He had heard about the party, and he wasn't sending him back to Trenton just yet. He knew what Roy was capable of, and he wanted to see him play sober. Elated that he had been spared from elimination, Roy grabbed a few hours of sleep in the Beaver Barracks and hit the ice that afternoon with guns blazing. Despite his initial resistance, he now realized the importance of this team and the gift he had been given in being chosen to try out. He wasn't about to waste this golden opportunity to be a part of something special, and he was determined to show that he was infused with the mettle to gain a place on the Olympic team.

With November coming to a close, air force headquarters formally announced Buck Boucher's tentative selection of thirteen of the seventeen members of Canada's Olympic hockey team. The list included Hubert Brooks, Patsy Guzzo, Red Gravelle, Roy Forbes, Irving Taylor, Andy Gilpin, and Ottawa defenceman Louis Lecompte. Spots for a goalie and two additional players were still open and waiting to be filled. Early in the new year the full complement of seventeen players, plus Frank Boucher as coach, Sandy Watson as manager, and George McFaul as trainer, would be bound for Europe to attend "the Games of Renewal" in St. Moritz. But if anyone thought a place on the team that day meant he could start packing his bags, he was quick to find out otherwise. In his statement to the press, Buck made it clear there were still no guarantees: "This is strictly a tentative selection, and if before the team sails, other players prove to be better than the ones named today, they will be taken to the Olympics." At the time, no one could have predicted how prophetic Buck's comment would turn out to be.

OLYMPIC NIGHT

☆

FEATURING

☆

☆   ☆

PRICE   PRICE

25c   25c

☆   ☆

R.C.A.F.   Flyers
Canadian Olympic Team
VS.
McGILL "RED MEN"
Added Attraction **"Barbara Ann Scott"**

OLYMPIC NIGHT

04

On the evening of Saturday, December 13, 1947, Ottawa was well into the grip of winter. Temperatures that night hovered around a bone-chilling minus twenty degrees Celsius. The night sky was crisp and sharp, and a full set of stars was on display. But the evening chill did nothing to dampen the spirits of the throng of people lining up under the lights at the corner of Argyle and O'Connor Streets in downtown Ottawa.

For that night was a momentous evening for sports fans, patriots, and politicians in the nation's capital. That night was Olympic Night at the Ottawa Auditorium. Over the past week newspapers had touted the extravaganza as a "must see" event. Brochures, placards, ads, and a glossy, colour-printed twenty-one-page program championed the spectacle as an event "not to be missed." Olympic Night presented hockey fans with an opportunity to come and catch their first glimpse of Canada's Olympic hockey ambassadors, the RCAF Flyers, in action as they played their first official exhibition game against the McGill Redmen. In just three weeks the Flyers would be heading off to Europe. These were the men Buck Boucher, Frank Boucher, and Sandy Watson had handpicked to carry Canada's Olympic hockey banner all the way to St. Moritz. Their opponents, the McGill Redmen, were leaders in the senior intercollegiate league. Recently the U.S. Olympic hockey team had played the Redmen and soundly beaten them. The prevailing thinking among the RCAF brass was that this exhibition match would showcase their team to their supporters and benefactors while providing their boys with a hot match to test themselves.

Spectators at Olympic Night would also be treated to two special features during the intermissions. Teenage figure skating sensation and gold medal hopeful Barbara Ann Scott was going to perform an exhibition of the routine she would be taking to the Olympics in between the first and second periods of the game. During the second intermission, her coach, Sheldon Galbraith, would present an additional figure skating demonstration. It was engineered to be a huge night, and the public relations machine churned up the media and well-wishers into a frenzy.

Nearly seven thousand spectators poured into the Ottawa Auditorium and filled the magnificent ice rink to the rafters. Each of the patrons had coughed up between $1.00 and $1.50

for coveted seats to witness the match. As a former Olympian himself, Tommy Gorman was a proud supporter of the Flyers. He had donated his rink for all their practices, and tonight he was also donating the proceeds of the event to help fund the Flyers' travel costs and operating expenses overseas.

Everyone who was anyone in Ottawa was there. His Excellency the Governor General and Lady Alexander, along with their family and aides, were in attendance. Sir Alexander Clutterbuck, the British high commissioner to Canada, was there with his wife, Lady Clutterbuck. Kurt Forcart, the Swiss chargé d'affaires representing the hosts of the 1948 Olympics, was there. Thirteen cabinet members, including Defence Minister Brooke Claxton and Health and Welfare Minister Paul Martin Sr., were there. The chiefs of staff of the three armed services were there, along with a gallery of war heroes, including ace fighter pilots Air Marshal "Billy" Bishop and Wing Commander "Johnny" Johnson. Between the two of them, Bishop and Johnson had shot down 110 enemy aircraft in the two world wars. Former Olympic greats from previous Games were there. Top brass from the Canadian Olympic Association, the Canadian Amateur Hockey Association, and the Canadian Figure Skating Association were there. The mayors of Ottawa and Hull were there. Even the internationally acclaimed RCAF Central Band was there to provide musical accompaniment and entertainment for the evening. As an added bonus the assistant bandmaster had composed an original march titled "On to Victory," which the band would play in dedication to inspire the Flyers and Barbara Ann Scott on their way to greatness. It was an over-the-top display of national pride and chest thumping. Now all the Flyers had to do was beat McGill!

The one man missing from this celebratory evening was Buck Boucher. Because of his paid job as head coach of the Ottawa Senators, Buck was unavailable to man the bench and coach the Flyers on Olympic Night. His obligations with the Senators were taking him on the road for a two-day trip to play against Boston and New York. His son, Frank, would take over the coaching reins for the night. But prior to leaving, Buck had a word with the press, telling them he felt the team was in fine shape and was reaching its peak form. He had every confidence in them.

Perhaps Buck was thinking about the Senators when he made those statements. From the puck drop the Flyers were totally outplayed and back on their heels. Wave after wave of McGill attackers buzzed the Flyers netminder, firing shots almost at will at Corporal Joe Tunney in between the posts. Meanwhile, the Flyers' sieve-like defence seemed incapable of setting up plays of their own, or of stopping the formidable McGill assault. After eighteen minutes of humiliation, McGill cracked the seal on the Flyers net, opened up their scoring streak, and never looked back.

The unrelenting McGill offensive continued throughout the second period. McGill dominated the ice and played rugged, aggressive hockey with solid displays of bodychecking and plenty of speed to spare. The Flyers, in contrast, looked weak, flat, disorganized, and unable to penetrate the solid wall of McGill's defence. When the buzzer sounded, signalling the end of the second period, the score had jumped to 5–0 in favour of McGill. But the score could have been much higher. It was only Joe Tunney's exemplary skills in net that held McGill's tally to five goals over the first two periods.

While Sheldon Galbraith entertained the crowd with his figure skating display during the second intermission, Governor General Viscount Alexander made a trip down to the Flyers dressing room to pay the boys a visit. He asked Frank Boucher point-blank, "What's the matter with my team?" Boucher answered, "Sir, if I knew, I'd fix it."

The highlight of Olympic Night was Barbara Ann Scott's impeccable figure skating performance. The crowd sat enthralled and in awe of the petite champion's sublime routine and display of skill. For those in attendance there was at least some consolation that in little Miss Scott, Canada clearly had one good chance of capturing a gold medal in Switzerland.

When the Flyers took to the ice for the third period, the ominous cloud hanging over them loomed even darker. McGill continued to pour on the power. They deftly backchecked any and all of the Flyers rushes and advances and kept their goalie supremely protected. For anyone watching the match, it was blatantly clear that McGill was the better-conditioned team and exhibited a cohesiveness and unity that was lacking in the Flyers lineup.

By the time the final buzzer sounded, the McGill Redmen had creamed the Olympic hopefuls 7–0 in a completely one-sided match. Humiliated, the men of the RCAF Flyers were left to skate off the ice with heads hanging low before the nearly seven thousand fans, including a litany of government dignitaries, military brass, and representatives of foreign allies. There was no question that McGill had been infinitely better that evening. Heads were certainly going to roll. And many in the press, the public, and the locker room questioned whether an air force team should be going to St. Moritz at all. Coach Frank Boucher later said, "I do not know who organized that exhibition game, but we weren't ready. We hadn't jelled as a team yet."

The day after the game the media reaction was swift and ravaging. *Ottawa Citizen* columnist Jack Koffman wrote: "The roof fell in on Canada's hockey representatives Saturday night and the gloom is thick in official circles. That seven-goal pasting at the hands of McGill Redmen has everyone worried. The airmen are bound to improve in the short time available for practice and exhibition games before sailing for the Olympic games. There is every indication though that they aren't going to improve sufficiently to give the Czechs, among others at the

Olympiad, a real scare. The Flyers' performance was extremely disappointing and the job facing young Frank Boucher as coach is a momentous one."

The rare hockey editorial in the evening edition of the *Ottawa Journal* sounded the alarm from coast to coast: "The folly of sending a hurriedly-organized RCAF hockey team to represent Canada at the Olympic games should have been obvious from the beginning. It became fully apparent when McGill University 'whitewashed' the Olympics by a lopsided score on Ottawa ice. This debacle reflects no discredit on the players, but it is no tribute to the wisdom of those who conceived or approved the idea that they should play for Canada. Unscrambling of this muddle is of national interest far beyond the limits of organized sports circles."

Under the headline "Team Proves Inadequate for Olympic Games," the sports editor at the *Montreal Gazette* continued the bloodletting with his article. "A perplexed RCAF hockey executive and an equally baffled CAHA were wondering today where they could find a hockey team to represent Canada in the Olympic Winter Games at St. Moritz in February. This was the result of the 7–0 pasting a fast-skating smoothly-working McGill hockey team plastered on the RCAF 'Olympic' representative here last night at the Auditorium. It wasn't so much the score that mattered but how badly the air force team looked in losing. Competent hockey observers who saw the game were unanimous in declaring that the air force side could not possibly represent Canada at the Olympics and added further that as the team is presently constituted it would mean complete replacement if the Dominion is to be adequately represented at the Olympics."

The resounding loss to McGill was a huge eye-opener, a very public embarrassment, and a tremendous shock. Maybe the guys were suffering from stage fright and jitters. Maybe they were outplayed because the McGill squad was already a well-oiled machine that had been playing together as a unit for half a season, whereas this group of Flyers had barely finished practising together. Regardless of the excuses, the Flyers' brain trust needed to get another quality exhibition match under its belt in order to adequately assess the merits of the current roster and figure out if the situation was as dire as it appeared. And they needed to do it fast.

On December 15, just two days after the loss to McGill, the Flyers were given a chance to quiet the furor whipped up in the press over their dismal showing at Olympic Night. A game against the strong army headquarters team of the Ottawa Senior Hockey League was arranged as part of a double bill at the auditorium. Norman Dawe, vice-president of the CAHA, was coming in from Montreal to attend the game. Buck Boucher was also back from his road trip with the Ottawa Senators. Together the two hockey titans were going to watch the match from the stands for a cold-hearted look at the Flyers. Then they would decide if help was needed and what could be done to improve the team. If the boys sporting the air force–blue jerseys could show determination and a high calibre of smooth and aggressive play, perhaps the pendulum of public opinion would swing back in their favour. Perhaps sweeping changes weren't in order, and they still had every right to be Canada's team.

For Frank Boucher, Sandy Watson, and the men of the Flyers, this was a chance at redemption. For the army it was an opportunity for public revenge for being shut out from consideration to represent Canada at the Olympics. There was no doubt the army boys were out for blood.

Although some in the media had already given up on the Flyers, *Ottawa Citizen* columnist Tommy Shields was still a fan. Prior to the match that evening, he reminded readers to keep some perspective: "Fashioning any kind of team from the candidates reporting here was a man's-sized job in itself. We do not argue that this team is good enough. But we like to remember that the Royal Canadian Air Force, in recent years, have had their wings shot full of holes on numerous occasions and still managed to come out on top. There may be a remedy in this case, and the RCAF should have the opportunity of finding that remedy before their plans and team are tossed in the discard."

Twenty-five hundred fans filed through the turnstiles of the Ottawa Auditorium that evening to witness the doubleheader on the slate. First up, the New Edinburgh Burghs were taking on the Hull Volants in regular league play. The RCAF Flyers' match against the army was second on the card. As the masses took to their seats in Tommy Gorman's ice palace, the streets in the capital region were blanketed under a few inches of freshly fallen snow. Meanwhile those without a care for hockey flitted around town making last-minute purchases in preparation for Christmas, which was coming up fast.

When the Flyers finally took to the ice late in the evening, the mercury had dipped below minus ten degrees Celsius outside. Inside the crowd of twenty-five hundred greeted the team with an equally frosty reception. There was no cheering, no RCAF bandfare, no fancy write-ups, no pomp and pageantry. The army attackers immediately took to the offensive and banged in an unanswered goal early in the first period. Under the gun, the Flyers responded tensely and struggled to find their groove against the hard-playing army team. As the first period continued, the army's superior forwards successfully tied up the Flyers snipers and prevented them from executing many of their set plays. Meanwhile, the Flyers defencemen were again woefully weak and unable to set up plays or clear the army forwards from buzzing around the Flyers net and relentlessly banging at loose pucks. By the end of the first period things were looking grim. The Flyers were trailing 3–0.

As the match progressed, the Flyers finally seemed to loosen up and make a game battle of it. They rallied in the second period when former bellhop Orval Gravelle capitalized on a hard shot directed at the army net by Hubert Brooks. Gravelle tipped in the rebound and got the Flyers on the board. Penalties flew on both sides in the rough, hard-fought game, but again the Flyers just didn't display the talent or ability to contend with the army players' clever passing and constant backchecking. The army goalie was a fixture in net and stonewalled the Flyers offence with a stellar performance. By the end of the second period, the Flyers had fallen behind 5–1 and were as good as done.

But in the third period the captains of the clouds showed promise. Andy Gilpin pocketed the team's second goal four minutes into the period, and the men in blue dominated control of the puck. Line after line of Flyers concentrated the action and attacks in the army's defensive zone, pressing hard. For a few fleeting moments it seemed as if the Flyers might claw their way back into contention. But the effort was too little, too late. The army defenders continually cleared the puck, and their hot goalie rebuffed any of the ensuing Flyers shots. With the spotlight blazing on them, the airmen went down in flames, 6–2 at the final buzzer. The body blow dealt by the army was their second high-profile loss in just two days. The reputation of the RCAF was getting hammered.

It was another huge embarrassment for the team. Deep-seated worry began setting in among the top brass. Had they bitten off more than they could chew? Would they need to withdraw from the competition? Air Marshal Wilf Curtis, chief of the air staff, was in the stands at both games and witnessed his team buckle under pressure. Incensed, he told reporters: "I'm sick with disappointment. We had such high hopes. There was such enthusiasm and support. The team is going to have to quickly strengthen itself immeasurably or it will have to be withdrawn. This thing is bigger than the RCAF, bigger than the CAHA; it's as big as Canada's prestige at the Olympics. I think we can still do it. We haven't much time, but there must be some players of required

(Left to right) Orval "Red" Gravelle, Pete Leichnitz, and Roy Forbes.

ability available somewhere, and we will find them. The defence was deplorable. Why I could have run down the ice faster than some of the players skated."

Obviously this was not the air force's finest hour. The Flyers knew this, the CAHA knew this, the press knew this, and the army knew this. In his interviews with journalists following the game, army coach Bill Cowley dug the knife in deep and roasted the Flyers with his comments: "My club is not in good condition. It may not have been so strong in the third period. But even at that, any Olympic team should be beating us. I could not figure out what hockey system or plays the air force was using."

It was now blatantly apparent to Frank Boucher, Sandy Watson, and Buck Boucher that their team was in deep trouble. They knew swift action was imperative in order to remedy the situation and quiet the outrage being directed at them from the upper levels of the air force, government officials, the Canadian Olympic Association, and a plethora of outside forces.

Immediately after the game, the entire RCAF Flyers management held heated behind-the-scenes brainstorming sessions with Norman Dawe of the CAHA. All agreed that drastic changes were in order. Starting from scratch was out of the question, and the CAHA was still solidly behind the air force team. The new plan called for the RCAF to forge ahead, auditioning more players while the CAHA scoured its ranks in search of a couple of eligible defencemen and at least one entire forward line to send over for tryouts. Many in the press, however, were calling for an entirely new team.

The remodelling got under way in earnest. Within days Sandy, Frank, and Buck had axed half the players who were currently shacking up at the Beaver Barracks. From initial tryouts of nearly two hundred airmen, only eight were deemed to have what was required to maintain a spot on the team. Hubert Brooks, Roy Forbes, Patsy Guzzo, Red Gravelle, and Irving Taylor were still standing, as were fellow airmen Louis Lecompte, Ross King, and Andy Gilpin.

Louis Lecompte was the oldest of the bunch. At thirty-three he was a big defenceman who played a tough and rough game. He grew up "the hard way" on Booth Street in Ottawa. Lecompte's dad was a shoe salesman and his mother cleaned office buildings. He gravitated to hockey at a young age and showed great promise on the Ottawa senior hockey scene.

Much as he loved hockey, Louis also had a love of photography. He signed up as a flight sergeant in the RCAF in 1935. During the war, he was posted overseas and worked in the RCAF's photographic unit as an aerial photographer capturing reconnaissance images.

Goalie Ross King and forward Andy Gilpin had both flown in to join the team from their station in Whitehorse, Yukon. King was a stellar goalie who had won the Memorial Cup when playing with the Portage la Prairie Terriers in 1942. Gilpin was an aircraft technician who grew up in Montreal playing Junior A hockey. As a young boy, Andy too knew about hard times. His father was gassed in World War I and spent much of his time in a veterans hospital. After Andy joined the RCAF in 1940, he played for air force teams wherever he was posted. He was smooth and fast on his skates, and he possessed incredible stickhandling skills.

Lecompte, King, Gilpin, and the others provided a strong core for the team, but if the RCAF Flyers had any hope of surviving at the Olympics, Manager Sandy Watson and Coach Frank Boucher desperately needed more manpower.

They had discovered their first batch of talented hopefuls right under their noses when they watched the New Edinburgh Burghs destroy the Hull Volants 6–1 in the first match of the doubleheader that evening at the auditorium. The RCAF power brokers couldn't help but notice the phenomenal skills of a number of standouts on the Burghs squad. Ted Hibberd, Ab Renaud, and Reg Schroeter had been playing together as one of the top-scoring lines in the league all year. Five of the six goals scored by the Burghs that night were slammed in courtesy of this trio. Pete Leichnitz was a solid, speedy centre who Watson and Boucher figured could easily slide onto an existing line or pair up with one of his Burghs mates. And Frank Dunster was a powerful defenceman who showed a penchant for crushing attackers on the blue line. For public relations purposes, Watson, Boucher, and the RCAF upper echelon were still hopeful they could pull from within the air force ranks. But it was starting to look as if they might have to find amateur players like these from outside the force.

Getting these five players into the RCAF blue jerseys could bring new scoring punch and defensive muscle to the Flyers lineup. But would they all meet the amateur eligibility requirements for competing at the Olympics? Furthermore, would they take a leave of absence from their jobs and current hockey team to join the air force and accompany the Flyers overseas for the next three months?

Christmas came early for Frank and Sandy. None of the guys had been paid to play hockey, so there were no issues with their amateur status. The ribbon on top was that Reg Schroeter, Ted Hibberd, Pete Leichnitz, and Frank Dunster were all former RCAF or currently in the RCAF reserve. So calling them back into service should be a snap. Ab Renaud was also a warrior, but he had served in the army during the war. When approached and offered the opportunity to try out for the Flyers, all five men were keen to give it a whirl.

Reg Schroeter was a true Ottawa boy who loved his country and loved the great outdoors. He played all his hockey growing up in Ottawa and, with his four brothers, was a fixture in the local hockey world. Known for his speed and agility, Reg also had a blistering shot and displayed great stickhandling skills. During the war Reg and all of his brothers served in the air force. Reg was a pilot, part of the air training unit—an extremely dangerous job. His war service didn't see him take to battle in the skies over Europe; rather, he and his colleagues were tasked with pushing trainees to the limit to get them up to speed for battle. It was a deadly assignment. Four thousand men died trying to get their wings in the British Commonwealth Air Training Plan.

After his stint in the RCAF, Reg was working with the federal government at the Department of Mines. His best friend and linemate, Ab Renaud, was also working in government, at the Department of Agriculture just across the road. The morning after the brass saw them tearing up the Hull Volants, both received calls from Minister of Defence Brooke Claxton's office to come down for a meeting. Getting your bosses to approve a three-month leave of absence was no problem when you worked for the government and had Brooke Claxton's seal of approval. By noon both of the guys had been shanghaied from their office jobs and were on the ice trying out for the Flyers. Within twenty-four hours of their game against the Volants, Schroeter and Renaud had been accepted onto the Flyers and were practising with the team.

For forward Ab Renaud, signing on as a Flyer meant he had to take a pay cut. During his time in the war with the army, Ab had served as a sergeant in the medical corps. If Ab was going to join the RCAF team, he would need to take an air force position at the rank of corporal. Although it meant a drop in rank and a drop in weekly wages, for a single guy with a passion for hockey and a love of his country, it was a no-brainer. He was in with both feet, and the Flyers gained a steady, 165-pound forward who never gave the puck away, never made mistakes, backchecked like a demon, and displayed consistent firepower as a goal scorer.

Young guns Pete Leichnitz and Ted Hibberd were both just twenty-one years old. They were childhood friends, and both had briefly served in the RCAF. By the time they were of age to sign up for the fight, much of the action overseas was already dying down. Neither of them pursued lifelong careers in the RCAF after the war.

When Sandy and Frank came calling, Ted was working as a clerk for Metropolitan Life. His buddy Pete was working for the federal government in the revenue department. They both happily accepted the offer to pull on the Flyers jersey and sign up as aircraftmen.

Defenceman Frank Dunster's path onto the Flyers was a little rockier. A tough guy to the core, Dunster was exceptionally gifted at throwing his chiselled frame around on defence. He won the Memorial Cup while playing with the Oshawa Generals in 1940 and was poised to continue climbing the hockey ranks. Known for guarding the blue line with a vengeance, Frank landed legendary hip checks and his straight-up open-ice hits were equally lethal at putting the brakes on approaching attackers. On the ice Dunster was a force to be reckoned with, and junior hockey reporters gave him the moniker "the Blue Line Masher." But Frank's dreams of pursuing a professional hockey career were cut short when he chose to serve his country at war.

Like Hubert Brooks, Dunster also served as a navigator in the RCAF. Dunster was in a Halifax bomber as part of the No. 6 Group, Canada's special Bomber Command delegation. Night after night Frank took to the skies as a member of 420 Squadron, nicknamed Snowy Owl. Their squadron's motto was "We Fight to the Finish." True to that motto, Dunster flew an astonishing thirty-seven missions in 1944, three of them during the devastating Battle of Berlin. When he came home from the war, Frank landed a job as a firefighter with the Ottawa Fire Department. It was decent, fulfilling work that allowed him to spend time with his growing family and continue to play the game he loved with the New Edinburgh Burghs.

When Sandy Watson and Frank Boucher offered Dunster a position on the Flyers, he was thrilled and eager to join up. But when Frank went to the Ottawa fire chief and asked for a three-month leave of absence, his request was instantly gunned down. The fire department wasn't prepared to allow Dunster to take time off to go and chase pucks around Europe. Moreover, he was told he wouldn't have a job to come back to if he chose to play for Canada.

Dunster relayed the bad news to Sandy Watson. Not one to ever give up, Sandy pulled some strings and secured an OK from the RCAF brass to re-enlist Frank at his old rank. For Frank it was like a gift from the gods. He could come back into the air force fold in a career he loved, plus he would be able to take advantage of the once-in-a-lifetime opportunity to play for Olympic gold. Filled with elation and buoyed by a sense of national pride, the Blue Line Masher leapt at the opportunity. He went in to see his bosses at the Ottawa Fire Department and told them to stuff it. He was heading back into the skies, and he was going to play his heart out for his country on the ice in Europe.

Individual team photos of (clockwise, from top left) Murray Dowey, Wally Halder, André Laperrière, and George Mara.

CALLING IN THE BIG GUNS

05

In the run-up to Christmas, the men on the RCAF Flyers hockey team continued their twice-daily practices at the Ottawa Auditorium as new recruits came and went. With one day off for Christmas, the boys were back on their blades the very next day. Bolstered by the five new players acquired from the Burghs, there was a contagious new spark in the lineup and an obvious and pleasant sharpening up of the team's overall play in practices. Lines were getting stronger, and the men were progressively jelling into a cohesive team. The warriors like Dunster, Brooks, and Forbes had an instant connection. Although they hadn't seen action together in the same units overseas, their shared experience provided a concrete foundation for a bond to take root and grow between the men with each passing day.

The improvement in play was encouraging to Buck, Frank, and Sandy, but with less than two weeks to go before departure day for Europe, they still had holes to fill, and they desperately needed a few more available, accessible, high-quality players. In order to assemble the best possible squad, Sandy and Frank were going to have to make some amendments to the original concept of an exclusively air force team. Using Buck's NHL connections, they contacted four of the top minds in hockey who were currently operating at the highest level—Frank Selke, senior general manager of the Montreal Canadiens; Jack Adams, general manager of the Detroit Red Wings; Walter Brown of the Boston Bruins; and Buck's brother Frank Boucher of the New York Rangers.

If anyone could identify untapped resources of amateur firepower that could fulfill the Flyers' needs, it was these four men. They had their collective finger on the pulse of all up-and-coming hockey talent across the nation. They unanimously encouraged the Flyers' management to go after three guys they had on their radar—Wally Halder, George Mara, and André Laperrière. CAHA executives were 100 percent in agreement with the recommendations.

Wally Halder and George Mara were both working in business in Toronto but moonlighted as high-scoring forwards with the Barker's Biscuits team in the Canadian Food Products division of the Toronto Mercantile League. And André Laperrière was a young, strapping defenceman in his second year of studies at the University of Montreal and playing on their hockey team in the intercollegiate hockey league. All of them were amateurs, and all of them had caught the attention of the big guys in charge of the big leagues.

Without question all agreed that Wally Halder was one of the best amateur hockey players in Canada not on contract with any of the big teams, although he could have played for virtually any of them. He was a big, strong, versatile, extremely gifted athlete with brains.

Born in Toronto on September 15, 1920, Wally was from a well-to-do family. It seemed that whatever Mr. Halder put his mind to, he could accomplish and then some. While studying at the University of Toronto, Wally was captain of and leading scorer for the Varsity Blues hockey team. He was also the national senior doubles tennis champion and a swimming and diving instructor.

On the ice, Wally was tough and fiercely competitive. A very fast skater, he also possessed an innate ability to stickhandle, read plays, and deliver a blazing shot with impeccable accuracy. At 185 pounds he was rock solid, hard to hit, and equally at ease operating as either a sniper on a forward line or a stay-at-home playmaker engineering the action from the blue line on defence.

During the war, Wally had signed up as an officer in training with the Royal Canadian Navy. He was an outstanding recruit and was voted by his peers to "receive the cuff links." This was a time-honoured award that recognized an all-around recruit who exhibited leadership skills, excellent aptitude in his studies, and enthusiasm for the unit. Wally was a natural-born leader who was friendly and jocular. He played all out, all the time, but was recognized as a guy who played the game cleanly. Although big, strong, aggressive, and rough, he never received a penalty throughout his entire time on the ice with the University of Toronto.

Wally and his good friend from the navy George Mara both played for navy teams while they were stationed in Canada and overseas during the war. When they returned home, both men were offered tryouts with the New York Rangers. Both impressed the pants off Rangers coach Frank Boucher, and both were offered lucrative no-trade, no-cut contracts to play for New York. They declined the offers, opting instead to stay in Toronto, where they could pursue their business careers and play for Barker's Biscuits in front of thousands of fans at Varsity Arena.

While many young men would have jumped at the opportunity to play in the NHL, Wally and George were from well-educated, well-connected backgrounds. They loved playing hockey, but a life in business offered a stable future and greater financial opportunities. The constant travel that was part and parcel of being an NHL player may have also contributed to their disinterest in a pro career. Perhaps they undertook the NHL tryouts simply to test themselves, to see if they could cut it against some of the best in the game. Whatever their reasoning, both men possessed the skills to play professional hockey at the highest level but had chosen to pursue more lucrative careers in business instead.

Like Wally, George Mara was born into a family of privilege in Toronto. George's father, William Mara, ran a very successful business as an importer of wine and liquor. The Wm Mara

Company was reputed to have the largest wine vaults in all of Canada. George's dad had also been a star football player with the Toronto Argonauts until he broke his ankle. His natural athleticism, leadership skills, and streak of independence clearly trickled down to young George.

While attending Upper Canada College, George was captain of their Junior B hockey team. At fifteen, he led the UCC Blues to an undefeated season and the league championship. His coach, retired Toronto Maple Leafs star "Gentleman" Joe Primeau, knew he had a gifted future professional under his wing. But George wasn't about to be pushed into pursuing a lifelong career as a paid athlete. He played for a love of the sport, pure and simple.

The Detroit Red Wings expressed an interest in young George when they spotted him playing for UCC and then for the Toronto Marlboros in Junior A hockey. They placed him as an up-and-comer on their negotiating list and invited him to formally sign with the team in 1942. George respectfully declined their offer and instead elected to volunteer for the Royal Canadian Navy as an officer in training. He served on a corvette in the North Atlantic, on a gate vessel out of Halifax, and on two minesweepers. He also performed sea duties as a lieutenant on the Newfoundland-to-Ireland run. While serving in the navy George played with Wally Halder, and the two became fast friends. When George was posted to a naval base in Saint-Hyacinthe, Quebec, Frank Selke tapped him to play for the Montreal Canadiens farm team, the Montreal Royals, but George was unable to because of his duties.

Like his best friend Wally Halder, George Mara was an exceptional stickhandler who had a great head for the game and a cannon for a shot. He had a well-honed talent for seeing the entire ice surface and an awareness of the movements of all players, which allowed him to make accurate, effective passes. At five foot ten and 180 pounds, he was a smooth, solid skater with golden hands. Colleagues and friends noted that Mara could also hang on to a puck forever if he wanted to.

When he returned home from the war, George was once again approached by the Detroit Red Wings to suit up. This time it was against Toronto in the Stanley Cup playoffs. Although he was excited by the offer, George was being groomed to take over the massive family importing business, and a professional hockey career in Detroit was not in his cards at the time. Now, an opportunity to play for Canada for Olympic gold was something entirely different. That was something George could steal away from the family business to be a part of for a few months. That was something of substance, where he could once again contribute and do his bit.

When George and Wally rolled up for their first practice at the Ottawa Auditorium on December 29, some of the other boys couldn't help but notice that these guys were clearly from a different social strata. They were impeccably dressed and both were driving beautiful, brand-new 1948 Buick convertibles. Money was definitely not an issue for either of these chaps. Neither Wally nor George wanted to temporarily enlist in the RCAF; nor did they have to. As long as they were amateurs, they were eligible to join the team. So Wally and George signed up as civilian volunteers who had served in the navy.

TWENTY-TWO-YEAR-OLD ANDRÉ LAPERRIÈRE was a bright-faced Frenchman with a warm, friendly smile and a shock of thick black hair. One of the younger men cherry-picked to try out for the Flyers, André was also the only French-speaking player on the squad. Born in the Montreal working-class neighbour-hood of Outremont, he started playing pickup games of shinny at the tender age of seven on scrappy patches of ice in local parks. It seemed like every boy in the neighbourhood was mad about hockey, and André was no exception. His first skates were four-bladers, just like the ones a young Roy Forbes had learned on in Portage la Prairie.

In those formative years André developed a passion for the game and spent hour after hour duking it out with thirty other kids, chasing a single puck around the frozen park. Young André was imbued with a burning desire to be on the ice every day—in snowstorms, in bitter sub-zero temperatures, even in torrential downpours of freezing rain. Crusted in ice, soaking wet, he would walk home a few hours later with a giant smile on his face. André felt as if hockey was a part of who he was, a key component of his essence. The instant he received new skates, shoulder pads, and gloves at Christmas, he had them out of the boxes and on his body. Brimming with glee, André then paraded around the living room modelling his new getup to the laughter of his younger sister, Renée.

There were no rink managers manicuring the ice for André and his neighbourhood buddies. The kids in Outremont brought their own shovels to clean the surface. They also made up their own teams and designed and knitted their own "team" sweaters. This was how André learned to play hockey. He never played on an organized team, never went to any tournaments, never had any lessons or formal coaches. Instead he and his friends created their own league, playing pickup matches in their homemade sweaters on ice they cleaned themselves around Montreal.

The big, strapping kid that Frank Selke wanted for the Montreal Canadiens and Frank Boucher wanted for the New York Rangers had never played an official game of hockey until he went away to Laval College boarding school at the age of sixteen. André hadn't been doing so well at his studies, so to improve his grades in preparation for university, his parents decided that he needed a stricter, more focused education. His father was a streetcar driver, and he wanted André to strive for greatness, for a university degree, and for a career that could take him places. So they sent him away to do his final years of high school in Saint-Vincent-de-Paul, Quebec.

Although the school was not too far from home, his parents were permitted to visit only on Sundays or special occasions. André spent his first night there feeling sad, alone, and depressed. He missed his family and he missed his friends. But when he awoke the next morning and looked outside his dorm room window, André saw they had a beautiful ice rink with actual wooden boards and real nets. That changed everything.

His boarding school had not only an outdoor rink but a proper hockey team with a coach as well. André skated every day and excelled on the ice and in his studies. He captained his team, playing centre. Already over six feet tall and nearly 160 pounds, André was one of the bigger boys on the team and stronger than many of his linemates. He had a knack for bowling over his opponents or simply having them bounce right off him. To spectators on the sidelines, it appeared as if his skates were glued to the ice. Laperrière had a hell of a shot and loved the physical roughness of the game and the closeness of working with his teammates.

Every Sunday André's family would drive out to Saint-Vincent-de-Paul and watch him play. (His mom also knitted toques for all fifteen of his teammates to keep the winter chill off the boys' freezing skulls.) It was at one of these Sunday matches that André was plucked from hockey oblivion and thrust into the spotlight. His line scored six goals in a game and got a write-up in the local paper. The next weekend a scout from the Verdun Terriers of the Quebec Junior Hockey League came sniffing for a look and spotted the imposing young centre. Blown away by the undiscovered talent, Verdun struck a deal with the boarding school to have André come and play for them. The Terriers arranged for a cab to chauffeur him to practices in Verdun and games at the cavernous Montreal Forum. André could finish out his studies at boarding school, but now he was lacing up in the premier hockey league in Quebec. Suddenly the kid from Outremont who had been playing in obscurity was on everyone's radar, one step away from the big time. André felt like a star.

By the time he finished high school, André was tipping the scales at 170 pounds solid and standing about six foot two. He still played centre, only now it was with the University of Montreal Carabins. A student at the university's École des Beaux-Arts, André was doing an arts degree, specializing in advertising, printing, and graphic design. Watching him play for the university team, his coach decided to try throwing André back on defence. Laperrière loved it and blossomed into a stellar rushing defenceman with a bullet for a shot and an impeccable skill at clearing the front of the net and protecting his goalie. Over two seasons André was a menacing force for the Carabins and helped captain his team to two Canadian Intercollegiate Hockey Union championships.

On the evening of December 28, André was taking a well-deserved rest from his second year of university studies, relaxing with his parents and younger sister in the buzz of post-Christmas celebrations. As he was clearing the plates from the dinner table at the family home in Outremont, the phone rang and his mother answered. The man on the other line was speaking English and asking for André.

André's English was pretty rough, but his mom's was non-existent so she handed the phone over to her son. The man on the other end of the line introduced himself as Sidney Dawes, president of the Canadian Olympic Association. He described the RCAF Flyers and said, "Listen, André, how would you like to join our team to represent Canada at the Olympics?" At first André thought it was a joke, someone from school playing a prank.

But Dawes was dead serious. Once he had composed himself, André told the head of the Canadian Olympic Association that he needed some time to think. Joining the team meant he would miss three months of school, essentially losing an entire year of his studies. Dawes's response was short and to the point: "I'll call you back in fifteen minutes. I need an answer tonight."

With his head swirling, André relayed the information to his incredulous parents and sister, who had been listening and waiting in curiosity. Elated, his father told him, "This is an offer you will never get again in your life. Your studies can wait. You can go back to university next year." Fifteen minutes later on the nose, Dawes called back with one question: "What's your answer?" André responded, "I would love to go." Dawes told him to get to Dorval airport for 7:00 a.m. sharp. A plane was coming to pick him up and bring him to Ottawa. At twenty-two years old, André had never even dreamed of visiting Europe, let alone playing hockey for his country on the world stage. He didn't sleep a wink all night.

At 6:00 a.m. the next morning, André caught a cab in the darkness and made his way out to Dorval. As he sat on a bench at the airport with thoughts ricocheting in his head, a young man dressed smartly in uniform approached, asked him his name, and ushered him out onto the tarmac, where a forty-seater DC-10 was waiting just for him. As a civilian André had no experience with planes or with the air force, and the bizarreness of a personal escort in a giant plane was not lost on him. In fact, he had never travelled anywhere before. While the DC-10 cut through the clouds from Montreal to Ottawa, André looked out of the window at the countryside racing below and thought, *What the hell is happening to me?*

With more than his fair share of butterflies, the big kid from Outremont hit the ice midway through the morning workout practice. There were about thirty other men being run through a series of drills and exercises under the watchful eyes of Buck and Frank Boucher. No one else spoke French, and many of the guys seemed to be friendly and getting along well. Immersed in a sea of English players, André felt like the odd man out. Fortunately he was in peak playing condition. He blazed into action, was impressive as all hell, and finished up the morning session feeling chuffed about his performance. At the end of the practice Buck Boucher called out name after name, and André's heart sank as he watched the other guys skate off the ice. Not quite up to speed on what was actually going on, André figured these guys were in and he was out. While he anxiously waited to hear his name roll off Buck's lips, he watched as the poor defenceman who had flown him out that morning was axed from the team and André was identified as his replacement. Moments later in the dressing room, Hubert Brooks dusted off his French, introduced himself to André, and welcomed him onto the team.

It all happened so fast it was like being in a dream. The night before, André was at home having supper with his family. A day later he was being inducted into the air force as an aircraftman level 2 and getting suited up to go to St. Moritz to play for his country in the Olympic Games.

* * *

AS THE CALENDAR TICKED OVER TO 1948, the final composition of the RCAF Flyers was finally announced. With eight days to go before the boys in air force blue were due to set sail for Europe, Sandy Watson and Frank Boucher had a team they could feel confident in. *Ottawa Citizen* sports editor Tommy Shields caught a glimpse of the Flyers in a hotly contested closed-door practice game against Buck Boucher's top-notch Ottawa Senators squad. In his column Round and About he wrote: "From having nothing at all, so to speak, the Airmen now have a hockey team. Changes and recent additions have raised the Olympics up from a lowly rating to a point where they now can be looked upon as a squad capable of representing Canada creditably in the coming Winter Games at St. Moritz. How good the team ultimately will be, or how far they will go in the Olympic tournament, is something which cannot be foretold."

In addition to their matches in St. Moritz, the men had signed up to play in a series of exhibition games before and after the Olympics. Their gruelling schedule had them ping-ponging by boat, train, plane, and bus through England, France, Switzerland, Czechoslovakia, Sweden, Holland, and Scotland. Quite simply, without the exhibition matches, the team could not afford to make the trip. Funds generated from their exhibition games were crucial to covering the costs of food, travel, and accommodations for the twenty-man contingent. As a bonus, though, the pre-Olympic matches would help give the newly minted team a few more chances to play together. The prep matches would also provide an opportunity for the men to get acclimatized to the European ice surfaces and to the higher altitude that came with playing in the Swiss Alps.

With last-minute practices under way in Ottawa, Manager Sandy Watson put together a list of supplies for the men to bring with them on their three-month odyssey through war-torn Europe. Since many of the spots they were going to hit on the old continent were still reeling from the devastations of war, the niceties of life could not be counted on. For the boys in blue it was almost like packing for an expedition. The items on Sandy's list were deemed "compulsory." They included a kit bag, a suitcase, an RCAF grey overcoat, a civilian overcoat, a civilian hat, an RCAF cap, the RCAF uniform, a lounge suit, a pair of light trousers, one pair of boots, one pair of shoes, one pair of overshoes, one pair of slippers, four RCAF shirts, four civilian shirts, RCAF and civilian ties, two suits of long underwear, four undershirts and shorts, a heavy sweater, RCAF and civilian gloves, six pairs of civilian socks, three pairs of RCAF socks, two pairs of flannelette pyjamas, one dressing gown, one woollen and one silk scarf, a dozen white and a half dozen RCAF handkerchiefs, a belt, braces, a parka, flying boots, a blazer, shoe polish, and button polish, which could be divided among several members. As well, Sandy made it very clear that toiletries must be packed. "As soap is on ration in many European countries, members must bring at least six large bars apiece. Towels are frequently not provided in European hotels at present. Each member should bring at least two towels. Many such hotels are not equipped for electric razors, hence it is advised to bring a safety razor and blades."

On January 6, 1948, just when everything seemed to be humming along with military efficiency, fate dealt Sandy Watson and Frank Boucher a progression of unkind blows. With two days to go before departure, all the players had to undergo a routine medical exam to be cleared for the extended trip overseas. The medical once-over included a series of inoculations. Wally Halder, Reg Schroeter, and George Mara all suffered violent reactions to their shots. Big André Laperrière hated needles and passed out when the nurse administered his. These were minor, temporary setbacks. In time all would recover well enough to hit the ice in Europe.

But the severest blow came a day later, on January 7, when doctors looked at the results of chest X-rays of the team's star goalie, Dick Ball. His chest plates indicated that Dick had a spot on his lungs, either an infection or potentially something worse. The questionable status of his lungs grounded Dick from travelling overseas. In the blink of an eye the Flyers lost their starting goaltender. Shocked, Sandy Watson immediately went into damage control. His team was due to catch a train to New York in just over twenty-four hours. There was no way he was going to allow everything he had pulled together over the past three and a half months to go up in flames. Ross King was a good backup goalie, but the Flyers needed a new starting goalie—and they needed him now!

ABOUT THREE HUNDRED MILES DOWN the road to the west, a young man by the name of Murray Dowey tucked himself into bed after a long day's work as a clerk and typist at the fledgling Toronto Transit Commission. As he put his head on the pillow that evening, Murray had never heard of the RCAF Flyers. He had no idea that earlier in December, the Flyers got whipped by the McGill Redmen and by the army hockey squad. And he had no idea that the next afternoon, the Flyers were heading off to Europe on a three-month road trip to play hockey for Canada.

At about 11:00 p.m. Murray and his wife were jolted out of a deep sleep by the hammering bell of the telephone on their night table. The man on the other end of the line introduced himself as Dr. Sandy Watson, manager of Canada's Olympic hockey team. Half asleep and stunned by this unknown late-night caller, Murray asked Dr. Watson, "What's this all about? Why are you calling me?" Sandy explained that Murray's Barker's Biscuits teammates George Mara and Wally Halder had said he was the best amateur goalie in the Toronto Mercantile League. As it turned out, the Flyers now needed him to join their ranks, if he was willing. Their existing goalkeeper had just failed his medical exam, and the team needed a new netminder to sign up for the air force and come to Switzerland to play in a series of games across Europe for a period of about ninety days. Oh, and they were leaving Ottawa for New York tomorrow afternoon in order to catch their boat to England.

Murray was honoured by the offer but gobsmacked by the audacity of the proposition. Although he was ecstatic about the concept of playing hockey for Canada, he couldn't see how he would be able to secure three months off work and be on a train the next day. In typical Sandy Watson fashion, the chief medical officer of the air force informed Murray, "No problem, leave it to me. I know Allan Lamport. He's the Toronto Transit commissioner. I'll call you back." Watson then called Lamport at home in the dead of night, got the green light for Murray's paid leave of absence from the TTC, and called him back at about 2:00 a.m. He told Murray to get to Downsview air base for 6:00 a.m. They were sending an RCAF plane to bring him to Ottawa. Watson reminded Dowey to pack for winter and for three months of travel. As for gear, Spalding had supplied the team with two sets of goalie equipment.

Without a wink of sleep, Murray scrambled to get it all together. When he got to Downsview Airport, the fog was so thick he could barely see in front of his face. All flights had been cancelled. In a panic Murray called Sandy and was told to get in a cab, get downtown to Union Station, and grab the first available train to Ottawa. Laden down with his bags and some of his own personal hockey gear, Murray blazed down to the heart of the city, slid onto a train, and slumped into his cabin chair with an exasperated sigh, only to realize he was on the milk run.

His train stopped at every tiny station between Toronto and Ottawa. Exhausted and bedraggled, Murray finally arrived at Sandy's office at RCAF headquarters on Elgin Street just after noon. He knocked on the door and shuffled into Sandy's office. There behind the desk was the man who had woken him up thirteen hours before and ordered him to make tracks with haste. Looking imposing in his RCAF uniform with the big stripes, Sandy looked

Murray up and down in both shock and surprise. "Who are you?" he barked. "Well, my name's Murray Dowey," replied Murray. "Murray Dowey! You look like that?" retorted a clearly disgruntled and perturbed Dr. Watson. Ragged and tired, Murray looked like something the cat had dragged in. Unimpressed, Watson couldn't fathom that the skinny, scraggly, pale-looking twenty-two-year-old was some kind of wizard in net.

But Frank Boucher and Sandy Watson had run out of time to find anyone else. Dowey was such a last-minute arrival that he missed the team's final practice session. Watson, Boucher, and the RCAF brass had to take a leap of faith. They wouldn't be able to judge what Murray was capable of between the posts until they got to Europe.

Over the span of a few lightning-fast hours, Murray was sworn in to the RCAF at the same aircraftman rank as young André Laperrière, kitted out in an air force uniform, and sent to the Canadian Pacific Railway sleeper train bound for New York. To get him into the official team photo, which had been taken a couple of days earlier, the pros at the RCAF photographic lab worked their magic by pasting Murray's head onto Dick Ball's body.

While chatting with Murray that afternoon, Watson discovered that Dowey's favourite sport wasn't even hockey—it was baseball. As a kid Murray had spent hours in the summer throwing and catching a ball against the wall behind his school in Toronto's Beaches neighbourhood. The end result: he had good hands and pretty quick reflexes. Murray started playing goalie because he wasn't a strong skater, and he figured being in net was something he could do. But baseball was his first love. He spent his summers pitching hardball for Tip Top Tailors in the Beaches fastball league. In the winter, he played hockey for Barker's Biscuits. Watson was riddled with concern that he had made a disastrous decision in selecting this skinny kid who loved baseball more than hockey. But it was too late to bring in someone else.

In the waning hours of daylight on Thursday, January 8, the team gathered at Ottawa's Union Station for a final send-off. After three months of headaches and being bashed in the media, it was finally time to get on with it. Although they had bolstered their ranks with some new talent, the Flyers were still considered low-flying hopefuls without much chance of a medal by many in the press. At best, some reporters placed them fourth; at worst, other writers posited that they would finish way down the pack. Internationally, Reuters reported that North American hockey domination was coming to an end. The Czechs were regarded as the gold medal favourites, with the Swedes pegged to capture silver. The Swiss were ranked as the team that would beat the Americans to grab the bronze. The Flyers were in the "also-ran" category with teams like Poland, Austria, Britain, and Italy. A local Ottawa sportswriter went so far as to suggest the RCAF Flyers were an embarrassment, and rather than champion the team upon their departure, he accused them of "folding their tents and sneaking away into the night."

But the RCAF and Chief of the Air Staff Wilf Curtis were not about to cater to negative opinions or let their team down. Curtis made sure the air force public relations machine whipped up a healthy contingent of military well-wishers and RCAF officials at the station to mount a rousing, boisterous, heartwarming send-off. Hundreds of family members and hockey fans crowded into the station, which was also packed with journalists. The same RCAF Central Band that had belted out tunes at Olympic Night a month earlier was there in full splendour. This time the musicians proudly blasted out "Royal Air Force March Past." It was an in-your-face gesture to the naysayers that buoyed the players' spirits and put smiles on all their faces.

You could not have asked for a better send-off. All the players except civilians Wally Halder and George Mara were sporting their RCAF uniforms. Tears were flowing as wives and girlfriends kissed their sweethearts goodbye, much as they had just a few years earlier when their warriors set off for foreign battlefields. Thankfully this time guns and kit bags had been replaced with hockey sticks and equipment bags.

Buck Boucher was the last person to shake hands with the players before they boarded the train on the first leg of their journey to the Olympic hockey wars. He told reporters: "Judging by the way the team has improved lately and the confidence of the players as a whole we may surprise a lot of people in Canada. They aren't in top shape at present, but they'll come around." As photographers and newsreel cameramen snapped pictures of the boys, little fireball Red Gravelle wore a smile a yard wide and commented, "We don't know just what sort of opposition we'll meet at the Olympics, but we all feel we can give them plenty of trouble." A jubilant and confident Frank Boucher wasn't about to go out on a limb, but he wasn't going to back down either. Normally quiet and reserved, the coach predicted: "The boys will scrap and I believe we have a good chance of winning it all at St. Moritz. Any team that beats us will have to show both hockey class and plenty of fight, of that, I'm sure."

Although the boys were under an immense amount of pressure, they weren't about to show it. As the train pulled out of the station, belching thick clouds of smoke into the crisp, wintery skies, they could put all the negativity and stress behind them. It was now time to hone their skills, to come together as a team, and to play the game they had all developed a passion and a talent for as children.

No matter where they had come from, the men on the train barrelling towards New York had hockey infused into every fibre of their beings. These were men who grew up without the distractions of the Internet, cell phones, video games, Facebook, or Twitter accounts. As children of the Depression, these men spent countless hours on outdoor ponds and rinks, wearing makeshift pads and borrowed skates. They had soldiered through a litany of hardships and challenges time and time again and developed the ability to overcome almost any obstacle.

Latest addition Murray Dowey was no exception. Born in Toronto's Cabbagetown neighbourhood in January 1926, Murray was a sickly kid who seemed to catch anything and everything going around. Whether it was the measles or the mumps, the flu or a common cold, young Murray would get slammed by the illness and be forced to spend time at home in bed recuperating. On average little Murray went to school just two or three days a week. He was plagued by asthma, food allergies, and a host of airborne allergies, such as hay fever and ragweed. It seemed as if Murray's lungs were somewhat challenged as he would easily get short-winded and had a history of bronchitis. As a result of his compromised constitution, young Murray was never a good eater and he developed into a slender boy with a light, lean, scrawny physique.

Murray's mom was always there at home to care for her little trooper, who was an only child. The doctor's house calls were a regular ritual at the Dowey household. On one such occasion Murray overheard the doctor telling his mother, "He'll never be able to run. He'll never be able to play any sports at all. Just be satisfied you got him, and love him the way he is." The doctor even went so far as to suggest that Murray's weak system would fare better if the Doweys could move to warmer, drier climes, like perhaps Arizona. But in the dark days of the Depression, on a postman's salary, there was no way the family could afford such a leap. Instead they made their way down to the city's Beaches area. It wasn't the toasty, arid desert of Arizona, but it was home at a time when many families were struggling just to get by.

Murray never let any of the wheezing, the coughing, or the shortness of breath stop him. He didn't care that he was skinnier than the other kids. It was all just part of who he was. Despite the doctor's warning, he knew he wasn't some sort of fragile ornament that was going to break.

Fortunately for Murray his teachers at Bulmer Road School were outgoing and athletic and encouraged all their students to play all kinds of sports, especially hockey and baseball. Every morning before school they would remove their dress shoes, put on running shoes, and fire up the kids to get outside and play. With Fairmount Park right next door to the school, there were plenty of opportunities for the kids to be active. In summer they played baseball and tennis, and in winter they watered down the park, creating an outdoor rink for those who were fortunate enough to have skates.

Playing road hockey in Toronto's east end was a near daily source of entertainment for young Murray. Too small for skates, little Murray and his buddies could always find some discarded newspapers to tie around their legs and use as goal pads. Magazines made for better protection, but they were more expensive and harder to come by, and you could always find a newspaper. Murray wrapped those papers around the bottom part of his legs with string, grabbed a few sticks and a ball, and played on the street with his friends until darkness fell and he was called in by his mom. When cars approached, the boys would hop up onto the sidewalk and then carry on after the cars drove by. Nobody bothered them, and that was their entertainment day after day for hours and hours.

Murray's first hockey sweater was an iconic red, white, and blue Montreal Canadiens jersey. When he was around seven or eight, he got his first pair of hand-me-down skates. He tried to be a forward, but his friends were a lot better at racing up and down the ice than he was. Murray just didn't have the wheels to skate as fast as the other boys. One day, as he watched another fellow playing net, he noticed that the other kids all scored pretty easily on him. Murray figured he could play goal just as well as that other guy. He boldly strode over to the coach and asked if he could try his hand in net. To his surprise, the coach said, "OK, we'll get the pads on you." Simple as that, Murray became a goal-tender. In net he found his niche and relished the pads, gloves, and heavy stick; he even enjoyed freezing his face off while guys fired pucks at him all afternoon.

It was his love of baseball that transformed Murray into a superstar in net. The move down to the Beaches neighbourhood exposed him to top-tier fastball and softball leagues, and Murray took a shine to playing ball. As soon as winter let go of its grasp on Toronto and spring rolled around, Murray began a new daily ritual. Every day he got a rubber ball, went over to the schoolyard, and threw the ball against the wall. He picked it up and threw it back against the wall. He did that by the hour, all day long, especially on Saturdays. After three or four hours he would grab a bite at home and get right back at it. The relentless hours playing solo wall ball helped Murray develop a strong glove hand and a rifle for his throwing arm. On the field playing organized fastball and softball, he excelled as a pitcher and played pretty much every infield position except catcher. Over time it was only natural that Murray would find a way to translate his baseball prowess into his hockey world as a goalie.

If a puck was rocketing towards Murray's head, his inclination was to try to catch it. Problem was, back then the goalkeeper's glove was basically just a finger glove with a flimsy pad, which made it virtually impossible and quite painful to attempt to grab the puck. Frustrated by the inadequacy of his gear, eleven-year-old Murray and his buddies got a first baseman's mitt, put some felt and cloth around it, and fashioned a crude goalie glove. Now when the puck was shot at Murray, he could catch it rather than try to stop it with his body, pads, or skates. Little Murray Dowey, the asthmatic kid who doctors had written off as a delicate flower, was one of the first to develop and master the trapper glove.

When Murray started playing for his middle school team, their big weekly outing was to pile into a few parents' cars and head out of town to practise in Markham. It was the treat of all treats. An old farmer had a giant barn with a beautiful pot-bellied stove that roared away in the corner. All winter the farmer hosed down the dirt floor of the barn, opened the massive barn doors and windows, and let the cold air blow through the rugged wooden structure. It created a perfect sheet of smooth, glassy ice that was protected from the elements yet infused with the sweet smell of crisp country air. For the princely sum of two dollars, the boys got to practise for hours in the farmer's rural ice palace, protected from the stinging winds and driving sleet and snow. Playing in the barn was like nirvana.

For a skinny little guy, Dowey had surprisingly fast reflexes. His legs and pad work were pretty decent, and his blocker and stick work were solid, but his catching hand was his secret weapon. Murray figured that as long as he could see a puck coming at him he could stop it. The thing that would irritate him the most was when his teammates were warming up and tried to rifle pucks at his head for fun. The head shots made things a little dicey when you had no mask. Despite the flimsy equipment, none of the injuries he got growing up were too serious. One time he took a puck off the head at a practice. Fortunately the coach of the team was a barber. He shaved the part of Murray's skull where he was cut so he could get a few stitches, and that was it. Now and again he got some cuts on his face and a broken nose, but for the most part Murray's time in net was relatively pain-free.

That is, until one day when he was fifteen and playing a game of shinny at Fairmount Park. There was a scramble in front of the net. A player let a stick go, and it hit Murray in his left eye. It pretty much closed right up. After that Murray never had great sight out of that eye. Eventually the left eye essentially gave up on him, and he went partially blind in it. Thing is, Murray never made that knowledge available to any of his friends, coaches, or employers. He didn't want his vision issues to affect the way people treated him in hockey or in the war.

Like Patsy Guzzo, Murray Dowey was a double threat on the ice and the baseball field. He may have been a little skinny, somewhat short-winded, and partially blind, but he could catch anything that flew. He was also one helluva great pitcher who had a rubber arm, pitched no-hitter games in both fastball and softball, and won three Bulova watches in the top fastball league in the country while pitching against American teams at the Canadian National Exhibition in Toronto.

* * *

EARLY DAYS FOR DEFENCEMAN FRANK DUNSTER, aka the Blue Line Masher, were equally riddled with challenges and obstacles. The fourth of seven children, Frank was born on March 24, 1921, in a tiny shack of a wooden house in Richmond, Ontario, on the outskirts of Ottawa. Frank's father was a farmer with a small patch of land and a lot of mouths to feed. He did his best to provide for the Dunster clan, but it seemed hardship pursued the family with a vengeance. When Frank was just a boy, one of his older brothers contracted tuberculosis and died. Living in the cramped quarters of the meagre farmhouse, one of his sisters also succumbed to the disease not long after.

In a desperate attempt to save the family, Frank's parents upped stakes and moved the remaining Dunster kids to Ottawa. Thankfully things started looking up when Frank's dad secured a job as a special constable with the RCMP. With a houseful of kids on a special constable's salary, there weren't a lot of new toys or fancy pieces of sports equipment kicking around. But playing sports and being active was part and parcel of growing up in the Dunster household. Frank gravitated towards the physical games of football and hockey, and quickly displayed a natural aptitude for both. But it was hockey that ignited a fire deep within him.

An outdoor rink just down the street from their house in the Glebe area became Frank's second home. He hit the ice with a fervour, using borrowed and hand-me-down equipment, and rapidly packed on the muscle and developed into a top-notch player. His physical strength and rough play encouraged the older kids to invite Frank to play with them. Unfortunately his time on the ice with the big kids didn't last long. In his early teens Frank was struck down by tuberculosis. It seemed the disease was doing its best to wipe out the entire Dunster family. For the better part of an entire year Frank was bedridden and engaged in a heated battle with the deadly disease. Racked with wicked chest pains, swollen glands, feverish chills, a hacking cough, and blood in his spit, Frank waged war with the vicious child killer as it ate away at his once strong and impressive frame. Whether it was the hand of God, a twist of fate, or Frank's iron will, somehow the disease did not win. Frank persevered and fought it off. He then immediately set his mind to rebuilding his body, getting back on the ice, and resuming his studies.

Smart as he was strong, Frank caught up quickly. He was quite gifted at school and did exceptionally well at mathematics. As for his physical rebirth, Frank launched himself back into hockey and earned a starting spot on his high school team, the Ottawa St. Pat's of the Ontario Junior Hockey League. At seventeen Frank helped lead the St. Pat's to the Canadian junior championship. The following year Frank made the jump to Junior A hockey and won the Memorial Cup while playing with the Oshawa Generals. Scouts and reporters in Oshawa took notice of Dunster's aggressive style of play, deft puckhandling skills, menacing hip checks, and tenacity at guarding the blue line. Frank was an intimidating force who played hard and possessed the skills to make it all the way to the big leagues.

When war hit, Frank put the brakes on his dreams of a hockey career in the NHL. Like so many of the young men of his generation, he felt a burning desire to do his part and sign up. For Frank this meant a war fought in the air. But he wasn't about to totally abandon the game he loved. He packed his beloved skates with him when he went overseas just in case he got a chance to grab a game of shinny, or perhaps even lace up with an air force team on one of the bases in Europe.

SEVENTEEN MEN MADE UP THE FINAL roster rocketing towards New York and then on to Europe. Only eight of them were from the original squad that got creamed in front of all those eyeballs on Olympic Night. Although the final seventeen had yet to play a game together, all the men now lacing up for the RCAF Flyers were guys who had learned to never give up—whether at home, on the ice, or in the air. They were all talented hockey players imbued with a passion for the sport who were accustomed to staring danger in the face, forming tight bonds, and doing their best when called on.

Maybe it wasn't so crazy for Sandy Watson and Frank Boucher to believe they could create a winning team out of this disparate group of guys in record time. Maybe it wasn't that far-fetched for them to be cautiously optimistic they now had the right combination of ingredients for success. If Sandy and Frank could build on the shared experiences and many commonalities of the boys speeding along on the train, perhaps they could get them to play as a cohesive, organic unit. Hopefully, as they did during the war, they could all take on the world and come back as champions.

Ready for action and sporting their practice jerseys.

PART TWO
Canada's Mystery Team

On the deck of the Queen Elizabeth. *Front row (left to right): Frank Dunster, Murray Dowey, Hubert Brooks, George McFaul, Orval Gravelle, Louis Lecompte.*
Middle row (left to right): Pete Leichnitz, Ab Renaud, Ted Hibberd, Patsy Guzzo, Irving Taylor, Frank Boucher, Roy Forbes. Back row (left to right): Wally Halder, Andy Gilpin, Dr. Sandy Watson, Reg Schroeter, Ross King, André Laperrière, George Mara.

EUROPE BOUND

06

Somewhere between Ottawa and Montreal, Patsy Guzzo sidled up beside newcomer Murray Dowey as the Canadian Pacific Railway sleeper train sped towards the Big Apple. Blustery winter temperatures frosted their windows with a sheen of ice as four inches of freshly fallen snow created banks alongside the train tracks. It was late in the evening on January 8, 1948. In just three weeks the opening ceremonies of the Winter Olympics were to commence and the boys were to play their first game against the number-two ranked Swedes.

Patsy was one of the first men to win over the coaching staff and earn a spot on the RCAF Flyers. Murray was the last. Although separated in age by more than a decade, Murray and Patsy found they had a few things in common. Both were married, both saw their military experience curtailed by health issues, and yet both of them were supreme athletes in hockey and in baseball. In fact, over the years they had squared off against each other more than a few times at various fastball tournaments when Murray pitched for Toronto's Tip Top Tailors team and Patsy pitched for the Ottawa clan. Murray was still getting the lay of the land and figuring out who the other folks on the Flyers were. He knew George Mara and Wally Halder, but the other guys were a total mystery to him.

As they careened through the countryside in the darkness of night, Patsy suppressed the inner fears that were bubbling to the surface. Just days earlier, his wife had suffered a miscarriage, and he was worried about leaving her at home alone with an infant daughter for three months. He had almost quit the team so he could stay back to help, but his mother-in-law insisted he go. She could manage the family just fine in his absence. A friend who drove Patsy to the station gave him a diary to take over to Europe in hopes that writing down his thoughts would ease his mind and help him feel more connected to home. Murray, on the other hand, had no problems leaving Toronto in the rear-view mirror, and he was brimming with elation to be along for the ride. He had never been to New York, he had never been on an ocean liner, and he was ecstatic to be heading overseas to see the world. For Murray, this was the beginning of the adventure of a lifetime.

When the train pulled into New York City at 8:00 a.m. on January 9, the boys had a few hours to enjoy the sights of the city before they had to board the *Queen Elizabeth* for a six-day

Atlantic crossing to Southampton, England. They grabbed breakfast at Churchill's restaurant across the street from Grand Central Station and hit the town to take in a Rockettes show at Radio City Music Hall. Next Sandy, the consummate scrounger, secured the boys a free lunch at NBC, where they tackled some public relations duties with a live radio broadcast before they saddled up in preparation for a suppertime departure on the high seas.

As the late-afternoon sun began its descent in the sky, the boys hauled their bags aboard the massive ship. Young André Laperrière and neophyte traveller Murray Dowey were in awe of the sheer size of the monstrous vessel. The RMS *Queen Elizabeth* was the world's largest passenger liner. With a gross tonnage of more than 83,000 ton she was akin to a floating city. Over 1,000 feet long and 230 feet high, she could carry more than twenty-two hundred passengers at a blistering speed of twenty-eight knots. Purpose-built by Cunard Steamship Lines to serve the needs of both well-heeled and budget travellers, she was pulled into service for troop transport during the war. She ferried close to a million troops safely back and forth during her time as a war horse, packed to the rafters with boys itching to join the fight. Her speed allowed her to outrun and outmaneuver German U-boats prowling the shipping lanes between the old world and the new.

Ocean voyages were familiar territory for most of the Flyers. Hubert Brooks and Frank Dunster had been crammed in like sardines swinging from hammocks with thousands of other warriors on their last sailings across the Atlantic. George Mara and Wally Halder were seasoned navy men. And as veteran bomb aimer Roy

Forbes made his way up the gangplank, he quipped to reporters, "This is a bit different from last time I was on the Lizzy—I was lugging a kit bag then."

With the New York skyline for a backdrop, the boys assembled on deck in full uniform for a series of team photos for North American newspapers and newsreel cameramen. Then it was time to wave goodbye to the Statue of Liberty. They weren't going to see her again until April, when they sailed back into New York City. They still had virtually no idea what they were up against. They knew the Americans had handily beaten McGill in an exhibition game, and they knew the Czechs, Swedes, and Swiss were very strong teams that had already played together for months, if not years, and were stacked with talented, skilled players. Aside from that, they were pretty much in the dark.

Accommodations for the Flyers on the *Queen Elizabeth* were far from luxurious. Strapped for cash, they travelled steerage class, as far belowdecks as you could go. They slept two to a room in bunk beds just up from the massive boilers and mechanics that kept the floating iron behemoth plowing ahead through rough seas. Forbes joked to the new guys to be careful where they put their feet. They were down so low, one misstep might send them through the bottom of the boat.

The American team was also on board, but unlike the boys sporting the air force woollen blues, they were travelling in first class. The Americans haughtily paraded around the upper decks wearing smart grey flannels, snazzy blazers with distinct U.S. Olympic crests, and fur-lined coats. While the Flyers were rocking away in steerage belowdecks, up in first class the Americans hobnobbed with movie celebrities like Burgess Meredith and his new wife, Paulette Goddard, as well as former Olympian and on-screen "Tarzan" Johnny Weissmuller. The American boys also dined and mingled with titans of industry and the wealthy elite, like car magnate Henry Ford.

Although the Flyers had to sleep belowdecks, they weren't relegated to staying down there for the entire voyage. But it seemed like whenever they stuck their heads up for a breath of fresh air, they invariably crossed paths with the cocky American players. The negative press from the Flyers' shellacking in the McGill and army games the previous month had preceded them. This provided plenty of fodder for the Americans to have a go at them. The Yanks leapt at every opportunity to mock and taunt the Canadians, insisting that the U.S. team was going to wipe them off the map. Many of the American players went so far as to challenge guys like Brooks, Forbes, Dowey, and Halder to a bet, promising to pay up if they didn't whitewash the Flyers by at least ten goals.

But the Canuck boys weren't about to take the bait. In fact, they couldn't have cared less about all the grandstanding and chose not to engage with the Americans. Brooks, Halder, Dowey, and the gang figured, *Let them shoot their mouths off. We'll do our talking when we meet them on the ice in St. Moritz!* If anything, the taunts and jeers from the American squad, much like the negative press from the newspapers at home, only fuelled their desire to silence the critics and prove everyone wrong. The men made the best of it and took advantage of the week-long crossing to recover from injuries, bond as a team, and enjoy some of the luxuries of peace-time travel on a ship like the *Queen Elizabeth*. They snuck into movie screenings in first class, enjoyed hot, well-cooked meals, attended mass in the lush first-class lounge, and settled into the daily ritual of ship life.

Those who weren't nursing injuries exercised lightly and did laps around the upper deck several times a day. Murray Dowey, Patsy Guzzo, and André Laperrière bundled up in their RCAF flying jackets and stood with arms open wide against the railings on the upper deck while the wind pelted their faces. This high up, with the ship cutting through the waves and nothing but open water as far as the eye could see, they almost felt as if they were flying. "We were living like kings and we didn't realize how lucky we were," recalled Dowey.

When the rolling seas weren't too bad the guys played shuf-fleboard or deck tennis and grabbed their sticks for a bit of deck hockey. Inside, they marvelled at the facilities their floating, over-sized hotel had on offer. The ship was equipped with running water and elevators. One of the prized features, especially at night or when the weather was bad, was a smoke room that doubled as a bar. Many of the Flyers took a shine to a parlour game the staff of the *Queen Elizabeth* hosted every day before dinner. Wooden horses with wooden jockeys on a stand that measured about two and a half feet high were placed at one end of a long carpet marked off with about thirty lines. Spectators downing drinks and sucking on cigars or cigarettes then chose their horses and placed their bets: one shilling, or twenty cents, a ticket. A young lady then placed a dice in a cup and gave it a roll. An officer of the ship read out the numbers, and two other young women moved the horses along the carpet. Some of the guys burned their two-pound daily allowance betting on the horses. Others took advantage of the fifteen-cent rum drinks and enjoyed themselves a little too much in the bar room on the upper deck, which the boys had dubbed "the Snake Pit."

In many ways a number of players seemed to be treating their time on the *Queen Elizabeth* like more of a holiday than preparation for an Olympic mission. Roy Forbes and a few of the guys were invited to party up top by high rollers Paulette Goddard, Burgess Meredith, and Johnny Weissmueller. They had a lot of fun drinking and dancing with the movie stars up in the Snake Pit and the smoke room. Various groupings of guys played impromptu games of rummy and poker, drank beer, strolled the decks, played bingo, watched movies or live concerts, and bet on the wooden horses. When the weather permitted they ventured out onto the deck to take in the heavy smell of the sea and marvel at the vastness of the ocean.

Roommates Sandy Watson and Frank Boucher were glad to see the new guys blending in with the old, but the drinking and gambling of some of the boys was going too far. By Wednesday, January 14, the men had travelled close to two thousand miles. The next day they would be approaching Cornwall, England, and the time for fun and frivolity was over. Sandy and Frank had given the boys a long leash to let loose and get to know each other, but now it was time to hunker down. Sandy appointed war hero Hubert Brooks to rally the men to a meeting in the ship's gymnasium and play the heavy as his aide-de-camp. There Sandy issued a stark warning: "The first one that drinks beer or liquor or engages in any gambling from the time we land until the Games are over is being sent back on the next boat." He went on to berate the boys and told them how disgusted he was with some of their behaviour. Frank Boucher didn't add a word but stood stone-faced beside Sandy. His silence spoke volumes, and his disappointment was plain for all to see. Clearly the two of them were dead serious.

The dressing-down didn't stop there. Sandy chastised the players for becoming swell-headed. He continued: "When photographers and newspapermen make a fuss over you, it isn't because of your individual talents; none of you is that good. It's because you are a member of the Canadian Olympic Team." The message was loud and clear. You are here for one reason—because we have picked you to play hockey for Canada. Toe the line from now on, or you're gone.

Not wanting the guys to lose focus, Sandy impressed the "big-ness" of the Olympic Games on his charges. "This is one of the greatest opportunities a hockey player could ever expect. There is a lot to gain, materially and otherwise. Win the Olympics, and our names will be remembered for generations." With that he outlined their itinerary for the week of exhibition matches to be played against excellent squads in Britain and France. The next day they would be docking in Southampton. There was no more time for messing around, and no more time for games. He wanted them to get their things together, get their heads on straight, and get down to business.

* * *

IN THE EARLY MORNING HOURS OF Thursday, January 15, local tugs belched out thick clouds of smoke as they pulled and pushed the massive *Queen Elizabeth* into her berth at the docks in Southampton, England. A few hours later, with a hearty breakfast in their bellies, the men disembarked and waded into a throng of fans cheering not for them but for the Hollywood celebrities and bigwigs coming out of first class.

While jockeying through customs and crowds to grab his luggage and get to their bus, Murray Dowey got the surprise of a lifetime when a sergeant major bellowed out to him, "You Murray Dowey?" Perplexed and somewhat uncertain as to why he was being singled out from among the other RCAF Flyers, Murray answered, "Yes, sir." The major pulled him aside, pointed over to a man standing amid the throng, and told him, "Your grandfather is here waiting to see you." Shocked and filled with elation, Murray enjoyed a few fleeting minutes with his grandfather. The last time Murray's granddad had seen him he was just a baby. Murray's grandfather had built homes in Canada during the Depression, but he left and returned to live on a farm in England not long after Murray was born. Murray's mom had somehow alerted his granddad about Murray's last-minute trip, and his granddad busted out all the stops to get to Southampton for a chance to once again hug the little grandson he had not set eyes on for decades.

The brief reunion was bittersweet for Murray. He longed to spend more time connecting with the grandfather he had just met, but he had to hop on the team bus, which was waiting to make tracks for London. Dowey recalls: "I remember the last words I said to him. I said, 'Grandpa, hopefully on the way back I'll be able to stop and have a few days with you.' But it never happened." Those few minutes on the dock in Southampton were the first and last time Murray ever got to see his granddad.

With their gear piled high in the back few rows of their bus, the boys headed for London, about eighty miles to the northeast. Bad luck once again beset the team when they were barely out of sight of the docks. About a mile into the journey a streetcar came barrelling through an intersection and slammed into the side of the Flyers' bus. The impact shattered the back windows and sent Patsy Guzzo and Wally Halder flying from their seats. Fortunately, the tram hit the back half of the bus, where their leather luggage cases and hockey kit bags were stacked floor to ceiling. A few more feet towards the middle, and the impact would have surely injured some of the players. As it was, Sandy Watson, Hubert Brooks, and many of the boys were picking glass fragments out of their hair and luggage for the next couple of hours. But no one was hurt.

After a brief encounter with the bobbies who surveyed the damage, they were back on their way with chuckles and shaking heads. It was a glorious welcome to Mother England.

More sobering than the crash, however, were the street scenes that welcomed the players. Two years after the war, stark evidence of the devastation wrought by German bombs was present in all directions. The bus passed bombed-out streets, destroyed cathedrals, and countless buildings wrapped in scaffolding as armies of men attempted to rebuild the shattered English infrastructure. Sandy had warned the men what to expect regarding meals and lodging overseas. London in January 1948 presented much bleaker offerings than the creature comforts enjoyed by the men back home in Canada. Here the effects of the war were still exerting a heavy toll in the areas hard hit by the turmoil; the men could expect power outages, shortages of food, and grim accommodations. For men like André Laperrière, Patsy Guzzo, and Murray Dowey, it was a shock to witness first-hand the aftermath of post-war England. But for others, like warriors Roy Forbes, Frank Dunster, and Hubert Brooks, this was familiar terrain that stirred up memories of hard-fought times.

Hubert Brooks during flight training.

INTO THE FIRE

07

Nearly seven years before Hubert Brooks made the trip to England as an Olympic hockey player, he had arrived in the port of Southampton to start his overseas military service. On September 29, 1941, he and his RCAF brethren spent their first night billeted at the Metropole Hotel in the centre of Bournemouth, just down the road from Southampton. There was no service or hotel staff at the Metropole. Instead, the young men coming over and readying for operational training units were greeted by damp, chilly rooms with communal toilets and crumbling plaster walls. Breakfast for the new RCAF recruits consisted of sad powdered eggs marooned on a slice of rock-hard toast, complemented with a tiny piece of grease-soaked Spam. Over the next few weeks

Brooks and his classmates were put through a battery of tests, training exercises, and medical checks. They took in aircraft recognition lectures, practised shooting skills, and were equipped with their battle dress and flying gear, which consisted of silk- and fleece-lined boots, chamois leather gloves, helmets, goggles, and new flying suits. From here it was on to the operational training unit as part of Bomber Command, and the young man who grew up on a homestead in Bluesky, Alberta, was one step closer to action in the air.

Brooks joined the 19th Operational Training Unit, whose motto was "Strike hard. Strike sure." Everything at the OTU was geared towards perfecting the trainees' individual skills while slamming home the crucial importance of working together as a team. Hubert and his air observer classmates performed countless navigation exercises, circuits and landings, single-engine flying, and practice bombing runs. They graduated from Anson aircraft to Whitley aircraft on their trajectory to the skies in the bigger Wellington and Halifax bombers.

Month after month was spent perfecting the art of high-level bombing. This required intense coordination between navigator/bomb aimer and pilot in order to successfully hit a fifty-foot target from an aircraft travelling at speeds in excess of two hundred feet per second. By the time Brooks had finished his training and joined the 419 Moose Squadron, he had accumulated 200 hours of daytime flying and 110 hours of nighttime flying. As a member of the 419, he became ensconced in a brotherhood of Canadian men who had developed a strong fighting spirit and an intense sense of comradeship. On April 5, 1942, it was time to put his training to use. His first mission was an attack on Le Havre. The four-and-a-half-hour round-trip flight went off without a hitch. Brooks and his crew dropped fourteen 250-pound bombs on their target and made it safely home to their base at Mildenhall in County Suffolk.

Just three nights later Brooks and his crewmates would take part in the biggest, most ambitious night raid of the war to date. Five hundred Allied aircraft were going to target Hitler's industrial centre at Hamburg in a concerted effort to bomb the mighty German war machine to bits. Unfortunately, things were about to go a lot less smoothly in Hubert's second mission.

In the waning light of April 8, Hubert Brooks and his crewmates readied for takeoff in a Wimpy Wellington aircraft that they had named *N for Nuts*. They were in the number-two position in the squadron, but just as they were about to go full throttle down the tarmac, skipper Art Crighton spotted a problem with one of his flight instruments. Their plane was pulled out of the stream for a last-minute fix. The panel got sorted and they eventually roared down the runway in thirteenth position at 22:00 hours. As they took to the night sky in "lucky" slot thirteen, superstition and feelings of uncertainty seeped into even the boldest of the crew. Lucky number thirteen—for Brooks this smelled of only one thing . . . disaster.

As he lay in the nose of *N for Nuts*, he readied his bomb sights and kept his eyes fixed on the approaching target of Hamburg's industrial complex. All around him German flak batteries lit up the night sky in a parade of exploding shells and massive blinding searchlights. On approach to the target the front gunner called out over the intercom, "Starboard engine's on fire!" Seconds later Brooks jettisoned the bomb load and gave skipper Art Crighton a course for home. But the boys were not having a good night. The automatic extinguishers were unable to tame the flames consuming the starboard engine. To make matters worse, mere moments later, the port engine also burst into flames. Initially the crew in the stricken bomber had hoped they could limp to the North Sea and make it to the safety of the Frisian Islands. But their plane was in major trouble. She was engulfed in fire and plummeting towards the earth. At 1:18 a.m. Captain Crighton ordered Hubert and his crewmates to bail out.

In a flurry of well-practised and co-ordinated movements, Brooks attached his parachute harness and dove out of the Wellington's escape hatch into the frigid night sky. He pulled the rip cord and shot upwards at a hundred miles per hour with only one thought racing through his mind: *Let me land on the right side of the border. Let me land in Holland, not Germany.*

FORTUNATELY FOR BROOKS THERE WERE NO German Focke-Wulf night fighters prowling the skies and picking off Allied targets as they descended to the ground that evening. Nonethless, his parachute landing was far from graceful. When he smacked down in a farmer's field, Brooks hit hard and injured his left leg. A nanosecond later his parachute pack smashed into his head, and one of the buckles opened up a gash in his skull that started pouring out blood. Undeterred, he successfully tore his parachute into strips, buried it, and then limped in the darkness in a north-west direction towards the North Sea.

Hubert hobbled across fields and scrambled into unseen strands of barbed wire that slashed his face. With his knee screaming at him and his face covered in blood, Brooks approached a farm-house in the early light of the morning. He was hoping to be received by some friendly Dutch folks. But lady luck had waved goodbye to the twenty-year-old back in Mildenhall. When he knocked on the farmhouse door, Brooks was greeted by the steely glare of a German farmer. While the farmer's wife dressed his wounds and made him some breakfast, the farmer's daughter bee-tled off to alert the local police. Shortly thereafter she returned home with a German soldier escort. By 8:00 a.m. Hubert Brooks was a prisoner of war.

From the moment he surrendered in the farmhouse kitchen, Brooks was emboldened by a single thought: escape.

That afternoon Brooks was reunited with most of his crew-mates from *N for Nuts* at the German air force field and detention barracks on the outskirts of Oldenburg. Amazingly, his buddies had managed to make the jump from their stricken bomber. All but rear gunner Ernest Howard. Ernest almost made it, but his parachute got jammed in the rear escape hatch and he had ridden the flaming bomber down to his death. Brooks vowed that what-ever it took, he was going to make it home alive.

The survivors were carted off to DuLag Luft, an interroga-tion camp near Oberursel, a stopgap en route to the main POW camps. DuLag Luft was run by the Luftwaffe air operations staff and the Abwehr, or German intelligence. Its main purpose was to extract as much information as possible from aircrews by a variety of means. The boys were strip-searched and had all their belongings taken from them. In the eyes of their German captors they became nothing more than numbers and information. Hubert Brooks was bestowed with POW number 24803.

Chucked for days into a solitary cell dubbed "the cooler," Brooks was grilled by interrogators seeking all kinds of information. They wanted to know his home address, the type of aircraft he had flown in, the bomb load, his point of departure, the name of his squadron, and information about his base commander; their thirst for any clues or bits of Allied knowledge seemed insatiable. But Hubert was a tough customer. He would give them only his name, rank, and serial number.

Although his captors had managed to find the special fly buttons and collar studs issued by the air force, Brooks was able to squirrel away a key item from his escape kit: a tiny compass that was about the size of a dime. Just before he was strip-searched, he hid the compass in his mouth for use when the opportunity presented itself. After four days of mental gymnastics in solitary confinement at DuLag Luft, he was shipped to Lamsdorf prison camp, also known as Stalag VIII-B.

Stalag VIII-B was a massive camp located deep in the heart of the Nazi-dominated region known as Silesia. The area was a centre of coal mining, steel manufacturing, and heavy industry that was vital to the military production of the Third Reich. Tucked away in the outer reaches of Germany, near the borders of Czechoslovakia and Poland, it was about as far from the front and neutral countries that an Allied fighter could find himself.

Hubert's first impression of Stalag VIII-B was that it was enormous, covering many acres of land. The entire camp was encircled by two barbed-wire fences. The inner fence was about twelve feet high, and the outer fence was slightly higher. In between the fences the Germans had placed coils of razor-sharp barbed wire. They had also positioned a tripwire perimeter about a dozen feet from the fences. If you somehow made it past the tripwire, you would be shot by the guards who were positioned around the clock in twenty-foot towers equipped with searchlights and machine guns. There were also constant foot patrols and guard dogs to contend with.

On April 15, 1942, Brooks came to the stark realization that he was captive in a veritable fortress: a fortress reputed to be the largest stalag in the entire Third Reich. Many of its prisoners had been taken at battles in Dunkirk and Crete. The main camp housed seven thousand men in the army compounds. A separate air force section held a smaller contingent of five hundred captured airmen. Thirteen thousand additional captives were registered with the camp, but they were away on work parties scattered around the countryside in smaller labour camps known as Arbeitskommandos.

Hubert recognized almost immediately that escaping from the main compound with its searchlight towers, machine-gun nests, warning wires, patrols, and guard dogs would be near impossible. But if he could get himself on a work party, with a bit of patience and planning, he might have a chance of success.

The Arbeitskommandos were set up to house and take advantage of the lower-ranking POWs by using them as grunt labour. This freed up young, strong German men to join the fight. The labour camps were less guarded than the main camp and had POWs working under guard in coal mines, quarries, factories, lumberyards, and railroads. In order to get himself on a work party, Brooks had to somehow bust himself out of the air force and into the army, and he had to become a lower-ranking soldier. The solution was simple: he needed to find an army boy who was willing to swap identities.

As Brooks hunted for his doppelgänger, his family back in Montreal received the news, via telegram and official letters from the Air Ministry and Department of National War Services, that Hubert was alive and being held as a POW at Stalag VIII-B. When Montreal reporters pressed his sister, Doris, for a comment about her brother's capture she quipped, "Good luck to the Nazis. Hubert is too full of the devil for them to hold him." She was right.

Brooks looked around for a soldier who was roughly the same age, height, and size as him. Ideally the man willing to swap identities with Hubert would have the same hair and eye colour as well. One day while he worked his way through a crowd of prisoners watching a soccer match, Brooks discovered a Kiwi soldier who fit the bill and was willing to make the switch. Private Frederick Cole of the New Zealand Infantry had just come back to the main camp after a long stint at an Arbeitskommando. He was less than keen to go back out for more hard labour. He would happily play the role of Flight Sergeant Hubert Brooks and exchange the hard grind of a soldier for a bump up to officer status.

Switching identities was remarkably easy. A few days after meeting, both Cole and Brooks feigned illness and got shipped off to the camp hospital. Once inside the bustling hospital they dodged into a washroom, where Brooks promptly peeled off his air force blues and Cole removed his khaki Kiwi battledress. Five minutes later Hubert Brooks was marching back to the army compounds as a New Zealand private.

Brooks immediately set about planning his first escape. He knew he couldn't do it alone. Thankfully, the POW who put together the work parties was a British sergeant major, so Brooks was able to essentially pick his posting. He engineered his way onto a work party in the biggest, deepest coal mine in the village of Bobrek, not far from the pre-war Polish border. For two weeks he slugged coal from dawn until dusk in the depths of the coal shaft. Amid the dust and the dirt he met an Irish soldier named Private Cross, and the two devised a plan to escape from their barracks on the upcoming Saturday night.

In the days leading up to Saturday, June 6, Brooks smuggled a pair of pliers back from the mine in a coffee can. He and Cross also cobbled together some food provisions from their Red Cross parcels. Brooks still had his dime-sized compass, as well as a tiny Union Jack taken from the wrapper of a mustard tin that the two men could use to identify themselves to friendlies. The plan was straightforward: cut through the barbed-wire enclosures of their camp in the darkness of night and trek to

Krakow, where they would try to liaise with members of the Polish Underground. The sleeping quarters at Bobrek were surrounded by two barbed-wire fences with floodlights in all four corners. The windows of their huts were also covered in barbed wire, and there was one armed guard at the main gate and another guard patrolling the perimeter.

Brooks and Cross chose Saturday at midnight for their breakout. They figured the guards would be distracted by checking the night shift from the mines back into camp. Plus on Saturdays the guards tended to have a beer or two. As an added bonus a violent thunderstorm hammered the camp with pelting rain that evening, providing Brooks and Cross with additional cover. Just after 10:00 p.m. they deftly clipped the barbed wire over their windows and then cut through the wire of the first fence in a spot cloaked in shadow. Soaked to the bone, they jumped a second six-foot-high fence, ran down the embankment to the railway line, and slipped off into the darkness. There were no blaring sirens, no searchlights, no gunfire, and no guard dogs chomping at their heels. They made it!

By foot they snaked their way for miles and miles along roads and railway lines headed for Krakow. The two escapees bolted from cover only at night. For sustenance they rationed their food supplies to six biscuits with a little butter and cheese and a small piece of chocolate every twenty-four hours. During the day, they slept shrouded in the woods. After a week on the run they made it to the border of occupied Poland. So far their escape had been uneventful. But now, on the threshold of freedom, both men were on edge. As they crawled along a creek on the outskirts of the city,

Brooks and Cross stopped dead in their tracks. Small glowing lights straight ahead hinted at the presence of border patrols or search parties. Slinking slowly towards the glowing lights, the fugitives realized that what they thought were cigarettes were actually only fireflies.

The next morning a cold rain teemed down onto Krakow as the two men wandered through the streets of the city, cautiously trying to make contact with a member of the underground. By nightfall they had failed to find a contact, so they headed to the outskirts of the city, picked an isolated house, and decided to rap on the door and try their luck. The instant the door opened they were toast. Three men answered the door, two of them with swastikas on their lapels. Hubert turned on his best Montreal accent in a vain attempt to spin a story that he and his friend were French peasants forced to work at a labour camp who simply wanted in out of the rain. But the pro-Nazi Poles turned them over to the local Gestapo agents, who quickly discovered their POW dog tags. The jig was up.

The Nazi agents kicked, slapped, and beat the snot out of Brooks and Cross, probing them for information about how they had escaped and who they were trying to connect with in Krakow. The boys gave them nothing, and on June 25 Hubert got shipped back to Stalag VIII-B.

The second he hit the massive POW camp, Brooks was re-interrogated and thrown into solitary confinement for fourteen days as punishment for his escape attempt. Fortunately his masquerade as Private Fred Cole of the New Zealand Army was still intact. Brooks still had hope for a second chance at escape. Already weak and malnourished after weeks on the run, he was fed only bread and water for ten days. Then his jailors softened up and gave him a couple of tiny potatoes, a ladleful of bland soup, and a couple of thin slices of black bread. His time on the lam had given Brooks serious blisters that became infected. The infection spread to the lymph nodes in his groin, and he required surgery and hospitalization.

While he was recuperating in his hospital bed, Hubert met another escapee, Wing Commander Douglas Bader, the legless Royal Air Force ace fighter pilot. Although Bader had lost both legs in a flying accident in 1931, he went on to become one of the Royal Air Force's top aces in World War II. Bader never allowed his physical challenges to slow him down. Despite being captured after bailing out of his stricken fighter during a dogfight over German-occupied France in 1941, Bader had attempted numerous escapes. The two men shared stories and discussed the intricacies of plotting a successful jailbreak.

A few weeks later, with his fake identity still intact, Brooks started working on his next escape. This time he set his eyes in a new direction. He would escape south across the Czech border, with the ultimate goal of reaching the south of France. He hooked up with a British sergeant named Joseph Sidi, who knew the Mediterranean well and was also game to bust out of Stalag VIII-B. Brooks and Sidi got themselves posted to a railroad work party not far from the Czech border. There were sixty men in the work camp, and upon his arrival Brooks quickly learned that quite a few of them were also itching to get out. After only two days on the railroad, Brooks and Sidi came up with a plan for their escape. Again it would be a midnight departure on a Saturday. This time around, four other prisoners were in on the breakout. The men would split off in pairs once they hit the ground.

The guards must have gotten wind that an escape was imminent. Every night when the prisoners returned from the railroad to the two-storey building where they were billeted, the guards took their pants and shoes and locked them away in a bolted room. But Brooks and the others had already figured out a workaround. They scheduled a fake boxing match in the mess hall to distract their captors. On Saturday night, while other prisoners throttled each other and men hooted and hollered, Brooks, Sidi, and the other fugitives used stolen hacksaws to slice through the window bars of the precious trouser room. They left the bars in position so as not to alert the guards. Later that evening, after the guards had made their final rounds, Brooks and company snuck back in, gathered up their pants and shoes, and knotted together a series of blankets. Using the "rope" made of blankets, they shimmied down the side of the building to the ground floor and stole off in pairs. Once again Hubert slipped away from his German keepers in the dead of night undetected.

The plan was for Brooks and Sidi to hoof it across the mountains towards Brunn and then make tracks for Lunenburg, thirty miles to the south, where Hubert figured they could sneak onto a freight train bound for Milan. It was a perfect plan. But in Brunn they almost got caught while raiding apples in an orchard. The irate owner and his guard dog pounced on Brooks, but when he and Sidi produced their mustard-tin Union Jack the Czech farmer called off his dog, loaded the men up with apples, and wished them well on their journey. The next night, while they crossed a railway bridge near Lunenburg, a German guard fired shots at them, but Brooks and Sidi tore off into the brush and evaded capture. They made their way to the Lunenburg marshalling yards and found an open freight car loaded with huge lumps of coal and destined for Milan.

In the murky light of pre-dawn they carefully burrowed down into the coal, making sure not to disturb a white line that was painted over the top for inspectors. Buried in their tiny cavern of coal, Brooks and Sidi rode the rails for an entire day, all the way to the outskirts of Vienna. Finally it seemed Brooks was on his way to freedom.

When the train pulled into the railway yards early the next morning, however, fate delivered a punishing blow. Their car was uncoupled from the engine and shunted off to a siding. The fugitives had no idea how long it might be parked there. Could be hours or even days. Brooks and Sidi crawled out of their coal cave and hid in the forest with plans to return at night. Hours later when they snuck back into the rail yard they couldn't find their coal train. After a half hour of searching they figured the next best bet was a lumber car they discovered that was bound for Trieste. They squeezed themselves in among the giant pieces of cut wood and settled in for the long ride to Italy. Just after midnight the train started moving, but their luck had run out. Before leaving the yard, the cars were shunted to an inspection platform that was lit up in a blaze of spotlights. Brooks and Sidi were yanked from their burrow by Austrian workers and railway police and handed over to a detachment of SS troops. The Germans were not pleased, and they didn't mess around.

In no time the two escapees found themselves face-deep in the mud at the bottom of a Straflager punishment cell on the grounds of a French POW camp outside Vienna. The cell was essentially a dugout with a barred door. After thirty hours there they received their first dribs of rations. Determined to escape, Brooks and Sidi spent the next four nights in the freezing muck of the Straflager, carefully working loose one of the bars. But while they were working on the second bar, they got caught red-handed. The German officer in charge exploded in rage. He told them, "Attempting to escape . . . this will be a lesson to both of you." For the next fifteen minutes the guards pummelled Brooks and Sidi with their rifle butts. When the guards tired of using their rifles, they kicked and punched the two escapees repeatedly. To Brooks it felt as if the beating lasted for hours. As he and Sidi lay wounded in the Straflager, extra guards were posted to watch them. With their dreams of a quick escape squashed, the two were shipped back to Stalag VIII-B within the week.

Upon his arrival at Lamsdorf, Brooks was once again thrown into solitary confinement for fourteen days and given a diet of just bread and water. His captors told him that if he tried another escape he'd be shot on sight. But Brooks wasn't rattled by the threats.

A few weeks after being released from solitary he met up with a red-headed Scotsman named Sergeant John Duncan of the 51st Gordon Highland Division. Like Brooks, Duncan was burning to get out and was bestowed with a fighting spirit. He was also a seasoned soldier who had made three attempted prison escapes, including one where he successfully spent fifteen months on the lam in France. Duncan had been caught and sent back to Stalag VIII-B only because a jealous lady friend squealed to the Nazis when she spotted him showing an interest in another woman.

Finally it seemed Brooks had found the perfect teammate. They devised a new bid for freedom. Both knew this was their last chance. If they got caught it was game over. They set their sights on Poland. Its hilly terrain and thick forests presented an ideal target for them to find asylum and seek out local help. On November 10, 1942, they got themselves posted to a small working camp of twenty prisoners at a sawmill in Tost, Silesia. Just a few days after their arrival, Brooks and Duncan got wind that there was a snitch among the POWs. But no one was going to spoil their plans. They quickly sniffed out the rat and confronted the man, who was working as the camp's interpreter. Getting him out of there was the only way for Brooks and Duncan to safely make a bid for freedom. He soon had "an accident" that required him to be shipped back to the hospital at Stalag VIII-B.

Although their snitch was now out of the way, the first snows of winter had already fallen. Brooks and Duncan decided to wait until spring to make their break. In the meantime Brooks worked his magic to gather as much information and as many materials as possible in preparation for their bolt for freedom.

He spent the entire winter as the helper on the mill's delivery truck, which dropped lumber pit props to all the mines in the area. Brooks and the German truck driver also made a few extra German marks by loading up their empty truck with coal and delivering it to local households around Tost. Hubert seized upon the opportunity to seek out friendly Poles and make contact. Every once in a while he put some dirt in the carburetor when the truck driver and the guard weren't looking. When the truck invariably broke down, Brooks volunteered to walk around and find Polish citizens to help get it going again. He used his ingenious series of truck "breakdowns" that winter to get his hands on two large maps of Europe as well as four maps of the Tost district and the entire region as far as Krakow. The icing on the cake was a friendly Pole who gave him the address of a Polish Underground contact in the city of Częstochowa.

By the time spring rolled around Brooks and Duncan were ready to mount their final escape. They had a stash of food supplies, maps, clothing, some rudimentary Polish language skills, a compass, and knowledge of the immediate terrain around their work camp. On Monday, May 10, 1943, Brooks and Duncan plunged their hacksaw blades into soap and cut through the window bars of their sleeping quarters. This time there was no raging thunderstorm or boisterous boxing match to mask their flight. Instead, a fellow POW sat on the steps and plucked his mandolin while a second man sang softly to the night sky. Just after midnight Brooks and Duncan vanished into the darkness.

Night after night they beat a path towards Częstochowa and stole a few hours of restless sleep while hiding in the woods during the day. About five days out they were shocked from their sleep by the rumbling wheels of a cart. As a farmer approached, Brooks and Duncan feared the worst. Maybe they were about to get shot; maybe they were about to get turned in. Whatever this man's intentions, there was zero doubt that he had spotted them and was coming straight at them. But sensing their tension the man called out, in broken German and Polish, "I am a good Pole. I saw you when I went to my fields early this morning and I said to myself, *Let them sleep*. Now I'm going into the village to fetch the schoolteacher and some food."

Just like that the pendulum had finally swung back in Brooks's favour. The generous farmer took them to his farmhouse, and two days later they were introduced to a pair of Polish smugglers who helped them sneak into German-occupied Poland, and from there on to Częstochowa and a meeting with the Polish Underground fighters.

It had been more than a year since Brooks and his crewmates bailed out of their stricken bomber. Instead of masquerading as a Kiwi soldier and attempting to escape from multiple prison camps, Hubert could have taken a correspondence course, learned to play piano, or studied Shakespeare in the officers' wing of the air force compound at Stalag VIII-B. But Brooks had joined up to fight. And so had John Duncan. Of the ten thousand British air force prisoners who were housed in permanent camps, fewer than thirty ever successfully escaped and made it back to Britain or neutral territory.

Getting back to their squadrons in England was virtually impossible. Their new friends in the Polish Underground presented them with three options. They could lie low, wait out the rest of the war, and depend on the generosity of a Polish family. They could join the civilian underground in the city. Or they could take to the hills and join the Polish partisans fighting with the Armia Krajowa, or AK. As far as Brooks and Duncan were concerned, the choice was obvious. A life as a guerilla fighter waging warfare against the occupying German army was their ticket back into the action. They chose to join the AK and fight in the hills.

Polish resistance fighters in stolen German uniforms.

FREEDOM FIGHTERS

08

June 1943. Before taking to the forests of the Carpathian Mountains, Hubert Brooks and John Duncan had to first develop a much better command of the Polish language. For the next three months they found themselves squirrelled away in the attic of a home occupied by a couple of Polish women. Their tutors were a duo of spry octogenarian sisters who had taught in Paris years earlier.

Day after day in the sweltering summer heat of the attic, the sisters brought them their meals and ran them through a series of language exercises using an old chalkboard. All summer long Brooks and Duncan had to stick to the confines of the attic and stay out of sight because a family of Nazi collaborators lived right next door. Although cooped up by day, every evening the fugitives slipped out into the garden to fill their lungs with fresh air and stretch their legs. But despite their confinement, Brooks and Duncan could never forget who and what they were preparing to fight. Every day, as the brave elderly ladies declined Polish verbs for them, they could hear the deadly chatter of machine guns ringing out during execution hour at a nearby Jewish concentration camp.

By August 1943 the two pupils were ready to join a unit of the Armia Krajowa in the vast mountainous forests of southern Poland. Brooks and Duncan criss-crossed their way from underground hideout to underground hideout. Finally, in October they made their way out to the foothills of the Carpathian Mountains. There, freedom fighters from the forest partisan unit took them to their new home, the Wilk, or Wolf, base camp. Snow already covered the peaks of the Carpathians, and the grasses of the mountain glades were crusted in evening frost.

Most of the forty Armia Krajowa fighters were busy eating supper when Brooks and Duncan walked into the Wilk camp. The two ravenous POWs nearly passed out from glee when they saw the massive portions of food on offer. Their plates were loaded with at least two pounds of beef stew. After a year in captivity on a steady diet of water, black bread, and meagre German rations, this was an incredible feast. An elated and appreciative Brooks exclaimed, "We can live like this for ever and ever!" His new partisan friends laughed and replied, "You'll be tired of meat before long."

The men of the Wilk forest unit that Brooks and Duncan had joined were a motley crew of amateur soldiers. Most wore civilian clothes, but some wore parts of uniforms. The youngest of the men in camp was still a teenager at seventeen. The oldest was the same age as Brooks's pal John Duncan, thirty-eight. The partisan fighters came from all walks of life. Some were university graduates; others were hardy farm stock and Goral mountain men from the nearby valleys. There were also some real soldiers among the group, as well as civilians who had fled the cities to join the fight in the mountains. All the men in the AK had one thing in common: each and every one of them was filled with a burning desire to repay the oppressive German forces for all the cruelty they had inflicted upon the helpless, innocent citizens of Poland.

The forest lair of the Wilk camp was carved into the Kudlon mountainside, in a densely forested area beside a deep ravine. A mountain stream just below camp provided fresh water. Wooden walls covered in thick turf were erected inside the dugout, and an iron stove sat on a large stone in one corner of the handmade cavern. Bunk beds were lined up along the dirt walls, and there were two small ventilation openings under the roof and door of the primitive hut. Thanks to the stove and the body heat of the forty men, it was toasty warm inside. From the outside the dugout blended in perfectly with its surroundings, making it virtually invisible to the untrained eye. Provisions were stored in another dugout nearby. Potatoes were buried to prevent rot, and meat was either salted to improve preservation or hung in the trees once the weather became cold enough.

The Wilk hideout high in the hills of the Gorge region was an excellent location to consolidate the resistance movement.

The Polish partisan unit Wilk *("Wolf") in Podhale, Poland.*

The region's steep overgrown slopes, wild backwoods, and deep ravines provided the perfect conditions to create dugout operating bases. From these concealed, rudimentary mountain camps the AK could plan and conduct a series of deadly sorties. They raided German food convoys, carried out assassinations of collaborators, blew up German installations, and liquidated SS officers and storm troopers.

The entire area reminded Brooks of the Laurentian Mountains back home in Quebec, where he had learned to ski as a youth. All those years of cross-country skiing back in Canada were now being put to use on the southern slopes and valleys of occupied Poland. Within the first few weeks, Brooks was strapping on the skis and racing down the hills for his early patrol missions. That first winter the AK carried out a number of successful raids and attacks, but there were also setbacks and some extremely tense situations.

On Christmas Eve Brooks and Duncan were invited to tag along with a couple of their partisan leaders to have supper with a family of friends who lived in a nearby village. As they walked along the road towards the town of Lipowka, they saw the head-lights of an approaching car. It had to be Germans as no Poles were allowed to drive or own vehicles. They dove for the ditch, cocked their weapons, and prepared to pounce, but the partisan leader named "Adam" shouted, "Nobody shoots until I take a shot!" As the car drove past, Brooks saw that it was filled with German soldiers and an officer. Adam was a tactician. He let the car pass without firing a shot, and the men crawled out of the ditch and carried on to celebrate Christmas at their friends' house.

Later that evening, after an enjoyable supper in pleasant company, Brooks hugged Adam and said, "Now I understand why we didn't shoot the Germans." Adam replied, "On a day like today I would not shoot even a German or my worst enemy." Brooks had learned an important lesson about guerilla warfare, strategy, timing, place, and planning. There were too many unknowns in that moment on the road. Three or four dead Germans that close to town would have exposed them all to greater dangers and would have certainly put the local civilian population at risk of a swift and wicked German retaliation. They would get the Germans, just not then and there.

Later that winter Brooks was involved in a raid on the Polish–German police station in the town of Ochotnica. The raid was retribution against the police from the garrison for an earlier attack on one of the partisan hideouts. It also served as an opportunity for the partisans to steal much-needed food, arms, and clothing from their enemies. On February 19, 1944, Brooks and thirty-one partisan fighters stormed the station and disarmed the policemen. In the melee the German station commander was killed, along with a Polish policeman and one of the partisans. Moments later a horde of German troops arrived and pinned down the partisans with heavy gunfire. Brooks and a slew of his men managed to bust free and escape, but over the next two days a bloody battle ensued in the nearby hills. Sixty German gendarmes attempted to squash the fourteen men in Brooks's unit. Although the AK lost five more of its boys, the Germans also lost at least six men, with an unknown number of wounded. The Germans called off their pursuit. Back in town they executed an additional forty hostages in retaliation for the partisan raid on the garrison.

While the Germans combed the area in a desperate hunt to extinguish the freedom fighters, the partisan unit retreated deeper into the forests and re-formed. By March their company had built up its numbers to 110 men, and Brooks was promoted to second lieutenant in command of a splinter platoon group of 40 men. John Duncan was Brooks's second-in-command.

In early spring Brooks and Duncan received their platoon's first liquidation assignment. There was a Gestapo informer who ran the lumber mill in the village of Lacko. The man was a traitorous Pole named Sikora. His treacherous dealings with the Germans had earned Sikora considerable wealth, and he was a constant source of danger for the AK. As a Gestapo collaborator he was personally responsible for tipping off the Nazis on numerous occasions, resulting in the extermination or deportation to concentration camps of many local families. Brooks's superiors wanted him to kill Sikora and to confiscate the large leather belts from the lumber mill. The partisan fighters could use the leather for much-needed repairs to their boot soles.

Armed with the necessary information on Sikora, Brooks planned the attack. He knew Sikora lived in a strongly built house with a large German shepherd as a watchdog. Sikora also had a stockpile of weapons, including a French Tommy gun, two rifles, a shotgun, and several grenades. Brooks decided against a full frontal assault. Instead, in the wee hours of the morning, he took Duncan and two of the Polish partisans with him as they crept down from the mountains to the outskirts of the village. There, by the side of the Dunajec River, they waited for Sikora to make his way down the main road that led to the mill. At 9:30 a.m., in broad daylight, Sikora approached. While Duncan and one of the partisans knocked out the phone lines in the village, Brooks and the other Pole sauntered straight up to Sikora and came face to face with him. Just as he passed by they wheeled around and shot him dead on the spot. They disarmed him, left him where he lay, and raced to his house. Brooks blazed past Sikora's startled wife, let the guard dog have a blast of bullets, and then seized Sikora's stash of weapons and high-powered battery radio. Sikora's wife called out, "What's my husband going to say when he comes back and finds what you've done?" Brooks replied, "I'm sorry, madam, your husband won't be coming back." And with that, they left. The Germans were in hot pursuit ten minutes later, but Brooks, Duncan, and the other two partisans were already in the wind.

In the spring of 1944 the situation in the Polish countryside was getting hotter and hotter as Brooks and his platoon engaged in several assaults on German positions. On May 12, they attacked a patrol of thirty men. They killed three and wounded five. On May 14, Brooks and four of his fighters ambushed a border patrol in the mountains and wounded four of the Germans. On May 25 his platoon mounted an audacious daylight ambush on a truck filled with storm troopers. They killed several of the storm troopers and captured a couple of them to use as bargaining chips and hostages. In a brilliant act of deception, they tricked the hostages into believing that the partisan unit was heavily armed and loaded with men. Next they sent one of the hostages into the village of Kamienica, where the SS had a stronghold. The hostage carried a message to his commander at the garrison to surrender. When Brooks and his men marched into Kamienica, the entire SS company was lined up outside the garrison waiting to turn themselves in. The bluff worked. Instead of liquidating the SS company then and there, the partisans decided to show the Germans that they were honourable soldiers, not barbarians. They took their weapons, food, and equipment, but they refrained from shooting any of the unarmed men.

Day after day, week after week, the various AK units continued their assault on the occupying German forces and those who collaborated with them. Brooks and his men ambushed more German patrols and vehicles; they destroyed bunkers and border posts, raided trains, and assassinated a slew of German officers and Nazi collaborators. As the heat of the summer intensified, so too did the engagements. Now more than ever, the freedom fighters needed to upgrade their armament and ammunition to contend with German armoured fighting vehicles, tanks, and fortified bunkers. Brooks was sent to work with a special Home Army troop known as the Pelikany, or Pelicans. His role was to help co-ordinate radio communications with the Allied forces in Italy, which were arranging airdrops of arms to supply the AK with beefier firepower to do battle against the Germans. Brooks not only helped coordinate the armament airdrops but also was the man on the ground responsible for retrieving the dropped "package" and transporting the precious goods back to base.

In early June Brooks, Duncan, and a team of partisans made their way to the drop zone on the slopes of the Slopnice Mountain. They got there early in the afternoon to make sure everything was ready to receive the nighttime airdrop. Suddenly they noticed two hunters had stumbled into the region. Although the men claimed they were hunting deer, Brooks and his team discovered when they searched the men's papers that one of them was a notorious Nazi collaborator, the vice-president of the Polish propaganda department of the General Government. Whether he and his colleague were actually there hunting deer or not, the men had wandered into the AK's drop zone. The fact that the vice-president was a traitor and Nazi collaborator sealed the men's fate. Brooks, Duncan, and one of their men promptly took the pair outside the zone and shot them immediately.

Later that night the plane dropped the first package right on schedule. Brooks and his team were ecstatic. It worked. Now they had what they needed to be more effective in their fight against the Germans. They gathered up seven long canisters filled with Bren guns, Sten guns, pistols, hand grenades, plastic explosives, detonators, radio transmitters, and medical supplies. Some of the boxes that were parachuted from the Allied plane were so heavy they plowed into the earth and had to be dug out. When the Germans eventually found out about the liquidation of the VP of the Polish propaganda department, they executed thirty Polish prisoners in Krakow as a reprisal. They also distributed posters with a price on the heads of the two British soldiers who engineered the liquidation of the high-rolling collaborator.

The supply drop of armaments helped infuse the men of the AK and the various partisan units with a sense of optimism and excitement. Instead of using old family rifles and stolen guns from patrol posts and police stations, they were now equipped with some serious firepower. For the next year Brooks continued to lead his platoon in battle after battle. Time and time again he narrowly averted death. He and his unit carried out a series of violent ambushes on German convoys and train stations. They also delivered swift justice to German officers as retribution for atrocious massacres like one at Porabka in July 1944. News of the atrocity incensed the partisans. The Germans had razed an entire village over suspicion the villagers had helped the AK. The Nazis had rounded up the village's forty unarmed men, women, and children, bayoneted them all, and tossed them on the flames of the burning town.

In August, Brooks, Duncan, and three partisans tracked down the German officer in charge of the massacre as he rolled along the countryside outside the village of Szczyrzyc. The commanding officer and another officer were busy overseeing the collection of food, beer, and supplies for the garrison back in town. Brooks and his men ensnared the German wagons in crossfire and riddled them with bullets. They gave the two Germans a quick burial by the roadside and were off.

All through summer and into the fall big battles raged as the Nazis pulled men and resources from the front lines in their attempt to control the region and extinguish the annoying rebel forces. Brooks and his unit joined six hundred AK fighters during an attack at Myślenice, near the villages of Lipnik and Wiśniowa. Vastly outnumbered by six thousand German troops, the rebels held their ground and fought off tanks, armoured cars, spotter aircraft, and heavy artillery. After two weeks the AK partisans pulled out and retreated to the hills to rest and regroup. Eighty German soldiers were killed in the battle. In retaliation, the Germans burned Lipnik to the ground. But that wasn't enough. All the Polish villagers they captured were forced into a large barn, tied to stakes, and set ablaze. From that day forth Brooks vowed to make sure he always had at least one bullet in his revolver, just in case he was ever captured.

He and Duncan were staying at the house of some friends about a mile from camp one night in the middle of September. Just before dawn he shot up like a bolt when a Polish friend woke him to warn him that a troop of Germans was approaching. Brooks raced out the back door, scampered down the gulley, and sussed out the large number of troops deployed along the highway with howitzers in position. He ran to camp and warned his commanding officer of the impending assault. Although it seemed they were surrounded, Brooks led a small scouting party to seek out a gap in the enemy's snare. While volleys of small arms fire and howitzer blasts poured onto the ridge all around them, Brooks deduced that there was an opening at the western end of the hill. He took fifty men with him and they broke through the German circle. Amazingly all the AK men made it out of the trap alive. For his heroic efforts that day, Brooks was later awarded the Polish Cross of Valour.

Brooks continued to fight with the AK right up until they disbanded in early 1945. Despite being regularly outnumbered and outgunned, the Polish partisan army had evolved into a strong, resilient force. From small skirmishes and ambushes to larger battles, they more than held their own and successfully thwarted the Germans from pacifying the area.

After not hearing from her son since the spring of 1942, Hubert's mother was finally informed in March 1945 that her boy was indeed still alive. It took a couple more months for Brooks to eventually make it home to Canada. Unfortunately, his homecoming was bittersweet. Upon his arrival he learned that his father,

Alfred, had died of a sudden heart attack in May 1944. Earlier that month Alfred had received news that suggested Hubert had been shot while attempting to escape and was presumed dead. The shocking news of Hubert's death was believed to be the cause of his father's heart attack. For Hubert, the sense of pride, excitement, and elation of coming home was offset by the heartbreaking news about his dad's passing.

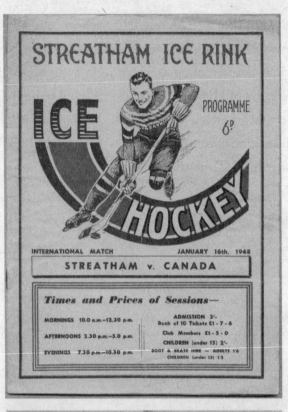

STREATHAM ICE RINK

ICE HOCKEY

PROGRAMME 6ᵈ

INTERNATIONAL MATCH   JANUARY 16th, 1948

STREATHAM v. CANADA

Times and Prices of Sessions—

MORNINGS 10.0 a.m.–12.30 p.m.

AFTERNOONS 2.30 p.m.–5.0 p.m.

EVENINGS 7.30 p.m.–10.30 p.m.

ADMISSION 3/-
Book of 10 Tickets £1 - 7 - 6
Club Members £1 - 5 - 0
CHILDREN (under 13) 2/-
BOOT & SKATE HIRE — ADULTS 1/6
CHILDREN (under 13) 1/3

TO-NIGHT'S LINE UP

FRIDAY, JANUARY 16th
1948

STREATHAM (BLUE RED AND WHITE)   INTERNATIONAL MATCH   **CANADA**

No.	Name	Position	Goals	Assts.	Pens.	No.	Name	Position	Goals	Assts.	Pens.
1.	M. Reynolds	Goal					Cpl. King	Goal			
11.	George Baillie	Defence					F'Sgt. Lacompte	Defence			
12.	G. Telkinnen	Defence					F'Officer Dunster	Defence			
13.	P. Ryan	Defence					AC2 Laperriere	Defence			
14.	D. Wilson	Defence					Cpl. Guzzo	Defence			
2.	Chuck Turner	Forward					Sgt. Ilpin	Forward			
3.	B. McEachren	Forward					Cpl. Taylor	Forward			
4.	A. Stinchcombe	Forward					LAC. Renaud	Forward			
5.	G. Drysdale	Forward					AC1 Hibberd	Forward			
6.	Norm Gardiner	Forward					F'Officer Schroeder	Forward			
7.	Ross Richardson	Forward					LAC. Forbes	Forward			
8.	Verne Gardiner	Forward					AC1 Gravelle	Forward			
9.	L. McKay	Forward					AC1 Leichnitz F'Officer Brooks	Forward			
10.	D. Miller	Forward					Mr. Holder Mr. Mara	Forward			

Team Coach: Red Stapleford

Manager: S'Ldr. A. Gardner-Watson   Coach: Sgt. F. Boucher   Trainer: Cpl. McFaul

Streatham versus Flyers program.

RAMPING UP IN EXHIBITION

09

The lady sitting behind the front desk at the Crofton Hotel that afternoon was dressed in full winter gear. She had on her fur coat, a warm hat, and a thick pair of gloves. It was about 2:00 p.m. on January 15, 1948. Inside the ancient hotel in downtown London the temperature hovered just above freezing. For the next four nights this would be home for the men of the RCAF Flyers while they got their land legs back and kicked off a series of exhibition games against a couple of top-tier British hockey clubs. After they dropped their gear and checked into their spartan, frigid rooms, the boys headed for the hotel dining room. They hadn't eaten a bite since breakfast on the *Queen Elizabeth* at 8:00 a.m. They were famished.

In a word, the food situation that greeted them at the Crofton Hotel was dire. Patsy Guzzo noted in his diary: "I shall never forget my first English lunch. The soup did everything to upset my stomach. I did not have to taste it; the aroma alone was sufficient. It reminded one of boiled fish eyes soup." This was a far cry from the pampering they had received on the *Queen Elizabeth*, even in steerage class. Reg Schroeter and Ab Renaud both got food poisoning within their first day at the Crofton. Even Hubert Brooks's iron gut couldn't handle whatever bizarre organisms were mutating in the questionable post-war food on offer at the hotel.

Most of the boys discovered they had absolutely no heat in their rooms. But Patsy Guzzo and his two roommates were the lucky ones. Aside from a couple of chairs, a sink, and a bathroom behind glass doors, their room also had a tiny coin-operated gas heater. For one shilling the little heater threw out puffs of warm air for a few blissful minutes. Once Patsy got his heater going, the noise of the humming contraption drew in about nine other players, who crowded into the room to catch a bit of warmth.

Of course not all the players were in quite the same position. Silver spoon boys George Mara and Wally Halder had the resources and the ability to spare themselves the discomfort of the Crofton. While they would have happily stayed with the rest of the guys, they weren't keen on spending the next four nights in the flea-bag, second-rate accommodations with the horrific food. As civilian volunteers, Wally and George checked themselves out of the Crofton and paid out of their own pockets to stay at the swankier

Dorchester Hotel on Park Lane. Sandy and Frank were none too pleased, but none of the players could blame them. If they had the cash and the freedom, they all would've done the same thing.

British newspapers welcomed the team's arrival in the United Kingdom and dubbed them "Canada's mystery team." Manager Sandy Watson, Coach Frank Boucher, and the boys on the RCAF Flyers squad were all amused. They were happy to keep the press and their opponents guessing. In fact, most of the other Olympic teams were dark horses just like the Flyers were.

From the moment the Flyers stepped off the boat in Southampton, all their travel and lodging arrangements were handled by a guy named John "Bunny" Ahearne. He also coordinated the team's European exhibition games. Like Sandy, Bunny had never really played hockey, but he possessed a deep love for the sport and he engineered his way to the top of the pyramid of amateur hockey in Europe.

Bunny was born in Ireland in 1901 and had served with the British Army in World War I. He was a man of action. He was crafty, he was cunning, and he was a risk-taker. He was also the owner of a massive travel agency, and more important, Bunny was the secretary of both the British Ice Hockey Association and the International Ice Hockey Federation. If there was anyone who knew everything going on in amateur hockey in Europe it was Bunny. He had his finger firmly on the pulse of the particulars of international hockey at the Olympics. For Sandy Watson and Frank Boucher, Bunny was a fount of indispensable insight and information.

Almost immediately after their arrival in London, Watson and Boucher held a team meeting at the Crofton during which Bunny gave them a few pointers about what to expect at St. Moritz. He told them about the bad refereeing, the inconsistent ice surfaces, the bizarre rules, and how the numbers game could be the difference between gold and silver. If at the end of the Olympics there were two teams with the same number of wins, the gold medal would be awarded to the team with the lowest goal average (goals scored divided by goals allowed). Bottom line: it was better to win a game 2–0 than 18–6. For Coach Frank Boucher, this was music to his ears. No matter what team he had played on he had always played defence. And he had always been a huge fan of playing a strong defensive game. In his mind, the best offence was a strong defence. Question was, Did he have the guys in the roster to pull it off?

Now that they were on the European leg of their tour, Boucher and Watson had just two weeks left to get this team of players they had thrown together to jell into a cohesive unit. They had six exhibition games lined up before they were to hit the ice at the Olympic Games. All crucial coaching decisions from now on were Frank's alone to make. The exhibition games would not only help him whip the boys into shape but also provide a window for him to test lines and figure out which players he would ultimately be calling on to lace up in St. Moritz.

Late afternoon on Friday, January 16, less than thirty-six hours after they had arrived in England, the Flyers boarded the bus and headed out into the ever-present London fog. The dimly lit streets of London were under an energy-conserving blackout, and that, coupled with the fog, made for a rather bleak and dreary drive. Their destination was Streatham rink to play against one of the best teams in the English National League. Most of the guys playing for Streatham were Canadians who had hung around after the war. It was well into the season in the European league, and the Streatham boys were already playing like a finely tuned machine.

The rink itself was larger than the ice surfaces the Flyers were used to playing on back home. They made their way up two flights of stairs and down a long carpeted hallway to their dressing room. After a pep talk and some reminders from Coach Boucher about the European rules of play, the boys were ready to hit the ice. For Murray Dowey it was his first shot to show Frank, Sandy, and the rest of the guys what he was made of. Only George Mara and Wally Halder had seen him play before.

Customarily as the goalie, whenever Murray played a game he had always been the first one to step out onto the ice with the puck. Then he'd throw it down and hit it with his stick as the rest of the players flew out onto the ice and fired warm-up shots at him before the initial puck drop. It was what all the other teams he had ever played on did. It was a sign of respect to have the goalie be the first man on your team to hit the ice. He was the one willing to take to the net and have guys fire pucks at his face. Quite simply, that was just how it was done.

But tonight, when Boucher told the guys to head for the ice, they all jumped up, bolted off, and left Murray sitting there all by himself. Sporting his thick pads and heavy gear, he was the last man out of the dressing room. He hobbled down the carpeted hallway and tried to catch up to the rest of the guys, mumbling to himself and thinking, *What the heck is going on? What kind of an outfit is this?* Clearly he was going to have to earn his new teammates' respect.

The Flyers hit the ice with guns blazing. Ted Hibberd and Wally Halder both banged in quick goals during the first period. The Streatham attackers tried to answer back, peppering Dowey with a barrage of shots, but Dowey was solid in between the pipes and stopped every blast the Streatham boys fired at him.

By the end of the first period, the Flyers were up 2–0. During intermission back in the carpeted dressing room, the boys congratulated Murray on his fine play. Just before they were about to head out for the second period, one of the guys yelled, "OK, Dowey, let's go!" Murray had passed muster. Up he went as the first man out of the dressing room. Buoyed by his new teammates' acceptance, he slid in between the posts for the second period and continued his rock-solid performance, catching shot after shot.

A few costly Flyers penalties allowed Streatham to tie the score. Midway through the second period, Wally Halder bagged his second goal of the evening. Shortly thereafter young Red Gravelle fired off a hard shot that beat Streatham's Canadian-born netminder. When winger Hubert Brooks worked his way in front of Streatham's net, he got slammed into the goalpost and popped a tooth. The Flyers battled to protect their lead, but fatigue set in. They faded in the final ten minutes of play and barely held on.

Murray Dowey's sterling play in net kept them from totally folding, and they squeaked out a 5–5 tie.

Boucher and Watson were far from elated, but they weren't too surprised by the team's performance either. In the post-game newspaper scrum, Frank Boucher told reporters: "It was only a fair show, but we will do better when we shake our sea legs."

Still cast as the underdogs, the mysterious Canadians had a secret weapon in their arsenal. A secret weapon that even Frank and Sandy couldn't fully appreciate yet. The underdog of all underdogs: lithe, nimble Murray Dowey.

MURRAY WAS JUST THIRTEEN WHEN World War II broke out in 1939. By 1944, when he was finally of age, he wanted to sign up and do his bit. His father had fought in World War I, and Murray was keen to prove that he too had something to contribute to his country. A friend who was associated with the Toronto Maple Leafs suggested Murray try for the navy, since it might give him a chance to get out to the East Coast to play some hockey. Murray wasn't too particular about what branch of the military he joined; he just wanted to offer his services and participate in the war effort.

He made his way down to Fort York, where doctors examined him and ran him through a battery of tests. He was 145 pounds dripping wet. He was slim, had hay fever and respiratory problems, and was asthmatic. When it was all said and done, the navy doctors outright rejected him. "No way, son. You're not going to be a sailor." Murray took it in stride, walked out the door, and figured he might as well try for the army. He was itching to be a paratrooper, but given that the navy had just rejected him, he assumed the army probably would as well. Nonetheless it was worth a shot.

The army doctors ran Murray through a full physical and a similar series of tests. Then a doctor pointed to a small piece of lead hanging from a rope in the ceiling. Murray had no idea why the small chunk of metal was hanging there. As the doctor pointed up, he said to Murray, "You see that string and lead? That's the only lead you can swing here, buddy." Dejected, Murray was putting his shirt back on and was about to make his way for the door when the doctor said, "You're in." Although there was no way he was fit enough to be a paratrooper, Murray Dowey had been accepted into the army fold. He couldn't believe they had a place for him, and he was ecstatic.

The army put him on a train and shipped him up to a base for processing. It was a scorching hot day in the middle of August 1944. As he rumbled along the tracks, Murray had no clue where he was going or what he was getting himself into. All he knew was that he had this huge kit bag filled with heavy equipment, and the train rolled to a stop at a training camp in Brantford. In a flash he and all the other new recruits were out on the parade square standing at attention when the regimental sergeant major suddenly barked out, "Private Dowey!" Startled, Murray's mind began reeling as he thought, *Oh, boy, what have I done now?* The regimental sergeant major was a lumbering hulk of a man. He came straight up to Murray's face, glowered at him, and said, "Come with me. The colonel wants to see you." He marched Murray into the colonel's office. As Dowey stood at attention in front of the desk, the colonel looked down at Murray's paperwork and said, "I understand you're a ballplayer." Murray replied, "Yes, sir, I am." The colonel ordered, "We're playing Newmarket this afternoon at 3:00 p.m. I expect a win. Dismissed." And that was it.

Murray had never imagined that his ball-playing abilities would serve a purpose in his military life. But he would not be the first or last man in the service to spend most of his days pitching or skating or dribbling a ball.

The role of sport in the military goes back centuries and continues to this day. They might not be fighting in the air or in the trenches, but organized sports teams contribute to the armed services by creating and boosting morale and cohesiveness within the military units. Athletics are a part of basic training and improve physical fitness. And sports teams not only provide men and women with something to do in addition to military duties, but during times of war, they also give troops relief from the tensions of armed conflict. Sports help create bragging rights, and they bolster competition from unit to unit and branch to branch. A night out to catch a game of army versus air force on the base or at the local hockey rink also provides great relief and entertainment for other service personnel.

When Murray hit the mound that afternoon, he pitched a great game against Newmarket and his team won. For the next two years he was stationed at Brantford, where he ended up playing baseball for his unit. The sickly, asthmatic kid from the

Beaches who had impaired vision in one of his eyes excelled as a pitcher for his army squad in both fastball and hardball. He ate everything and did everything. Miraculously, the boy who never made it through a week of school because of allergies or illness never got sick in the army. In fact, it was the healthiest two years of his life.

Murray was not only a dynamo for the army in baseball but also a star goalie for his hockey team on the base. He was willing to fight overseas in whatever branch to do his bit for the war, but this is where he landed and where his superiors figured he was of best use. Twice a week during the winter months, he and the other army boys on the hockey team piled into an open-roof truck and headed over to London or North Bay or Hamilton for a night game to boost morale. The next day he was back in an office performing his military duties. Because he had fast hands and was adept at typing and shorthand, he was made a stenographer and put in the steno pool. That's how Murray Dowey, the underdog, rode out the war: either behind a desk in the orderly room or out on the baseball field and in the hockey rinks entertaining troops.

ON SATURDAY, JANUARY 17, 1948, MURRAY and the rest of the RCAF Flyers got to play tourists for a night. They pulled on their parkas and ventured out into the driving London rain to take the Tube and catch a game at Wembley Arena between the Wembley Monarchs and Streatham. For guys like Patsy Guzzo, Murray Dowey, and André Laperrière, a ride on the subway was the first in a lifetime.

When they got to Wembley Arena they were treated to a feast for the eyes. The rink was a lavish establishment, designed for maximum enjoyment. There were no pillars or posts to obstruct the sightlines for fans. Aside from the regular seating, which was in itself quite special, there was a glassed-in VIP section. Here fans could sit down at a table, order themselves a thick, juicy steak and a fine drink, and tuck into their A1 meal, enjoying the game in style. While the boys sat in the regular seats, Sandy and Bunny Ahearne were in the luxurious VIP section. A full orchestra played music throughout the game, and the arena even had its own resident cartoonist. Periodically, the artist drew game statistics, coming attractions, and caricatures of the players, which were then projected onto a giant screen at one end of the rink. It was quite the spectacle, and the boys had an entertaining and relaxing night out.

Playing spectators for the night also gave them the opportunity to witness some of the European rules in action. They saw that there was no icing regardless of the number of men on the ice. When a player finished serving a penalty, he had to skate back to his own blue line before re-entering the game. It was also quite obvious that bodychecking was severely restricted.

After the game the boys were treated to sandwiches and tea, and they grabbed a quick sightseeing tour from the top of a double-decker bus. Then it was back on the Tube to grab some sleep in the frigid rooms of the Crofton Hotel.

Next stop en route to Switzerland and the Olympics was France for an exhibition match against Le Club Racing de Paris. For the duration of the tour, Sandy Watson carried around a small leather briefcase chock full of the team's cash. It was their $5,000 bankroll courtesy of Tommy Gorman and their cut from the receipts of Olympic Night. Back in Ottawa Sandy had told the boys that the safety of his briefcase was the responsibility of the entire team. If he happened to forget it somewhere, he wanted the other nineteen sets of eyeballs on it or they would all be left high and dry. The night before the boys left for France, Sandy waltzed out of a restaurant and forgot his bag on a chair. A quick-thinking Patsy Guzzo spotted Sandy's empty hands. He raced back in and grabbed the bag before any stranger had a chance to take off with the team's entire travel fund.

The Flyers left London for Paris in style, aboard a Viking twin-engine airplane named *Violet*. For veteran airmen like Brooks, Forbes, and Dunster it was comforting to slip back into the clouds and travel by air. When they landed, the players were whisked off to Paris City Hall for a champagne reception and meeting with Mayor Pierre de Gaulle, brother of the famous Charles. Later in the afternoon, they posed for pictures for the press machine and enjoyed a few seconds of celebrity status as Pierre de Gaulle presented them with the keys to the city.

With city hall in the rear-view mirror, they bused past the Arc de Triomphe and the Eiffel Tower to their lodgings. Once again, the high-flying Olympic hopefuls found that Bunny Ahearne had them shacking up in the lowest of the low. The Victoria Hotel was located in the student quarter of the city and looked presentable from the outside. But when the boys got inside they were intro-duced to a whole other world. No heat, stinky rooms, and grotty beds. Ahearne had arranged for the lads to eat their meals at a nearby restaurant. Just like at the Crofton, the culinary choices offered to the Flyers left much to be desired. The main course for dinner was horsemeat. Sandy threw a fit and demanded some proper food. When the waiter brought him eggs as a substitute, Sandy was convinced they were in fact ducks' eggs, and he refused to eat a bite.

A day after they arrived in France the Flyers faced off against the strongest hockey team in Europe, Le Club Racing de Paris. Once again, their pre-game meal was horsemeat. And once again, their opponents were virtually all top-notch Canadian professional players who were moonlighting in France. Le Club Racing de Paris had not lost a game in nearly a year and a half.

As darkness fell over the massive Palais des Sports, Canada's reputation as a hockey powerhouse brought out spectators by the boatload. Sixteen thousand Parisians scrambled into the streets and jammed the subways hoping to witness their "French" pros whip the mighty Canadians. Although the puck drop was set for 9:00 p.m., the game was delayed by more than an hour because the subway simply could not cope with all the people rushing to the arena.

As the boys waited in their carpeted dressing room at one end of the rink, the noisy crowd flooded into and packed the arena. Just before the match, Le Club de Racing's brass came over and talked to Sandy about making sure the Flyers played a clean game, this being an exhibition match and all. But from the puck drop, the Paris club proceeded to do everything but chop the Flyers' heads off. Patsy Guzzo got smashed in the face with an elbow and came off with a beautiful shiner. Ab Renaud got clipped by a high stick and was awarded with a juicy cut over his eye. And Roy Forbes got a nasty slash in the face that opened up a big gash. While Frank Boucher was busy on the bench barking orders and tweaking lines to deal with the assault, Dr. Sandy Watson and trainer George McFaul were stitching and sewing up the boys' faces.

Although battered and bruised, the Flyers were up 1–0 by the end of the first period. In the early half of the second period they continued to pour on the pressure and leapt ahead 3–0 when Wally Halder and Reg Schroeter slammed in a couple of nifty goals. Then the wheels started to fall off. The Flyers made a few boneheaded defensive plays, and the Racers pounced and beat Murray Dowey with two quick goals. The Paris club clamoured back into contention, slashing and bashing. Tempers flared and a mittful of penalties were handed out as the players mixed it up.

About midway through the game, Hubert Brooks vaulted over the boards and tore across the ice on a mission. He lined up one of the Frenchmen and laced him with a vicious bodycheck that sent his opponent flying over the boards face first. The referee stopped the game and threw Brooks off the ice with a game misconduct. In the final period the Flyers simply ran out of gas. They went down 5–3 in front of the massive crowd of sixteen thousand spectators.

Sandy Watson was gutted. The Canadian success he had imagined was not materializing. Despite all the last-minute changes made in Canada, Coach Frank Boucher was also left wondering whether his team could get it in gear to compete at the Olympics, or whether they would be bowled over by the stiff competition. With the Olympic Winter Games just a week away, newspaper reporters for the Canadian Press were harbouring even bleaker thoughts. On January 22, CP reporter Jack Sullivan outlined his predictions in black and white for all to see. Czechoslovakia was favoured to snag first place, Sweden was pegged for second, and Switzerland was slated for third. Canada's RCAF Flyers were not even seen as contenders. They were counted out by the odds-makers and considered an also-ran.

But the men on the RCAF Flyers, like bomb aimer Roy Forbes, weren't about to be rattled by some bad press and a few losses on the road to the Olympics. They still had a full week of practices and exhibition games to work themselves into winning shape. This was just hockey. It was a game. These were men who had overcome countless life-and-death situations. These were men who had survived some of the darkest days of World War II and come out on top.

Elsie Forbes gives her son Roy his wings.

ON THE RUN

10

At 22:20 on June 12, 1944, Roy Forbes sidled up beside his pilot and friend "Root" Lacey as Root steered their Lancaster bomber down the runway at Middleton, St. George. Roy liked to sit up front while the engines roared and the massive bomber pulled away from the earth and took to the skies. Once they were well on their way, Roy made his way down to his bomb aimer's bay and lay in position so he could spot for the navigator, watch for night fighters, and prep for his bomb drop. This was their twelfth mission together. Lacey and Forbes were both prairie boys and had become fast friends and drinking buddies from the day they met, when they shared a Quonset hut in flight school many months before. Like Roy, Root was a farm boy, but he was a lot bigger than

Roy, and he whipped the Lanc around like it was nobody's business. When it was time to pick their crewmates, Roy and Root found a couple of likeable farm boys from Dauphin, Manitoba, to be their gunners. Their flight engineer was a Brit. Everyone else was Canadian.

The entire crew of seven was like a family. Ranks were a forgotten thing. The boys in the Lanc that was humming through the night sky towards the south of France loved each other like brothers. They drank together, they bunked together, and they fought together. Tonight their mission was to bomb the snot out of the rail yards at Cambrai.

At around midnight their bomber stream was high above a thick cloud cover and about an hour away from their target. As Forbes lay in the bomb aimer's bay with his eyes scanning for enemy night fighters, the curtain of cloud suddenly opened. He called out to his skipper over the intercom, "Jeez, Root, look at that. There's something down there." Ten thousand feet below, in the blackness of night, the sea was lit up by the twinkling lights of hundreds of Allied ships that were also heading towards France. It was a bizarre and surreal sight of different coloured lights, some with crosses. The bomber stream was flying over an advancing fleet of reinforcements sent to burst through the Atlantic wall as part of the invasion of Normandy. After a few minutes the clouds closed in again and swallowed up the flotilla. About half an hour later their Lancaster began to make its way down to bombing height.

Amid a wailing barrage of ground fire from anti-aircraft guns, Lacey took the Lancaster in low. Accuracy was a must. Bomber

Command wanted the boys to break everything up at the rail yards. They made it to their target, and from about a thousand feet up, Forbes unleashed hell on the infrastructure below. As they pulled up and started climbing for home, the massive German ground guns blew a hole in the wing. Two motors ignited in a wall of fire. In an instant, the fuselage and the engines were engulfed in flames. Lacey was in a death grip with the controls as he struggled to keep the Lancaster from keeling over and rocketing to the ground. It all happened so fast. Seconds later, Lacey called out to the boys, "Get out, get out! We've had it! Bail out!"

Forbes grabbed his parachute and threw it on his back. Fortunately he was still in the bomb aimer's bay and near the escape hatch. Just as he popped the door and leapt out into the abyss, he felt the hand of the flight engineer on his shoulder for a fleeting second. Forbes tumbled into the dark and looked up to see the stricken Lancaster in flames and going down fast. He figured he was only about eight hundred feet from the ground, far too low for a safe jump. To make matters worse, as he pulled the rip cord he nearly got spun upside down. One half of his chute got tangled, and it only partially opened. With virtually no control over his descent, he dropped fast and spiralled towards the rapidly approaching ground. In the seconds before impact Roy's thoughts raced back to home. He was certain he wasn't going to make it. He thought about his mom, Elsie, and his fiancée, Jeannie. They would both be so sad when they got the news. Then he hit, and he hit hard. He smacked into the earth on his side and mashed up his shoulder and his leg.

But Roy was lucky. He didn't get impaled on a tree and he didn't slam into a house or a rock. Instead, fate delivered him to a recently plowed farmer's field. The freshly tilled earth saved his life. Roy had no idea where the flight engineer was or if he had landed safely.

With his ears ringing and his shoulder and leg screaming at him, Forbes looked up from the dirt just in time to witness his beloved plane, which was carrying five of his best friends, explode in an enormous fireball as it piled into the earth a few miles away.

With no time to mourn the loss of his friends, Forbes limped from the open field and scrambled to a distant stand of trees and bushes. He buried his harness, his silk parachute, and his Mae West. He slunk over to the next field, collapsed, and waited in the bushes for daylight.

While he sat there in the dark, Roy thought about his situation. He knew he was in enemy-occupied France. It was highly likely that German spotters had seen him and the engineer leap from their burning Lancaster. They would be looking for them in no time. But Forbes was a fighter. There was no way he was going to surrender. Based on the bombing run, Roy figured he was around a hundred miles from the advancing Allied army forces. If he walked north he should be able to connect with them within two weeks. If Roy was going to survive he needed to get out of his uniform and boots and into some other clothes. It was about 2:00 a.m. He knew he needed help and he needed to take a chance.

Opportunity knocked a few hours later, when the sun poked its head up on the horizon. Roy spotted a farmer in the next field over who was working his horses and churning up the rich French soil. Forbes skirted to the edge of the trees and watched and waited as the farmer diligently led his team of horses around and around plowing his field. When the farmer made it to the edge of his pasture Roy whispered from the shadows, "Air force, air force, Canadian."

The farmer could have been a sympathizer; he could have turned Forbes in to the Germans. But introducing himself to this complete stranger was a risk that Roy had to take. He also knew the farmer would be putting his life on the line if he agreed to help Roy. The Germans were all over the place, and they didn't hesitate to shoot locals who helped downed Allied pilots.

The two men used a combination of hand signals and the odd word of French and English to communicate. The farmer had seen the plane go down the night before, and he understood that Roy wasn't a German. He was a friend and he agreed to help. The impoverished farmer left Roy in the field and went back into his house. He returned moments later with some ratty old clothes, a few scraps of food, and a pair of worn-out shoes that sported a giant hole in the sole and were three sizes too big for Roy. It wasn't much, but it was all Roy needed to blend in and look like a poor Frenchman if he was spotted by any Germans from a distance.

For the next two weeks Roy evaded capture as he made his way north to link up with the Allies. He stayed as far away from people as possible and avoided spots like bridges or roads where the Germans might be watching or other people might be travelling.

Under the cover of darkness Roy trudged through fields and forests and skittered along sad, dusty back roads. When it was feasible he swam across rivers and creeks and forded through swampy streams. After a few days his feet were bloody and raw from his nasty, hole-riddled shoes.

During the daytime Forbes grabbed fitful catnaps in fields, ditches, and trees. On rare occasions he allowed himself to catch a few hours of shut-eye in a barn. But barns were easy places to get caught inside, so he tended to sleep outside in a hidden spot.

With no food supplies, he stole carrots and potatoes from farmers' fields in the dead of night. When he approached a town, he was even more on edge. The towns were crawling with Germans, and the threat of being spotted by a German soldier or a Nazi collaborator consumed Roy. Out there all alone, with no maps and no weapon, he was scared. He was scared as hell.

Late one evening, as he headed down a dirt back road in search of a safe place to put his head down, he heard the ominous sound of a number of heavy machines and a dozen German voices approaching. Roy launched himself into the ditch and hid face down in the muck. For a few agonizing minutes he was certain his escape was over. But the unit rumbled by, and the boy from Portage la Prairie crawled away to safety.

Mile after mile Forbes worked his way across the French countryside. The holes in the bottom of his shoes were getting bigger and bigger with each passing night. Before he swam across a river he stopped to wash the blood off his feet. As soon as he took a shoe off, his blood ran out of it by the cupful.

After two weeks on the lam Roy was worn out. It was early Sunday morning, and he hardly even realized he had hit the edge of a little village. His feet were bleeding profusely and looked like raw, mashed meat. His body was still racked with pain from his fall from the sky. He was sleep-deprived and malnourished, having eaten only grass for the past few days. He couldn't keep his food down, and his head was spinning. He needed a miracle, or it was time to turn himself in.

As he sat down to get some water from a small hand pump at the side of the road, he heard church bells in the distance. Forbes jumped up and hobbled through the streets until he saw a troop of seven nuns walking down the road. They were heading back to the nunnery after mass. This was it. All or nothing. He scrambled up behind them and whispered, "Air force, British. Airplane, Canada." The nuns more or less ignored Roy, averted their eyes from him, and continued hustling towards their home. He followed and continued whispering, "Air force, British. Airplane, Canada." At the gates of the nunnery they signalled him to follow them in.

Roy was ushered into the Mother Superior's office. She barely spoke English and wasn't too pleased to have this strange, dirty man inside the nunnery. She told him she would introduce him to another woman who spoke English—someone who could help connect him with the French Resistance—and then she left. Roy had no idea if he was about to be turned over to the Germans, but he remembered being told in training that Catholics weren't too keen on helping the Nazis, and he was hopeful these French nuns were on the good side. Twenty minutes later he watched through the window as both the Mother Superior and another woman returned on bicycles.

The English-speaking woman was highly suspicious and put Forbes through the paces. She peppered him with questions about his "Canadian" identity and asked him about Canadian geography. She even tested his pronunciation and asked him to say words like "potatoes" and "tomatoes." When the interview was over, Roy was put into another room and given a bite to eat. Then another man showed up by bicycle. He was clean-cut, about five foot five, and all business. Just like that, Roy was staring down the barrel of the gun of an operative of the French Forces of the Interior. The man on the other side of the revolver said that if he believed Roy was a German, he would shoot him on the spot. If he believed Roy was a Canadian, there was a bike waiting outside and he'd be welcomed into the underground.

Roy passed the test and was accepted into the fold. He hopped on his bike and winced through the pain as he and the Frenchman pedalled like mad for a home in the countryside. About a week later a British air force unit prepared to mount a rescue attempt using a two-person glider to swoop in and fly him out. While Roy waited anxiously in the field for his glider to arrive, bad weather on the other end scrapped the mission. After that, Forbes was made to keep a low profile and stay in hiding.

He spent the next four months being passed along the French–Belgian escape underground. The resistance put him up in the attic of a pub and gave him a fake identification card that listed him as a deaf-mute. While he was staying at another safe house, he joined the local resistance forces on a clandestine night mission and helped them blow up a series of bridges. Eventually Forbes linked up with a Scottish Highland armoured unit, and his time in hiding was over. All told, he was on the run for nearly five months after leaping out of the flaming bomber. When the little scrapper from the prairies reconnected with the RCAF, he went straight back into operational duties doing airdrops of supplies until the end of the war. Three years later, here he was on the verge of accomplishing something he had never dreamed of—playing hockey on the Olympic stage for the eyes of the world.

Flyers versus Davos in exhibition.

TUNING UP IN EUROPE

11

As the RCAF Flyers' bus rumbled down the highway headed for Le Bourget airport, a thick ceiling of clouds enveloped the Parisian skies. It was time for the team to say goodbye to France and set off for Switzerland.

That day, as Sandy Watson stared out at the runway, a feeling of uneasiness washed over him. Although he had spent years in the RCAF, he actually hated flying. It was midday on Thursday, January 22, 1948, and the ominous carpet of clouds hugging the mountains had Sandy on edge. Two Dakota airplanes were slated to transport the RCAF Flyers and their gear to Zurich for their next pre-Olympic exhibition match. One Dakota was arranged to take all the players. It hadn't arrived yet. The other Dakota was booked to take Dr. Watson; the trainer, George McFaul; and all the team's gear. It was already on the runway and ready to go. But the pilot for Sandy's plane told the guys there was no way he was flying to Zurich, for a number of reasons. One, he had never actually flown to Switzerland before—he was with the Air Ministry from London. But more important, the Dakotas weren't capable of flying over the mountain ranges along their route. Rather, their flight path to Zurich took them *through* the mountains. With today's low clouds and three-thousand-foot ceiling, the pilot was very concerned about slamming into the side of a mountain on the way in.

Some of the boys with a lot of hours in the air tried to lighten the mood and joked with their manager about crashes and such, but Dr. Watson wasn't having any of it. The stern, tough disciplinarian with a penchant for jujubes was shaking in his boots. When the pilot for the second Dakota finally arrived, there was a burst of heated discussions. Thankfully this guy knew the landscape, he knew the route, and he had threaded the needle many times. A plan was devised for the two planes to make it to Switzerland. The seasoned Swiss pilot would fly lead in the boys' plane, and Sandy's pilot would follow on his heels as he slipped and skirted in between the mountains. Even Roy Forbes, with seven hundred hours in the air, had a few butterflies when the two Dakotas hummed down the runway and took to the skies at 2:00 p.m.

That night Patsy Guzzo pencilled some reflections into his diary: "I still don't know how Doc got the nerve to go. McFaul reported later that he shook the whole trip over. Poor Doc. We were up about 12,000 feet because of the high mountains, but on the way in it appeared as though we were skimming the treetops. Just before landing the pilot dipped a wing and we roared over the hockey rink."

Unscathed and happy to be planted back on terra firma, the boys felt like they had finally arrived and were poised on the doorstep of their mission. Not only that, the beautiful Swiss mountains and crisp, clean atmosphere of Zurich seemed like an alternative universe in comparison to their grim accommodations in England and France. After a long, slow bus ride up a very steep hill, the Flyers checked in at the ornate Dolder Grand Hotel, tucked into the woods on the German–Swiss border.

The boys were delighted. Their rooms were spotlessly clean and decked out with thick, lustrous carpets, large comfortable couches, double beds, double sinks, thick comforters, and glorious heat. The food in Zurich was also beyond compare. They treated themselves to delicious cakes and pastries and were amazed to find that real Coca-Cola was available for the first time since they'd left New York. After a soothing night's sleep they feasted on bacon and eggs for breakfast and felt as if they were ready to take on the world. Things were definitely looking up.

The first order of business for Frank and Sandy was to get the boys back on their skates. They had planned to use this final full week of practices and exhibition matches to tune up the guys before the Olympics. After a short walk through the woods at the Dolder Grand Hotel, they hit the ice for an early morning practice. Immediately the guys noticed how quickly they got winded while tearing around the ice at this high altitude. They also couldn't help but notice that the boards were only about sixteen inches high and six inches thick. You couldn't play the puck or the body off the boards like you could back home. Moreover, if you happened to shove your opponent or get shoved yourself, the rules in Europe dictated that you could hop the boards, run in the snow beside the ice, and then jump back over the boards and pick up playing right where you had left off. Some of the boys, like Forbes, Dunster, and Mara, practised hurdling the boards, skittering along in the snow, and leaping back onto the ice.

None of this was a surprise to Frank Boucher. He knew that with time his players would get acclimated to the thinner air. He worked them hard in practice and continued toying with strategies and tweaking his lines and defensive pairings in his hunt for the perfect formula.

Time on the road and on the ice solidified the friendships and bonds that were developing among the men. Warriors like Frank Dunster, Hubert Brooks, Roy Forbes, and Louis Lecompte had a natural affinity for each other. Longtime linemates Ab Renaud, Reg Schroeter, and Ted Hibberd had already developed a shorthand that came from months of time together on the ice and off. Wally Halder and George Mara were like two peas in a pod. Patsy Guzzo chummed around with newbies Murray Dowey and André Laperrière. Although Patsy was by far the most religious of the trio, they often went to mass together whenever the chance arose. Slowly but surely the entire team was jelling into a cohesive unit.

Murray Dowey and André Laperrière had hit it off from day one, when they shared a room on the *Queen Elizabeth* coming over. That first night on the massive ocean liner, Murray had presented André with a somewhat unique and unorthodox request. As they prepared to tuck in for the evening he said, "André, I got something special to ask you." André wondered, *OK, what the heck does this guy want?* Murray continued, "You know, back home, my wife always does my hair for me. I can't do it myself. Would you mind washing my hair for me?"

It was the kind of moment that could either make or break a relationship. For a second André thought Murray was having a go at him, but then he realized his new teammate was serious. He started to laugh. Murray chuckled along. "Yeah, sure," said André.

From that day forward the two strangers became the best of friends. Murray and André roomed together for the remainder of the trip, and André became an expert at washing Murray's hair. They maintained a lasting friendship long after the Olympics.

ON FRIDAY, JANUARY 23, 1948, the boys in blue laced up in their hotel rooms for an afternoon game against the Swiss national team at the Dolder rink. Decked out in full gear, they hopped on the bus and snaked their way through the streets to the rickety outdoor rink. Fully fifteen thousand Swiss fans braved a steady pounding rain and near freezing temperatures to catch a glimpse of the Canadian boys in action. The small wooden stands were jammed to capacity. A sea of spectators held newspapers and umbrellas over their heads while the players took to the ice. Others crowded onto nearby rooftops. Some of the braver souls clawed their way up into the treetops and perched themselves precariously on extended branches.

Although the rink had artificial ice, the teeming rain had created giant pools of water and slush. The surface was a total mess from the get-go. Undeterred, the Flyers launched into the match with gusto as if they were playing on an outdoor rink back at home. Ab Renaud led the attack with a pair of goals. Patsy Guzzo, Wally Halder, and George Mara also banged in nice goals despite the brutal playing conditions. In between the posts, Murray Dowey stunned the Swiss as he snagged shot after shot in his custom-made mitt. With a few minutes to go in the final period, the Swiss pulled their goalie and added another attacker to the ice. But a strong Flyers defence and Murray's hot hands kept the Swiss puck out of the net. At the final buzzer the game ended 6–3 in favour of the Flyers. Coach Frank Boucher told reporters: "The conditions were very bad but it turned out to be a pretty fair game and the boys looked good."

Players from both teams were soaked to the skin. Throngs of spectators choked the Flyers' access to their bus, so the Canadian lads walked back to their hotel shivering in the cold, with blue lips and short of breath. When they got back to their cushy digs at the Dolder, there were hot baths waiting for all of them. As an added bonus, Sandy ordered each of the guys to have a shot of cognac before bed to stave off a cold. The cognac came courtesy of George Mara's liquor empire contacts.

Buoyed by their victory against the strong Swiss contenders, Sandy Watson and Frank Boucher were pleased to see their team finally coming together. Not only that, but they were blown away by the scrawny last-minute surprise from the Beaches. Quite simply, Murray Dowey was like a magician in net. He possessed an extraordinary glove hand and lightning-fast reflexes. Boucher had never seen anything like it. The rest of boys on the Flyers bestowed Murray with a new nickname. From then on they called him "Fast Hands."

Watson and Boucher homed in on a revised strategy. They needed goals to win games. Thankfully their attackers and snipers were beginning to find their groove. But if they focused on teamwork built around defence, backchecking, and Dowey's prowess in between the pipes, they might have a chance to win it all. Boucher told his boys that their top priority was defence. His mantra was "Defence, defence, defence." If the other teams couldn't score, they couldn't win.

That love of baseball that Dr. Watson was so worried about when he first met Murray back in Ottawa was shaping up to be the Flyers' secret weapon. Murray's goaltending style was very different from that of other netminders. Most goalies tended to play the pads, go down, and try to block or smother shots. Sure Murray could block, but if the puck was in the air, he was going to catch it. The Europeans had never seen a goalie catch a puck before.

With just a few days to go before the opening ceremonies of the Olympic Games, the Flyers packed up their gear and checked out of the Dolder Hotel for another exhibition match against the

Swiss national team in the mountain town of Basel. Like everything else in Switzerland the train station was spotless. The train itself was clean, comfortable—and electric. It seemed to transport them effortlessly through the mountain passes. The boys marvelled at it all. Unlike Britain and France, this place felt completely untouched by the war.

The Swiss team and their coach, Wyn Cook, were on the same train. The Flyers hung out with the Swiss players, taking the opportunity to get to know a little more about their competitors. Cook was an old friend of Roy Forbes's from Winnipeg, and the two spent the train ride catching up and reminiscing. Once they arrived in Basel, both teams settled into separate hotels and tried to grab some rest after playing through that frigid deluge back in Zurich.

On Sunday, January 25, the sun was shining, thick snowflakes cascaded down, and the town was picture-postcard perfect. Patsy Guzzo got up bright and early to go to church with André Laperrière before the day's game. The mass was in German, and they didn't understand a word, but it still felt good to get to church.

That afternoon a dark cloud began to loom over the Flyers. As the boys got suited up in their hotel rooms, many of them were feeling light-headed from the high altitude. Others were developing colds and feeling run ragged from the travel and Friday's game in the rain. Most figured that once they hit the ice and the crisp mountain air, however, all would be good.

They piled into a fleet of taxis and made their way to the outdoor rink. An army of more than sixteen thousand rabid

Swiss fans encircled the ice. They were jammed into the wooden stands and spilling out onto the streets. Standing shoulder to shoulder the cheering crowds blanketed multiple blocks. Hundreds of others crowded onto nearby hills for a bird's-eye view of the rink. Swiss coach Wyn Cook now knew what his boys were facing in Canada's "mystery team." His players were the bronze-medal favourites, they were on home turf, and they weren't about to turtle to the boys in blue who had beaten them back in Zurich.

After the usual formalities both teams got off to a fast start. The Swiss got on the board first with an early goal. Patsy Guzzo answered back and tied things up. By the end of the first period the score was deadlocked 2–2. Then, in a complete reversal of form, the Flyers fell to pieces and the Swiss poured on the pressure. The lighter Swiss players were too much for the fast-tiring Canadians. Time and time again the Canadians were penalized for physical play and bodychecks that would never have been called back in Canada. Meanwhile the Swiss trotted out the European habits of holding, hooking, and taking dives, without any repercussions. Even the spears and jabs they deftly delivered to the Flyers went unpenalized.

All game long the short twelve-inch boards of the figure skating rink plagued the Canadians. They repeatedly fired pucks over the pint-sized boards into the snow. The Swiss, on the other hand, had no such problems and used the boards to bank their passes to great effect. They scored two more unanswered goals in the second period and jumped ahead 4–2. The Flyers attempted to bounce back in the third, but it was too little, too late. Tired, winded, and outplayed, they bowed down to the Swiss and lost 8–5. The massive hometown crowd poured onto the streets, cheering and chanting in exultation. Even though this was just an exhibition match, beating the mighty Canadians, from the country that gave birth to the sport, felt like winning Olympic gold to the legions of Swiss fans.

The loss to the Swiss national team was a heartbreaker for Sandy Watson and Frank Boucher. This was not the result they were hoping for with the Olympics right around the corner. With the exception of a few stars, the Flyers played terribly. After the game Hubert Brooks said it was like a punch in the guts for him and most of the guys. Roy Forbes said every guy on the ice was working like hell, but they were misfiring and couldn't find their groove. Maybe the press was right. Maybe this team was destined to embarrass the nation.

From all angles, the sad performance against the Swiss team on the eve of the Olympics was a shocking wake-up call for the boys. They had to play better, get used to the high altitude, and buy into Coach Boucher's defensive strategy. They had to stop playing like a bunch of individuals. And they had to do it now!

The pressure was also on Boucher to deal with the archaic rule of dressing only eleven players. Although the Flyers were travelling with seventeen bodies, Olympic rules dictated that each team was allowed to dress only eleven players plus a backup goaltender for each game. The rest of the guys would have to sit out the games and ride the bench.

With all the new blood and last-minute shuffling back in Ottawa, Frank had seen these boys play as a team in only a handful of exhibition games in England, France, and Switzerland. He wasn't ready to pick his starting eleven. He was still assessing the new guys and juggling line arrangements and defensive pairings. He told the players, "I have to pick eleven. It's no knock against anyone else. Once I pick the lineup, I'm going to stay with it until we lose."

No one knew yet who was going to sit out and who was going to play. Snow fell heavily in the mountains, and some of the boys grabbed a cable car for a scenic late-night jaunt to the top of the nearby ski runs. Eventually they all made it back to their hotel rooms. Murray Dowey tucked into a game of cards, playing rummy with Patsy Guzzo and Red Gravelle before retiring to bed. In the morning they were up early to pack their things and head off to St. Moritz, winter playground for the rich and famous.

Before they hustled off to the train station, Frank Boucher held a light morning skate for another look at his options. Snow had continued to fall throughout the night and all morning, so the boys did as much shovelling as they did skating.

To get to St. Moritz they needed to hop a couple of trains. When they hauled their bags onto the final train for the last leg of their journey, both the American and the English hockey teams were already on board. The Yanks and the Brits had snatched up all the available seats and weren't about to budge for the Canadians. The Flyers stood the entire ninety-minute ride as the train slowly wound its way through the steep mountains to St. Moritz at six thousand feet above sea level. This was it. Four and a half months before, Sandy Watson read a newspaper article back in Ottawa and hit the roof. Now, he and the band of brothers he had assembled were finally at the threshold of the Olympics.

AT THE 1948 GAMES OF RENEWAL, Olympic hockey was a round-robin competition. There were no playoffs. There was no sudden death and no shootouts. The gold medal would be awarded to the team that won the most games. Back in England, Bunny Ahearne had advised the guys to hammer in the goals but to be very mindful of the goals against just in case it came down to a tie. In the case of a tie, the medals would be determined by the teams' goal average: essentially goals scored divided by goals allowed. If a team scored fifty goals during the tournament and let in twenty goals, they would have a quotient of 2.5. Whereas a team that scored thirty goals and let in only three would have a quotient of 10. The team with the highest quotient would win. So although it was important to accumulate goals, keeping your opponents from scoring was even more critical. The Flyers had to stick to Boucher's game plan: defence, defence, defence.

IT WAS MIDAFTERNOON ON JANUARY 28 when the train pulled into the railway station tucked into the Swiss Alps. A cacophony of station bells heralded their arrival while porters, dressed in smart uniforms with the names of their respective hotels emblazoned on their caps, greeted their new guests. It was as if the Flyers had been transported into a winter wonderland. A thick carpet of snow at least five feet deep blanketed the entire resort village. The tinkling bells of horse-drawn sleigh taxis floated through the air. Villagers going about their business dodged visiting skiers as they raced along the snowlined streets. In the distance two giant mountains, the Languard and the Julian, reared up out of the earth and loomed larger than life.

Wealthy boys like George Mara and Wally Halder had already been exposed to this kind of lavish world. But for the rest of the Flyers it was as if they had been plopped onto a movie set. This was a village far removed from the bump and grind and noise and grime of any normal city. Rather, this idyllic, peaceful town oozed wealth and consisted almost entirely of luxurious hotels and shops.

Spared the kind of destruction that had scarred England, France, Poland, Italy, and other parts of Europe, St. Moritz still boasted many magnificent buildings and venues. War, however, had decimated the once-bustling tourist trade that was a major component of the town's lifeblood. Until recently many of the hotels had been closed and boarded up. With the arrival of the world's athletes, the Olympics presented St. Moritz with an opportunity to open its doors wide once again.

A who's who of the world's wealthy elite and royal society had flocked to the alpine playground to take in the Games and enjoy being pampered at one of the swanky hotels. The boys saw the familiar faces of celebrities they had rubbed shoulders with ever so briefly up in first class on the *Queen Elizabeth*. Movie star Paulette Goddard and her husband, Burgess Meredith, were there, as were Johnny Weissmuller and Henry Ford. A long list of princes, dukes, kings, duchesses, lords, and other notables had also come to St. Moritz.

But what was obviously absent were the masses of working-class spectators from other countries. Aside from the athletes, the delegates, the media, the wealthy elite, and those from nearby towns and villages, St. Moritz was far beyond the reach of most people's pocketbooks. Post-war travel restrictions and currency exchange restrictions also limited the number of tourists capable of making the journey to witness the Games.

One of the spectators who was able to dig deep and make her way to St. Moritz on her own dime was Bea Grontved. She had come to St. Moritz to get married. Her soon-to-be husband was none other than Hubert Brooks. Hubert and Bea had met a few years earlier, when he was searching for downed airmen in Copenhagen as part of the Missing Research and Enquiry Service. Bea was working for the American occupation forces in Germany. They met at a party when she was home in Denmark visiting with her family, and they fell madly in love. Bea and Hubert spent every minute possible together and got engaged while he was working overseas. When he was reposted back to Canada, the two made plans for Bea to immigrate and join him in Ottawa. The instant Brooks made it onto the RCAF Flyers hockey team, the lovebirds set in motion a new plan to tie the knot in St. Moritz right after the Olympics, win or lose.

Bea was staying at the Park Hotel on the edge of town. The boys were staying at the Stahlbad Hotel, a short walk away. A slew of athletes from other countries were also staying at the Stahlbad. The Czechs, Norwegians, Romanians, Yugoslavs, English, Poles, and Swedes all raced down the halls, piled into their rooms, and basically took over the hotel.

The Flyers cozied into their lush rooms at the Stahlbad. Like the earlier Swiss hotels they had stayed in, the Stahlbad was head and shoulders above the establishments they'd been subjected to in England and France. Old roommates Murray Dowey and André Laperrière settled in for a two-week stay. Patsy Guzzo roomed with Andy Gilpin and trainer George McFaul in a massive suite that had a salon with a chesterfield and lounge chairs. It also happened to be the only room on the floor with a phone in it. The boys quickly christened it as the de facto hangout spot for card games. Although Hubert's fiancée, Bea, was just down the road at the Park Hotel, he roomed with fellow warrior and defenceman Frank Dunster.

Although it was hockey that had brought them all together for the journey to Switzerland, the men of the RCAF Flyers were bound by the shared experience of war and the darkest days of the Depression. So far they had been unimpressive on the ice and were routinely lambasted by the press and their opponents. On the eve of the Olympics, with the eyes of the world watching, could they each reach down again to harness that fortitude for another sort of battle?

The Allied air war was a brutal campaign with devastating results for both sides. For the men of the RCAF, survival rates were grim. If you made it through ten missions you were considered lucky. Of the 125,000 Australian, Canadian, New Zealand, and British aircrew who served in Bomber Command, almost 55,000 were killed. If you made it to thirty missions you had completed your full service and could go home.

Although Frank Dunster was one of the lucky ones who survived his first full tour of duty, he wasn't about to leave the battle. Between February 15 and December 2, 1944, Dunster flew thirty-seven missions against the heaviest of heavy targets, night after night after night. Berlin, Essen, Cologne, Nuremburg . . .

His love of trigonometry landed Dunster in the navigator seat of his Halifax bomber—the odds were against him and the job required nerves of steel. The Halifax was a workhorse capable of delivering a serious payload of bombs, but she was light on armour, was light on guns, and had a tendency to go into a tailspin or lose control if she was flung around for evasive manoeuvres to avoid night fighters and flak.

Over his thirty-seven sorties, there were lots of near misses and harrowing experiences. Late one evening just after takeoff, Frank and his crewmates narrowly avoided a mid-air collision right over England with another bomber from 420 Squadron. With hundreds of these giant metal beasts cueing up to head off in tight formation into the night, collisions were inevitable. Heavy losses played a toll on Frank's mind. After some missions, it was a struggle to keep a brave face when people you'd had breakfast with in the morning were simply gone the next day. You didn't have to do anything wrong to get shot down; you just had to be at the wrong spot at the wrong time. It was just a question of luck.

On March 30, 1944, Frank's Halifax was one of nearly eight hundred Allied bombers that took to the night skies for an all-out assault on Nuremburg. Weather reports had indicated a protective light covering of cloud all the way over to the target. But as the bomber stream made its way across the Atlantic the clouds dissipated, leaving the bombers illuminated by a glowing full moon. From the ground below, the Lancasters, Halifaxes, and Mosquitoes were silhouetted against the moonlight. As they lumbered through the cool, crisp sky, the heat from their massive engines left huge contrails and provided the Luftwaffe fighter pilots and ground batteries with a bead on the hapless behemoths from miles away. They waited for the approach and then unleashed a world of hell upon the bomber stream. One by one bombers exploded in flames and dropped from the sky.

The mission to Nuremberg became an aerial massacre. The night fighters had time to attack the front of the bomber stream full force, then land, rearm, and fly up to attack the rear. Eighty-two Lancasters and Halifaxes were lost en route to the target. An additional thirteen went down over Nuremburg and on the way home. Nearly a thousand Allied airmen died in the span of a few hours.

Dunster and his mates in 420 Squadron were among the fortunate ones. They happened to be in the middle of the bomber stream. The bombers at the front and at the back bore the brunt of the Axis attack. Again it was luck of the draw. A week later, Frank was in the air again.

Back at the base in between sorties, Frank enjoyed beer with his mates and time on the nearby rink. He never knew when his number was going to be called. He had brought his skates with him from Canada, not because he was looking to play organized hockey or anything, but for pickup games with his buddies and a much-needed distraction from the horrors of war.

On a mission to destroy the shipyards in Kiel, Dunster's Halifax lost an engine to German anti-aircraft gunners, who also shot up the fuel tank and knocked out the navigation equipment. Unable to limp back to their own base, Dunster somehow guided his crew to the safety of an American air base, where they made an emergency landing. They spent the rest of the night there and had their plane repaired. Back at home base everybody thought Frank and his crew had been shot down. When they arrived home the next day, Dunster found his locker had been cleared out and his most valued possession—his skates—were gone. A friend from Ottawa took them believing Frank was dead.

For his incredible feats of flying, Frank Dunster was awarded the Distinguished Flying Cross. On his official commendation for meritorious service, W.G. Phelan, wing commander for 420 Squadron, remarked: "F/O Dunster has proved himself a most capable navigator who has always displayed outstanding determination and coolness." His group captain, L.H. Lecomte, added: "F/O Dunster, by his outstanding skill as a Navigator, was largely responsible for the successful completion of a tour of operations by his crew. His courage and skill have at all times been an example to the other members of his squadron."

Frank made it through the war. He was the consummate team player who did his duty and did it well. He rarely spoke about his experiences to his family when he came home. There was too much death, and the bad memories seemed to overwhelm the good ones. But the bonds that were formed from shared experience between the captains of the clouds ran deep. Here in St. Moritz it was time once again to show the world what Canadian boys were made of.

Game 1. The Flyers in action against the Swedes.

PART THREE
Showtime

Marching through St. Moritz in the opening parade.

LET THE GAMES BEGIN

12

At the crack of dawn on January 29, 1948, Hubert Brooks looked out his window in the Stahlbad Hotel. Wave after wave of thick, heavy snowflakes whirled through the air and added more layers to the five-foot-deep snowcake already on the ground. St. Moritz was in the final throes of a blizzard. In the run-up to the Olympics the mountain paradise had received the heaviest snowfalls since the pre-war years. It created the perfect conditions for the skiing and sledding venues but was not so ideal for the next day's opening ceremonies and ice hockey matches. From his cozy room in the Stahlbad, Brooks watched as teams of workers frantically wielded shovels to clear the fresh snow from various venues and spectator stands. If they weren't going to have a skate that morning, Brooks figured he could get in a visit with his fiancée. Meanwhile, some of the other guys headed into town for some window shopping.

It took half a day for the Swiss workers to shovel the snow, scrape the ice, and then water the surface by hand before the guys could lace up for their first practice. Refreshed, re-energized, and loaded up with wholesome food, the boys ran through a series of drills and exercises as Coach Frank Boucher ruminated over his final selections. For the most part the team was looking good, and Frank seemed pleased. Only a few of the guys were still suffering from high-altitude headaches, dizziness, and shortness of breath.

After the practice Frank and Sandy held a team meeting for a final discussion about Frank's strategy for success. Boucher wanted to hammer home a number of key points for the boys to keep in mind. They had to go all out and score as many goals as possible. That being said, they also had to remember to play smart and conserve their energy, considering the high elevation. They had to backcheck hard and play a tight defence. He could not over-emphasize the importance of defence. They had to be conscious of the European rules and the somewhat sketchy refereeing. He also reminded the guys that the spotlight was focused on them. Canadians had claimed the gold medal in ice hockey at all but one of the previous Winter Olympic Games. Yes, the press had slammed them. Yes, they had their detractors. Yes, most outsiders didn't think they had a hope in hell of winning a medal. This was their chance to prove them all wrong. Tomorrow was the big day, opening ceremonies followed by their first match against the rough-and-ready Swedes. Manager Sandy Watson ordered them all to get to bed by 9:00 p.m.

Meanwhile a firestorm of controversy swirled around the Games and threatened to derail the entire Olympic hockey program. Two teams claiming to be the official representatives of the United States had arrived in St. Moritz ready to play. The team whose players had badgered the Flyers on the *Queen Elizabeth* was sponsored by the Amateur Hockey Association. The other team was sponsored by the Amateur Athletic Union and the United States Olympic Committee. The Flyers had never seen the AAU boys before. The AAU team had really travelled to Europe in style. They had flown over on American Overseas Airlines.

As far as the Canadian boys were concerned, the showdown between these two American sports organizations was background noise and political posturing. They figured surely the situation would resolve itself before the Games began. But here they were on the eve of the Olympics and the two American camps were still fighting it out. If the two American contingents, the Swiss Olympic Committee, and the International Olympic Committee could not come to a resolution, the Flyers might be playing for a world championship title instead of an official Olympic medal. Sandy and Frank advised their players to put the entire debacle out of their minds and not interfere with the two teams. It would sort itself out. The Canadians were there to represent their country, pure and simple. The boys couldn't agree more.

Opening day, Friday, January 30, was one of those wintery mountain days when low grey clouds hang heavy in the sky, creating an eerie stillness in the air. The temperature hovered just below freezing. The atmosphere was electric. The entire town—twenty-five hundred locals—and about ten thousand spectators had turned out to watch the festivities. Many of the well-heeled guests stood on their hotel balconies with a fine Scotch in hand and fur throws draped over their shoulders. Dozens of reporters and newsreel cameramen blazed around in Jeeps as they jockeyed for the best position to capture images of the procession of athletes. Visitors jumped into local horse-drawn sleighs instead of trudging through the deep snow to find a spot to view the ceremonial procession.

At 10:15 a.m., 915 citizens of the world representing twenty-eight countries assembled in front of the luxurious Kulm Hotel in the centre of town for the traditional five-block march to the Olympic Stadium. Following protocol of the previous Olympic Games, the representatives from Greece were to lead the procession. For diplomatic reasons, countries were then lined up in alphabetical order, with Canada marching in fifth position, behind Greece, Argentina, Austria, and Belgium. The long parade of coloured flags and participants stretched and snaked along the snowy streets of town for two miles.

War hero Hubert Brooks was chosen to be Canada's flag-bearer and stood proudly at the front of the entire Canadian contingent of forty-one athletes and officials. As the boys lined up and everyone darted into position, Brooks could barely contain himself. He vibrated with excitement and was filled with pride. Trainer George McFaul was ten feet in front of Brooks. George marched with the small black-and-white "Canada" name placard hoisted above his head on a simple metal pole. The rest of the players, along with Frank Boucher, were at the back of the Canadian entourage, decked out in their woollen overcoats and regular RCAF service uniforms. They all sported toothy smiles and held their heads high as they marched in unison, three abreast. Manager Sandy Watson was setting the tempo a few steps in front of the lads, his arms swinging. Just ahead of Sandy were the speed skaters in their Canada sport jackets, their long blades tucked under their arms. Everyone was beaming, and the giant lightbox in the sky created the perfect marching conditions.

Up at the front of the Canadian procession, members of the ski team waved to the crowds with one hand while they held their skis over their shoulders with the other. Next came the figure skating component and the media darling of the Olympics, Barbara Ann Scott. The young teenager from Ottawa had recently graced the cover of *Time* magazine. Here in St. Moritz it appeared as if every single reporter, photographer, and newsreel cameraman wanted a piece of her as they scrambled over one another in the hunt for the ultimate close-up. Poised and calm she paid little attention to the media barrage and marched on with her teammates as she waved and grinned to the cheering crowds.

Barbara Ann and her fellow skaters were decked out in blue blazers with toasty ski pants and heavy boots. They all carried their skates in one hand and waved to the adoring fans with the other. As the Canadians paraded down the hill towards the stadium, the crowd of spectators grew thicker and thicker, with thousands crammed into the stands. Thousands more packed the surrounding hills that overlooked the stadium. The bravest of the bunch stood precariously in the thigh-deep snow on cliffs and ledges to get a bird's-eye view of the spectacle that played out below.

Remarkably, both American hockey teams marched in the parade. Neither side had capitulated yet. The AHA team sported blue coats, hats, and fur-lined aviator boots. The AAU team wore plush white winter jackets and matching hats. Tempers flared and a few of the AAU boys and the AHA boys got into fisticuffs en route to the stadium. Ultimately, at the last minute, the AHA team was chosen to represent the United States on the ice. After all the political posturing and arguing about which teams would be accorded official Olympic status, the AHA got the nod. But there was a caveat: they were to receive no official ranking in the tournament. If they were to win at the Olympics, they would be ineligible to take home a medal. However, as this hockey tournament was also the world championships, the AHA team would be crowned world champions if they were to win.

As far as the Flyers were concerned it was a political quagmire. They could not have cared less which American team they faced in the coming days. Right now they had their minds focused squarely on the upcoming match against the Swedes.

Once all the nations had arrived and lined up in the stadium, Brooks and his fellow flag carriers marched to the centre of the podium and encircled it. After a series of proceedings and speeches the Olympic flame was lit, and Enrico Celio, president of the

Swiss Olympic Federation, declared "the Fifth Winter Games as part of the modern Olympic Games to have begun." Brooks planted his flag in the snowbank beside those of the other twenty-seven nations and went to join his teammates.

The Flyers had a few hours to kill. Their first match against Sweden wasn't scheduled until 2:00 p.m. Frank and Sandy had very few scouting reports on the Swedes. They knew they had a few big defencemen and were reportedly one of the toughest teams in Europe. They were also favourites to win the silver medal. Watson wanted his players rested, fed, and ready for the afternoon game. The boys hopped into a few horse-drawn sleds for a ride back to the Stahlbad. Ten minutes later and twelve dollars lighter, they pulled up to their luxurious accommodations and made tracks for the dining lounge.

After a quick feast at the hotel, Coach Frank Boucher sat down in his room and stared long and hard at a blank sheet of paper. It was decision time. One by one he scribbled out his starting lineup for that day's game. He had seventeen capable players to choose from, but only eleven plus a backup goalie could dress for the match against Sweden. The rest of the players would have to ride the bench as reserve men. In the event of an injury or suspension, Frank could pull from his reserves list for the next match.

A few of the boys were obvious standouts. Murray Dowey was a shoe-in for starting goaltender. Last-minute additions Wally Halder, George Mara, and André Laperrière had lived up to their glowing recommendations. New Edinburgh Burghs linemates Ab Renaud, Reg Schroeter, and Ted Hibberd were on fire. Tough guy Frank Dunster, Patsy Guzzo, Irving Taylor, and defenceman Louis Lecompte all had years of high-level playoff experience under their belts.

The rest of the lineup consisted of a handful of young guns and tried-and-true veteran players. Frank felt he was spoiled for choice, but he could dress only so many guys. Warriors Hubert Brooks and Roy Forbes were among the five men who did not make the list. They joined teammates Pete Leichnitz, Red Gravelle, and Andy Gilpin on the bench, along with backup goalie Ross King. They were all first-rate players totally capable of lacing up against the best, but they fell victim to the numbers game. Boucher called them his "Black Aces." The boys who didn't make the starting lineup were gutted, but they understood the rationale. They might not have been called on for that day's battle on the ice, but they were all there to win as a team. And they were ready for action if they got tapped to suit up for the next game.

At 2:00 p.m. "the chosen ones" hit the ice for the pre-game warm-up. Murray was out first, and as the rest of the boys floated around the surface they peppered him with shots. Like the spectators in Basel, the St. Moritz fans were amazed that Murray caught almost every puck that was fired at him. None of the fans had ever seen a goalie catch a puck before. Bewildered and mystified, the spectators leapt to their feet with mouths agape and cheered as the nimble Canadian snagged puck after puck from the air. Coach Frank Boucher pulled the boys in close to the bench for a last-minute huddle. As always he didn't yell or get loud but made his point clearly and concisely to his men. He reminded them to keep the goals down and quietly repeated two words over and over: "Backchecking and defence, backchecking and defence."

Hubert Brooks was disappointed to be on the bench, but he was buzzing with excitement beside Frank and Sandy. He noted in his journal later that night: "This is what we'd been building up to. To say that the pressure was intense would be an understatement. We wanted to win. We wanted to prove the naysayers in the press, who had hounded us all the way to Europe, wrong. This team had something to prove!"

By the time Murray and the boys lined up for the opening faceoff, a couple of thousand fans had settled into their seats. About a thousand more stood in the deep snow and lined the hills and cliffs that overlooked the outdoor rink. Cameras started whirring as reporters and newsreel cameramen took up their positions beside the boards at ice level, in the stands, and up on the cliffs.

From the puck drop, the first line of Flyers started off jittery and uncertain. The Swedes, however, mounted a bold and aggressive attack. Like the Canadians, the Swedes enjoyed hitting, but they also wielded their hockey sticks like weapons. After three punishing minutes of play, the brawny boys from Sweden muscled in the first goal of the game. Once again the Flyers found themselves trailing.

This time the early Swedish goal didn't deflate the Canadians. They didn't fold as they had in their games back in Ottawa against McGill, or back in Paris against Le Club Racing, or back in Basel against the Swiss national team. This time, the Flyers reacted by

The Swedes take the puck in Game 1.

pouring on the power. Less than two minutes later, Patsy Guzzo delivered a beautiful pass to George Mara, who slammed it home and tied up the score. Mara's goal put wind in their sails and fire in their eyes. The boys in blue were infused with confidence and skated with an infectious purpose that rippled through their ranks.

For the remainder of the first period both teams played a tough and scrappy game. "Sticks flew and tempers flared," wrote Canadian reporter Jack Sullivan. Patsy Guzzo received a vicious, deliberate kick in the leg from a Swedish player who was sporting a baseball mask. As Patsy hit the ice and grabbed his leg, the Swede turned around, looked down, and asked him, "OK?" The refs either didn't notice or didn't care to call it. After the first period of play the score was still tied 1–1. The Canadians were holding their own against the silver-medal favourites.

In the early minutes of the second period both teams continued to battle it out. Then big gunner Wally Halder took a pass from Ab Renaud and rifled in the Flyers' second goal. The Swedes responded with full vigour, but none of their shots were getting by "Fast Hands" Murray Dowey. On the blue line, Frank "the Masher" Dunster laced one Swedish winger time and time again as the Swede attempted to skirt past him in between the boards. Dunster later remarked, "I hit him three times and it was hurting me more than it was hurting the Swede! This guy wouldn't give up. He just kept coming and coming!"

The boys in blue held on to their lead for the remainder of the second period. They were still getting used to the low boards, and Murray continued to dazzle and amaze the crowd—and his opponents—by stopping shot after shot with his homemade trapper glove.

When the third period kicked off the Flyers again took to the offensive. Thirty-five seconds after the faceoff, Reg Schroeter buried the insurance goal and gave the Flyers a commanding 3–1 lead over the Swedes. Now trailing by two goals, the rough-and-ready Swedes turned up their heated attacks. A few minutes after Schroeter's goal, one of the Swedes cut Wally Halder down with a brutal hatchet chop to the head. Wally hit the ice like a stone and didn't move for what seemed like an eternity. Eventually he got up under his own power, ran his hand along the back of his bloodied head, and skated off to the bench. Incensed, the Flyers had had it with the dirty play.

The final ten minutes of the game turned into what the press characterized as a "free-for-all" and a "near-riotous imbroglio."

The Swedes slashed, hooked, and speared almost at will in their attempts to claw their way back onto the scoreboard. André Laperrière hammered a big Swedish attacker and was rewarded with a penalty. Moments later Dunster unloaded on yet another Swede and also got sent to the box. The Swedes continued their vicious stick play and, with their one-man advantage, fired salvo after salvo at Murray Dowey. But the kid from the Beaches was like an octopus in net.

With an upset within sight and less than a minute to go until the end of the game, Murray caught a shot and casually threw it out to defenceman André Laperrière right in front of him. It was something Murray had done thousands of times over the years. The ref blew his whistle, stopped the play, and waved Dowey off to "la prison" for a two-minute penalty. Murray was dumbfounded. According to Olympic rules, the puck must be dropped and then put into play. Murray was in violation for "throwing" the puck forward.

As Murray skated by the Flyers bench on his way to the penalty box, Frank Boucher grabbed his goal stick. He shook his head disapprovingly and chastised Dowey quietly, telling him, "You shouldn't have done that. You shouldn't have done that." Murray's toss could very well cost the Flyers the win. The Swedes pulled their goalie and prepared to pounce with six attackers on the ice.

The pressure was on the Flyers to maintain their lead and preserve a victory. Although backup goalie Ross King was standing by and physically able to play, the rules dictated that Boucher was allowed to dress only one goalie per game. Boucher had to leave the net empty or pull from one of his ten remaining dressed players.

He called the boys to the bench and rallied for one of them to slide in between the posts. He leaned in close and said, "This is it, do or die. Who's going to play goalie?" Nobody said a word. Nobody stepped forward. Again Frank asked, "Come on, guys. Somebody has to go in net!" Again he was met with dead silence. None of them were willing to volunteer and shoulder that burden. Meanwhile the ref skated over and told Boucher, "If you don't make up your mind, I'm giving the win to the Swedes."

André Laperrière, Murray's best friend and roommate, grabbed the goal stick and made his way to the net. André had never played goalie and was terrified the Swedes would score on him and he'd let his team down. But as a defenceman he felt it was his duty to at least try. The six-foot-two Laperrière crouched down in net with a death grip on Murray's stick and waited for the impending Swiss assault. But André's teammates weren't about to turtle now. The Flyers took it to the Swedish attackers and played a tight, strong defence. They controlled the puck and stifled the six Swedish attackers from firing anything of substance at André as he quivered in the net. The young defence-man had only to deal with a flimsy shot from a distance. Victory was sealed. The underdogs handily defeated the second-ranked Swedes in what reporters described as a "tough, bruising contest."

Back in Ottawa the headlines read: "Spring Surprise at the Olympic Games." Sandy Watson and Frank Boucher were elated.

For the boys on the team, the battle with the Swedes was an eye-opener to the kind of refereeing they could expect for the remainder of the Games. Any body contact they delivered seemed to draw a penalty, whereas European stick wizardry appeared to go unpunished.

As the boys inhaled their dinners in the dining room at the Stahlbad, they were ecstatic. Despite all the bad press and all the negativity that was heaped onto their backs at home, they knew they had the capacity to take on the best and persevere. Since they weren't playing the next day, Sandy approved a bus trip into the centre of town so the boys could do some shopping and soak up the heady atmosphere on display. Cafes and restaurants like Hanselman's, Steffani's, the Palace Bar, and Chesa Veglia were chock full of visitors enjoying a vast assortment of luscious pastries, cakes, specialty coffees, and drinks. St. Moritz was more packed than it had been in decades. The town was abuzz as spectators rubbed shoulders in the packed streets and cafes with Hollywood movie stars like Joan Crawford and Jennifer Jones. To accommodate the swelling crowds, some hotels had converted reading rooms and other public spaces into temporary bedrooms. Others had even set up temporary overnight beds in the public bathrooms. Back at the Stahlbad the boys learned that their hotel had been closed for the past ten years. It had reopened only recently to accommodate the onslaught of visitors for the Winter Olympic Games.

The players explored the town and peered into the windows of various high-end jewellery shops and watchmakers looking for mementos and potential gifts to bring back to their wives and sweethearts. Many of the local shops also plastered giant pictures of the day's activities in their windows. Local photographers attempting to make a quick handful of francs offered freshly printed custom postcards from snapshots they had captured earlier in the day. Reg Schroeter, Red Gravelle, and Hubert Brooks had cameras and figured they would come back during the daylight to snap some candid pictures of their own.

Throughout the village a number of massive, elaborate three-storey snow sculptures adorned the outside of posh hotels and the odd street corner. While the boys wandered about, buying a few souvenirs and joking with one another about the shenanigans from the game, trainer George McFaul was already asleep back at the hotel. He had a pre-dawn train ride ahead of him the next day to get the boys' skates sharpened. The nearest available spot was in the town of Davos, about forty miles away.

That night the Flyers hit their pillows and dared to allow fleeting images of Olympic gold to run through their dreams. No doubt the Czechoslovakian top guns had similar thoughts as they tucked into their beds on a separate floor at the Stahlbad. In the Czechs' first game they had smothered Italy 22–3. As far as the top team in Europe was concerned, the gold medal was as good as theirs.

The next morning a bright sun and blue skies greeted the citizens of St. Moritz. It was a glorious winter day. Temperatures hovered around minus nine degrees Celsius, snow conditions were excellent, and the skies were crystal clear. It was Day 2 of official competition, but for the men on the Flyers it was a day off. After a hearty breakfast the boys flitted around to the four outdoor rinks so they could check out some of the other teams they'd be playing against over the coming week. They watched as England defeated the Austrians 5–4, the Swiss destroyed Italy 16–0, the United States obliterated Poland 24–3, and the Czechs took down Sweden 6–3. A few of the teams were clearly head and shoulders better than the rest. The Czechs, Swiss, and AHA American squad were impressive teams on the ice. Patsy Guzzo confided in his journal: "There is no doubt that it's going to be a tough battle all the way."

Hubert Brooks took advantage of the down day to cozy up with his fiancée. Together they spent some time with two of Bea's friends, Canadian figure skater Marilyn Ruth and Austrian figure skater Eva Pawlik. Brooks was also on hand to help Sandy with the many language hurdles the manager faced in St. Moritz. As a unilingual anglophone, Watson often relied on Hubert, with his mastery of French, Polish, Russian, German, Czechoslovakian, and Ukrainian, to help him communicate with foreign officials and various representatives for team business matters. Since Brooks wasn't likely to be lacing up for the Olympic matches, Watson formally made him his aide-de-camp. Meanwhile, Coach Frank Boucher thought long and hard about his lineup. Although he was pleased with the Flyers' opening match against the Swedes, Frank decided on a single change: Irving Taylor was out and Red Gravelle was in. Some of the boys speculated it was because Irving tended to hang on to the puck a bit too much. Frank Boucher never disclosed his reasoning.

First thing Sunday morning Patsy Guzzo bolted out of bed and headed into town to attend mass at St. Karl Church. It was Day 3 of the Winter Olympic Games, and the Flyers were slated to play Britain at the Palace rink in a couple of hours. Yesterday's blue skies were a thing of the past, and wintery weather had once again rolled into the pristine mountain village.

By the time Patsy made it back to the Stahlbad, most of the other guys were almost finished getting suited up in full equipment in their rooms. They paraded through the hallways and climbed onto a waiting bus that took them and the British team over to the Palace. Under a steady snowfall, two thousand fans filtered into the stands and lined up four-deep along the boards. Others scrambled up onto the hills in their thick woollen jackets and caps to stake out a spot in the knee-deep snow.

This was a big game for the Flyers and for the nation. It had been twelve long years since the last Winter Olympics, when Britain essentially stole the gold medal from Canada in Garmisch-Partenkirchen using a roster full of Canadian-raised players. Up until 1936 Canada had always claimed the gold medal in hockey at the Winter Olympics. It was time for the boys in blue to take on the defending Olympic champions and reclaim Canada's place at the pinnacle of hockey supremacy.

After the pre-game warm-up Boucher pulled in his boys for a last-minute reminder. He ordered them to go out fast and go out hard, with five men attacking from the opening whistle. The

Flyers went on the offensive right from the start. Boucher's strategy paid off. The Flyers dominated, taking control of the puck. One minute and eight seconds into the first period, Reg Schroeter fielded a nifty pass from his buddy Ab Renaud and let lose a bullet that beat the British netminder.

As the unrelenting snow swirled around the rink and converted the ice into a slushy mess, the Flyers continued to pour on the pressure. Wally Halder and Ab Renaud both rang pucks off the British goalpost and narrowly missed out on adding to the Flyers' tally.

Despite the heavy and consistent snowfall, the Flyers and the British team both played at a fast clip, but the blinding snow coupled with some incompetent refereeing quickly turned the game into a farce. At times the players could barely see the puck through the squalls, and the referees began to call penalties for questionable offences almost on a whim. The pace of the game slowed to a crawl as the referees stopped game play five separate times in the first period alone and sent players from both clubs to the penalty box. Canadian Press reporter Jack Sullivan wrote: "The march to the penalty box was a joke among players of both clubs." After the first few penalties the fans began a chorus of hooting and yodelling with each new ludicrous penalty call. The players, too, began to crack jokes with one another as the penalties became more and more baffling.

Roy Forbes and some of the other boys who had been warming the benches on both sides joined the action and wielded snow shovels to help clear the growing snowdrifts that clogged the ice surface. Slowly but surely, the game lumbered on. At four minutes into the second period George Mara stickhandled his way through the British defence and popped in the Flyers' second goal of the game. Again the boys shovelled the rink, and again the refs called penalty after penalty while the two-thousand-plus spectators whistled, hooted, and howled with laughter.

Nine more penalties were called in the second period despite the cleanly played match. This was nothing like the rough and scrappy game against the Swedes, and the boys on the Flyers could not make head or tail of what the refs were calling or why. When Wally Halder took a pass from Reg Schroeter and deftly beat the British goalie with a sweet backhand, the Swiss goal judge claimed the puck never entered the net. Players from both teams argued with the refs. Even the British players were saying it was a perfectly legal goal. Sandy Watson was livid. He stormed over to the IOC officials and formally protested to have the Swiss goal judge replaced.

By the time the boys faced off at the start of the third period, the game was already well over two hours on. The barrage of snow was turning into a full-on driving snowstorm and yet the game continued. The parade to the penalty box intensified at a dizzying pace, with the refs calling seven more penalties. At the sixteen-minute mark of the final period, Wally Halder took a pass at his own blue line and drove in through the blinding snow to score the Flyers' third goal of the game. The British fought hard in the dying minutes, but Fast Hands Dowey was simply unbeatable, and the Flyers' consistent backchecking dismantled the British attackers' scoring attempts.

After nearly three and a half hours, the marathon match limped to a close under whiteout conditions, and a swirling blizzard overtook the region. The Flyers chalked up their second win in a row, and star goalie Murray Dowey grabbed a shutout in the 3–0 win. On their way back to the hotel Murray and the boys joked with one another about the terrible ice conditions and the mind-boggling parade to the penalty box. When all was said and done, the refs had called twenty-one penalties even though it was a clean game. From the sidelines Roy Forbes figured they would have beaten the Brits by a good ten goals if the game had been played on decent ice with solid refereeing. For most of the guys it hardly felt like a hockey game at all, but nonetheless they were all pleased with the win.

Back in Canada their two-game winning streak was surprising news. The team that was condemned at every turn and verbally torn apart before departure was performing incredibly well. So far the Flyers were far from a national embarrassment; rather, they were proving to be worthy representatives of what Canada as a nation had become.

Suddenly, the underdogs' Olympic run for the podium struck a chord with the masses back at home, and congratulatory telegrams began to trickle in to the hotel in St. Moritz. Those who were close to the team had never wavered in their faith of what the boys in blue were capable of. André Laperrière's father was riveted to the family radio in their living room back in Montreal.

André's sister, Renée, remembers her dad listening to the news reports with his ear pressed so tight to the coils on the box that she thought he was going to go right through it. He was ecstatic and kept chanting over and over to Renée and her mother, "Oh, they're going to make it, they're going to make it!"

Benchside with the boys as they enjoy tea service during an Olympic match.

IN THE THICK OF IT

13

A baking hot sun blazed down onto St. Moritz first thing Monday, February 2. The previous day's oppressive curtain of snowy skies was replaced with a cloudless robin's egg blue. Murray Dowey, Patsy Guzzo, Andy Gilpin, and trainer George McFaul headed out from the Stahlbad bright and early to play spectators and take in the speed skating and figure skating events. There was no morning practice, and the boys wanted to soak up a few of the festivities and go shout and cheer for the Canadian skaters.

Other spectators flocked to the hills to watch the men's downhill followed by the winter pentathlon. While visitors slowly made their way to the bottom of the slopes, many of the locals chose a more efficient mode of transportation and simply cross-country skied through the thick, sticky snow. It was Day 4 of the Olympics, and the Flyers didn't have to take to the ice for their match against Poland until 3:00 p.m.

The picturesque mountain town with its luxurious shops and wealthy visitors made it easy to forget that just a few years earlier, the world had been embroiled in chaotic and bloody combat. But like England and France, many countries were still deeply scarred by the war. Poland, for example, a country that had been invaded and occupied by both the Germans and the Russians, lost a fifth of its population during the war—the highest percentage of any country involved. What's more, it also lost a fifth of its territory when the peacetime borders were redrawn. Now a smaller country as well as a Soviet satellite, Poland was trying to rebuild its devastated cities and feed its long-suffering population. And yet, out of the ashes of battle, somehow the Poles had managed to pull together a hockey team to bring to St. Moritz. And they were next to challenge the Flyers.

As the day wore on, the direct heat from the winter sun had begun to melt and soften the ice. By the time the Flyers and the Poles arrived at the Suvretta ice rink, dressed and ready for their match, pools of water and slush had turned the surface into a sticky mess. Both teams hunkered down and waited for the sun to drop—and pull down the temperature with it—so the ice would have a chance to harden up. About half an hour later the ice, though far from perfect, was good enough to give it a go.

The boys warmed up in front of a thinned-out crowd of about two hundred people. True to form, Coach Frank Boucher again lectured his team about the importance of scoring a lot of goals while playing a tight defence. Running up a big score against a weaker team went against all the tenets of good sportsmanship. But it was a painful necessity. If in the end it all came down to their goal average, they had to make sure they had blasted in enough pucks to stay in contention with the high-scoring Czech team. Just a day earlier, the Czechs had fleeced the Poles 13–2.

From the puck drop the Flyers completely overwhelmed and outclassed their Polish opponents. The Poles played with heart, but they were no match for the Canadians. Back in the Flyers net, Murray Dowey was thankful the temperature wasn't too cold. He occupied his time by skating back and forth from side to side through his goal crease, marking up the ice around his net just the way he liked it. He kept a watchful eye on the play in front of him, but he barely faced one shot in the opening twenty minutes of play. By the end of the first period the Flyers were already up 5–0.

Many of the Canadians felt terrible for the Polish players with their ill-fitting skates and equipment, especially former Polish resistance fighter Hubert Brooks. He had lived and fought side by side with the Poles for a couple of years, and he had a deep connection to and affinity for his Polish brothers. Without the help of friendly Polish allies, Hubert would have likely languished in a POW camp or been killed by his German captors. But this wasn't life or death. Here on the ice in St. Moritz, the Canadians had come to play a game. And they had come to reclaim the title of Olympic champions.

Brooks's conscience was eased by the fact that although the Flyers dominated control of the puck, men from both teams played a classy game. Opposing players helped each other up off the ice, and there were no cheap shots, heavy hits, or aggressive body blows throughout the game. Line after line, the men of the Flyers simply outskated and outplayed the inferior Polish team.

Chivalry and goodwill were also on display in good measure. In between periods George McFaul served fresh hot tea with lemons to players on both squads. When the Polish goalie got a cut on his nose courtesy of a deflected shot, Sandy Watson pulled out his medical kit and stitched him up as he sat on the Flyers bench.

After two periods of action the Flyers had leapt ahead by another six goals. Even young defenceman André Laperrière banged in a goal. Murray Dowey continued doing his side-shuffle in an attempt to keep his blood flowing and stave off the dropping temperature. Over the course of the entire game the Poles managed to fire a half dozen shots at Murray, but he had no trouble at all handling them. Reg Schroeter, George Mara, and Wally Halder were the big scorers, with Patsy Guzzo and Red Gravelle also harvesting a few goals in the win.

By the end of the match the Flyers had plastered the Poles 15–0. It was their third consecutive win and Murray's second shutout. Big gun Wally Halder later told reporters: "We hated doing it. It runs against all Canadian ideals of sportsmanship. But we had to do it to stay in this league against such competition as the Czechs and the Swiss." Halder, team captain George

Mara, and the rest of the boys would have preferred to build up a comfortable five-goal lead and then let the Polish team mess around with the puck for a while. But with all the other countries scrambling to register as many goals as possible, the Canadians had to resist being kind-hearted.

BACK AT THE STAHLBAD, SANDY WATSON wanted his team to hit the sack early. They had a 10:00 a.m. match against Italy scheduled for the next morning, and Sandy and Frank wanted to ensure the boys were well rested. They also didn't want their easy win against the Poles to lull the team into a false sense of security. It was still early days in the tournament, and the Americans were winning games, the Swiss were winning games, and the Czechs were winning games.

Boucher's boys played a few hands of cards, wrote some letters home to their loved ones, and tucked in for yet another early and rather boring evening. Because of the prevalence of the warm winds of the Swiss *föhn* and the warming sun, Olympic officials had decided to try to schedule all future hockey games early in the morning, when the ice was at its hardest. Regardless of any future weather postponements, the Olympics would be coming to an end at 4:00 p.m. on Sunday, February 8. By scheduling all the remaining hockey matches for the mornings, officials were optimistic they could beat the weather and complete the series of games.

Although Frank and Sandy knew going in that playing outdoors would be a factor the boys would have to contend with, they underestimated how frustrating the ever-changing climatic conditions would be. Some days the boys had to trudge into town from their hotel on the outskirts in a blinding snowstorm. Other days they had to sit for hours gear under a blazing sun fully suited up in gear. So far, the ice they were playing on left much to be desired. But the Flyers weren't alone in facing these challenges. It was all merely part and parcel of being there. George McFaul noticed that both the Swiss and the Italian goalkeepers sported flat caps. On one of his skate-sharpening trips to Davos, he picked up a baseball hat with a large bill for Murray Dowey, to help keep the low winter sun from his eyes.

As Frank Boucher drifted off to sleep that night, he grappled with his decision to stick with his lineup. On the ice, his chosen ones were getting more and more acquainted with one another. Three games in and they were coalescing into a fine unit, as he had predicted. But he had five more talented, able-bodied players who had sacrificed three months of their lives to come and play for their country on the Olympic stage. Feelings of guilt for denying them the chance to play in St. Moritz washed over him and did battle with his resolve to stick to his game plan. The lineup was working. He had told them he would stick with it until it stopped working. Why shuffle the deck now? Why risk messing things up when winning gold was why they were all there? He knew the smart move was to stay the course, but he couldn't help but feel bad for some of the guys.

Roy Forbes and a few of the other boys who had ridden the bench over the first three games were harbouring similar thoughts as they lay in bed that night. Although they hadn't gotten to dress yet, many of Frank's Black Aces were hoping that perhaps their coach might shuffle them in against a team like Italy. Resentment started to bubble to the surface for some of them. Even some of the guys who had played in all three Olympic matches to date, like Patsy Guzzo, felt that too much confidence was being placed in the newcomers and not enough encouragement was being given to originals like Forbes, Brooks, Gilpin, and King. Most of the Black Aces had been with the team since day one back in Ottawa. Yet here, in the moment of glory, they were relegated to the sidelines. Roy Forbes kept his disappointment bottled up inside, but it felt like a slap in the face. He burned to get on the ice and play his heart out, but it just wasn't happening.

TUESDAY, FEBRUARY 3, STARTED OUT LIKE a carbon copy of Monday, February 2. Crisp azure skies and a blazing sun greeted the boys when they looked out of their windows at the Stahlbad Hotel. When they got to the rink for their early morning match, they joined the Italians for a cup of tea and some friendly conversation as they waited for the OK from Olympic officials to take to the ice. Remarkably, just a few years earlier many of these men would have been wartime enemies. But here on the sunny terraces of St. Moritz, sport and civility were bringing them together in the spirit of the Olympics.

Patsy Guzzo thoroughly enjoyed his conversations with the Italian goalkeeper, and André Laperrière found a fellow French-speaking member of the Italian squad to have tea with as they sat on benches and waited.

Like the Poles, the Italians reflected their country's wartime suffering. The war and the Fascist government's loss had left the economy in ruins. Here at the Games, the country's devastated resources were evidenced in the hockey team's ill-fitting equipment and sad-looking skates. Guzzo, Brooks, and Forbes all reckoned they were the worst-looking skates they had ever seen. When both teams finally hit the ice, there was little surprise that the Italians were no match for the Canadians.

A mere seventy-five spectators hung around to cheer for the Italians whenever they gained possession of the puck. But the yelling was short-lived, and despite the once again slushy ice, the Canadians easily stole the rubber disc and controlled the action throughout the game. Shift after shift, the Flyers sent five men up and boxed in the Italians behind their own blue line. Then it was simply a case of which Flyer would score. Every Canadian in the lineup except for Murray Dowey fired in a goal or two. Even tough guy Frank Dunster got on the board when he hammered in the second goal. The Canadian Press reported: "It was a massacre and the Canadians were only half trying." By the end of the first period the score was 11–0.

Patsy Guzzo pocketed three goals and a couple of assists as well as carrying on chats with many members of the Italian squad during play on the ice. Somehow André Laperrière managed to pick up a couple of penalties, the only player who made the trek to the penalty box that day. Despite the fact that Wally Halder played a clean game, Italian reporters zeroed in on the big Canadian. When Italian players repeatedly tried to check

Wally, they simply bounced off him, so Italian reporters nicknamed him "the Brute."

After two periods, the score was 17–0. Partway through the third period it had jumped to 19–0 as the Flyers continued to steamroll the Italians. For Murray Dowey, all alone in net, the game versus Italy marked one of the lowest moments of his career. Up until this point in the match he hadn't faced a single shot. For almost two and a half periods he skated back and forth in his crease and attempted to maintain his concentration while at the far end of the ice his teammates toyed with the Italians like a cat batting around a mouse.

At about eight minutes into the third period, Enrico Menardi of the Italian team scooped up a loose puck around the Flyers blue line and sent a feeble shot bouncing off the boards just behind Murray. Unfazed by the dribbling shot, Murray slid over to jam his skate against the goalpost as he had done a thousand times before. Only this time, for some unknown reason—perhaps it was a lapse in concentration; perhaps it was because of sheer boredom—Murray didn't quite get his skate to the post. The weak Italian bank shot bounced off Murray's skate and trickled into the Flyers net, shattering the young dynamo's shutout streak.

Murray was so disappointed in himself he felt like crying on the spot. Frank Boucher hit the other end of the spectrum and was steaming. How could Murray let in such a pathetic goal? At these Olympics, if it all came down to a tie, that one simple goal could mean the difference between gold and silver.

The Flyers finished off the Italians with a final score of 21–1. That was the one and only shot Murray had faced in the entire blowout. If it weren't for his lapse in concentration, he would have earned his third shutout in a row.

Four games in and the no-hope misfits had crushed Sweden, Britain, Poland, and Italy. Despite their impressive wins, observers still considered the Czechs the team to beat. Poland and Italy were walkovers. The Flyers were still facing tough competition ahead with games against serious teams like the Swiss, the Czechs, and the highly touted AHA American team. Many in the press gallery assumed the Canadians' run of wins was about to come to an end.

That night Patsy Guzzo confided in his journal: "Tomorrow is one of our big tests against the USA at 8 a.m." Someone else in St. Moritz spent the evening having a little fun in the dead of night. No one knew for sure who did it, but a brazen souvenir hunter decided to sneak out under the cover of darkness and steal the historic Olympic flag from its mast over the Olympic Stadium. Many suspected an American GI was behind the heist, but it was never proven.

THE NEXT MORNING THE BOYS AWOKE at 6:30, fired up to take on the trash-talking Americans. They shovelled in their breakfast of eggs, bacon, and fresh pastries, suited up in full gear, and hopped on the bus to the Palace rink for their 8:00 a.m. match. They were pumped and ready for action.

When they got there it was as if the gods were having a go at them. Once again, the warm winds of the Swiss *föhn* had ruined the ice. Giant pools of water had formed all over the rink and created a soft, squishy surface. With sweat dripping off their brows, the boys had to sit on the bus and wait while officials checked the weather reports and conferred about postponing the game. A full hour ticked by. George McFaul took advantage of the warm sun and delayed start to darn players' socks and repair gear while he sat outside in the fresh mountain air. Eventually Sandy Watson tore off the bus and laid into the Swiss organizing committee.

With no signs of cooler temperatures coming, the game was cancelled until the next day. The Olympic press bureau issued a hopeful "weather getting colder" statement, and the boys went back to their rooms at the Stahlbad. They got changed, explored the town, wrote more letters home, received telegrams from their loved ones, lounged about on the comfy plush couches, played more games of rummy, and twiddled their thumbs in frustration.

Day 7. Thursday, February 5, 1948. Game day dawned cold and crisp. Although the sun was shining, temperatures hovered around freezing and the ice at the Suvretta rink was smooth, perfect, and glassy. Finally, conditions were ideal for the highly anticipated matchup between the Canadians and the Americans. The U.S. press, which had earlier slammed the Flyers, now billed this as the feature match of the tournament.

A month earlier, the two teams had butted heads on the same ocean liner on the voyage over to Europe. The Americans had travelled in first class; the Flyers were down below in steerage. None of the boys on the Flyers had forgotten the taunting, boasting, and cocky insults the American players had bombarded them with day after day at sea. They said they would beat the Canadians by at least ten goals. They said the Canadians didn't belong at the Olympics. They mocked them and wanted to place bets on how deep they were going to bury the Canadians. Everyone in the Flyers camp was hopped up and itching to make the Yanks eat their words.

As Murray Dowey skated out on the beautiful sheet of glass and took his place in between the posts, he remembered what Wally Halder and George Mara had said to him back on the *Queen Elizabeth*. When Murray had asked his pals, "Gee, I wonder what kind of a team they've got?" both guys gritted their teeth and shook their heads, and Wally replied, "If we don't win anything I just want to beat those Americans."

A thousand fans jostled for position in the makeshift wooden bleachers behind the massive stone hotel. At 9:00 a.m. the Americans lined up on their blue line and belted out a boisterous team cheer. They chanted and smacked their sticks on the ice and raised them in the air above their heads in an attempt to intimidate the Flyers. Unimpressed, Reg Schroeter squared up at centre ice for the opening faceoff. Wally Halder and Ab Renaud calmly took their spots on the wings.

Less than thirty seconds from the puck drop, Wally Halder let loose a cannon of a wrist shot from thirty-five feet out. U.S. goalie Goodwin Harding barely had a chance to register it, and the puck whizzed by his waist and slammed into the mesh behind him. Just like that, the Flyers were ahead 1–0, and the Americans instantly realized they were in for the fight of their lives.

The Canuck boys were on fire. They played fast and hard but were mindful to stick to Frank's game plan and play a strong defensive game. The American boys were husky and fast skaters. But the Canadians were out for blood. Defenceman Frank Dunster harboured no love for his neighbours to the south. He lined up attacker after attacker and was punishing on the blue line.

"It was one of our better games and all the boys played well. Dunster threw his 150 pounds around with devastating results," wrote Patsy Guzzo in his journal. Patsy was determined to stick to his opponent like glue and protect Murray from any American onslaught. Throughout the entire match, Patsy stifled every one of his opposing wingers from firing a shot at Murray.

Wally Halder, George Mara, and the rest of the boys in blue pounced on their American opponents with a vengeance. They were not only outplaying the Americans but also hammering them physically. The Flyers got called on three penalties in the first period, whereas the Americans had none. Despite playing short-handed for six minutes, the Flyers scored two more goals and were up 3–1.

Thirty seconds into the second period, Wally Halder repeated his first-period performance, smashing another quick goal past the American netminder. With the Yanks on the ropes, the unrelenting Canadian attack did not abate. Louis Lecompte, George Mara, and Wally Halder scored three more unanswered goals inside the next five minutes as the Flyers continued to lay the body against their neighbours to the south.

Sandy Watson sutured up American and Canadian players on the bench as the fast, hard action persisted. The European press dubbed Sandy a butcher for his bloody "operations," sewing up players with no anaesthetic. But Sandy knew the guys were essentially numb anyway, so he could stitch them up and send them back in. After forty minutes of dominating play, the Flyers had the game locked up 7–1.

As they took to the bench for a quick intermission, there were no feelings of guilt or thoughts of easing up against these particular opponents. The Flyers hit the ice for the third period and poured on their attack. The Americans answered back and snuck a goal past Murray in a scramble that broke out in front of the Flyers net. Wally Halder promptly responded with two brilliant back-to-back single-handed goals.

From the starting whistle through to the end of the game, the Flyers laid it all on the line. They flew across the slick, smooth ice with surprising speed and endurance and displayed superb stick-handling skills combined with a rabid, ruthless defence.

Nine penalties were handed out during the physical match, seven of them to the Flyers. Despite the short-handed play, the no-hope Canadians silenced the American guns to just thirteen shots against Murray Dowey. On the ice at St. Moritz, Boucher's boys handed the Americans their worst defeat in U.S. Olympic hockey history. The misfits from Canada had annihilated the Americans 12–3.

In the aftermath, Hubert Brooks and the rest of the boys allowed themselves a smile. There was no point in rubbing their clear and decisive victory in the Americans' faces. There was comfort in the quiet satisfaction that things had come full circle. Sure, the boys on the AHA squad had shot off their mouths and denigrated the Flyers. But they had also been through plenty themselves with all the infighting with the AAU team before the Games.

Murray Dowey had never imagined they would beat the Americans so handily. He thought it would be a closer game. But the boys in front of him played phenomenal hockey. They had made up their minds to take no prisoners, and it seemed there was no stopping the Flyers freight train from plowing through all comers.

Frank Boucher and Sandy Watson were exceptionally pleased. Frank had considered the United States the team to beat. Finally, after all the effort, their dreams and hopes were coming to fruition. The Flyers were playing exactly as Frank and Sandy had wished and hoped for. That night back at the hotel, a feeling of euphoria began to percolate within the guys that they just might have a chance to take it all. All they had to do was keep on scoring and keep that puck out of their net.

The boys in blue in action against the Austrians.

THE MIGHTY CZECHS

14

The Games of Renewal were now well past the halfway point. With three games to go, the boys were starting to see light at the end of the tunnel. In five consecutive Olympic matches, they remained undefeated and were now regarded as gold-medal contenders. But their gear and their bodies were also taking a bashing. Their stack of Northland sticks was dwindling at an alarming rate. George McFaul was repairing pads and sewing socks night and day. With all the gear and guys splayed about, the massive suite that Patsy Guzzo and Andy Gilpin shared with McFaul at the Stahlbad was starting to look less like a fancy hotel room and more like a cross between a locker room and a flophouse.

Doing laundry at the various posh digs in Switzerland cost a fortune. Sandy got hosed for $5.00 to have a few shirts, a pair of underwear, a set of pyjamas, and two pairs of socks cleaned. Irving Taylor got stiffed $1.75 to have a single suit pressed. The boys often resorted to draping their wet clothes and shirts over the lamps in their hotel rooms to dry them out. One evening, Ted Hibberd and André Laperrière rushed into Patsy's room to find his hockey socks smoking away on top of a lamp.

Hubert Brooks and Bea Grontved were buzzing as they finalized their storybook wedding plans. In just three days the two were set to tie the knot in a chapel overlooking the idyllic mountain town. Hubert cabled home via marconigram to inform his mother that all was coming together swimmingly for his big day.

At 6:00 a.m. on Friday, February 6, the boys in blue were up and at it in preparation for their 8:00 a.m. game against the mighty Czechoslovakian squad. Once again the air in the Swiss mountain village was crisp and cold. A thick mass of harmless clouds enveloped the sky in a wall of white and kept the sun from melting the ice. Dawn heralded a perfect day for an outdoor hockey match. The ice surface was hard as a rock: smooth, glassy, and fast.

Coached by Canadian Mike Buckna, the Czechs were the current world champions and heavily favoured to capture the gold medal. Buckna was no slouch at the game of hockey. Born in 1913 in Trail, British Columbia, he was an exceptional athlete who played with and coached the Trail Smoke Eaters when they won the world championships back in 1939. Buckna was courted by the Chicago Black Hawks to play for them in the NHL, but he turned them down.

Known as the Father of Czechoslovakian Hockey, Buckna was not only the coach of the national team but also the coordinator of the entire Czech hockey system. He revolutionized the game for the Czechs by teaching them how to play "Canadian" style. He pioneered clinics and introduced the Czechs to the kind of conditioning, passing, and playmaking required to master the sport. As a result of his guidance, the Czechs had risen from the cellar to become a world hockey superpower in just a few short years.

The Czech lineup at St. Moritz was stocked with world-class players. Under Buckna's direction the Czechs had produced a few tremendous NHL-calibre stars. Team captain Vladimir Zabrodsky was a mountain of a man. He stood six foot four and was an outstanding centre with a blazing shot. His free-skating style and tricky playmaking skills delighted fans. So far at these Olympic Games, Zabrodsky was at the top of the scoring chart. Although he was a hulk, he wasn't a big hitter, and he could fly on the ice. His colleague Jaroslav Drobny ran a close second to Zabrodsky. Drobny was fast and stocky and also possessed exceptional stickhandling skills and a cannon for a shot. Unlike Zabrodsky, he liked to mix it up and played a rough game. He was also a gifted multi-sport athlete and a Davis Cup–winning tennis star. In the 1950s Drobny would win the men's singles at Wimbledon. Rounding out the triple threat in the Czech lineup was goalie Bohumil Modry. With wicked fast reflexes, Modry was considered by many in the news media to be the best goalie in Europe. From what the Flyers could see, Modry didn't have Murray Dowey's quick hands, but he was fast on his feet and deftly used his entire body, pads, and stick to guard his net.

Just after 7:00 a.m., both teams thumped down the hallways of the Stahlbad in full equipment and boarded the same bus to the rink. Zabrodsky sat with the Canadian boys and engaged in some light-hearted discussions through broken English. It was a make-or-break match. The players of whichever power-house prevailed that morning would likely be listening to their national anthem with a gold medal around their necks in just a few days.

Coach Frank Boucher was grappling with a tough decision about his lineup. So far, the guys had excelled and performed exactly as he'd hoped. But this morning the Flyers' top scorer, Wally Halder, was seriously under the weather. Wally still wanted to play, but Frank wasn't sure if he should sit him out or keep him in.

About twenty-five hundred fans crammed into the stands at the Olympic Stadium. The ice surface was sheer perfection. Several members of the Canadian ski and skating teams cheered on the boys in the warm-up and nervously waited for the opening faceoff. Boucher pulled his boys in close. He instructed them to play a physical game; the Czechs were big and fast and had a few snipers, but they didn't like to be hit. He told them that neutralizing the big Czech gunners and protecting Murray was the top priority. If they allowed the Czechoslovakians to open up on them, their Cinderella run for a medal would be over.

The tension in the air was thick. Although both teams had racehorses revved up at the gate, the opening minutes started out at half speed. Both teams were playing cautious, defensive hockey. They danced with each other like boxers in the ring, waiting to see who would throw the first punch. Forwards on both squads resisted the urge to rush, take chances, or make risky passes. Halfway through the first period the taps were turned on. Wally Halder, Reg Schroeter, and Louis Lecompte rushed the Czechs and fired three rapid-fire shots in one shift at Bohumil Modry. The Czech goalie rebuffed them all. Moments later the Czech snipers skated the length of the ice and returned fire at Murray Dowey, but Fast Hands had no trouble containing the assault.

Back on the blue line, defenceman André Laperrière played heads-up hockey and did a superb job of breaking up the Czech plays and stopping shots. André threw a bit of the body around, but it was Frank Dunster who levelled the Czechs when they dared get close and had them shaking in their skates. After a couple of solid hits, the big Czech attackers tended to avoid trying to cross the Flyers' blue line with the puck and instead played five men back, opting to dump the puck into the Flyers' zone instead of pressing for an attack.

In the dying minutes of the first period, the Flyers again buzzed Modry and peppered him with a flurry of shots. The boys on the bench leapt to their feet and were screaming for a goal. But the Czech netminder once again stonewalled the Flyers' barrage of shots and kept the score deadlocked at 0–0.

With the first period in the rear-view mirror, the Flyers had outshot the Czechs nine to four. At the opening of the second period the Canadians again took to the offensive. They boxed in the Czechs in their own end and continued pressing with a series of shots and smart passes. When the Czechs stole the puck, the Flyers defence was like an iron curtain, and the forwards followed Boucher's plan to a T. They backchecked like men possessed. Midway through the second period, George Mara grabbed a loose puck inside the Czech zone and blasted a sizzler that was screaming for the right-hand corner of the Czech net. Modry barely managed to get a piece of it and the Flyers pounced on the rebound. They bombarded Modry with a volley of eight shots over the next few minutes, but the bewildered Czechs held on until the refs blew the whistle and stopped the action.

After two periods of play, the Canadians had fired twenty shots at Bohumil Modry. The Czechs had managed to direct only nine at Murray Dowey. Still, the score remained 0–0. Heading into the final period, both teams ratcheted up the heat. Over on the Czechoslovakian bench, captain Vladimir Zabrodsky pressed Coach Mike Buckna to let them play a more wide-open style of hockey. Zabrodsky wanted to go all out and wage a full frontal attack. The Czechs hit the ice going full tilt. Jaroslav Drobny unleashed a howitzer from the Flyers blue line that almost beat Murray Dowey. He blocked the shot but coughed up a rebound that bounced right out into the danger zone directly in front of his net. The Czech attackers scrambled to bang it in and slapped three quick shots at Murray. But the kid from the Beaches deftly handled each salvo, and his defencemen closed in, bunched up the crease, and muzzled the Czechs.

Murray was ecstatic with the protection his team provided him. Their Czechoslovakian opponents were solid skaters, they were fast, and they had some exceptional shots. But the punishing body blows being delivered by the Canucks continued to stop them in their tracks. All match long, Vladimir Zabrodsky was constantly looking over his shoulder.

Midway through the third period Zabrodsky grabbed the puck and tried to race past the Blue Line Masher. Dunster lined up the giant speeding Czech in his sights and crushed him into the boards. Zabrodsky dropped like a rock, his stick and glove flying through the air. Back in the Flyers net, Murray could not believe what happened next. The towering leading goal scorer at the Olympics stood up and started to cry. Maybe his hand got pinched, maybe he was frustrated—only Vladimir knew why—but he stood there and let tears roll down his cheeks. Murray later joked that perhaps it was because his tennis hand got hurt by the Masher. Zabrodsky, like Drobny, also played a mean game for the lawn tennis club in Prague.

The intense, hard-fought game carried on. The tables started to turn when the Flyers began taking penalties. George Mara got sent to the box for interference. Czech coach Mike Buckna ordered a five-man attack. But the boys in blue reached down deep and smothered the Czech power play. Dunster and Laperrière were airtight on defence. Not a single shot was directed at Murray while they were short-handed. On the next shift at full strength, Patsy Guzzo raced the length of the ice and almost squeezed in the winning goal. The Czechs rebounded and stormed back, pressing hard around the Flyers net. With less than five minutes left in the game, Frank Dunster drew a minor penalty that once again gave the Czechs an excruciating two-minute man advantage. Buckna sent in his attackers and they swarmed Murray. This time they unleashed four rapid-fire blasts. The blond, asthmatic kid from Toronto was unbeatable. Under immense pressure he staved off every attack and silenced the Czech gunners.

In the waning minutes of the game, frustrations ran high and ultimately bubbled over when George Mara and Jaroslav Drobny collided on the sidelines. The two heavies instantly got up and started throwing punches at each other. The refs skated in to break up the fight, and the crowd erupted into boos and cheers when they separated the pair.

At the final whistle the game ended in a scoreless tie. The "hopeless, inadequate" team that was skewered by the press when they left Canada had more than held their own against the reigning world champions. The unofficial British United Press scoresheet figured the Canadians had outplayed the Czechs based on tries throughout the match. The first and second periods were dominated by the Canucks, while the Czechs held the advantage in the third. Bohumil Modry stared down twenty-six shots from the Flyers. Murray Dowey repelled seventeen from the Czechs. After the game, Coach Mike Buckna told reporters, "It's real playoff hockey." When pressed for his thoughts, Coach Frank Boucher remarked, "I think we have a good chance of taking it."

As the two teams skated off the now rutted and pitted ice, the crowd gave the boys a big round of applause for a well-fought, well-played match. Their repeated chants of "Canada!" were like music to Murray Dowey's ears. In the 0–0 tie, Murray registered his third shutout in six games. After his disappointing lapse in concentration against the Italians, he felt elated about his performance that day in battle with the top-notch Czechoslovakians. If the Flyers could win their final two matches against the Austrians and the Swiss, they were in contention to win it all.

A FEW HOURS LATER CANADIAN TEEN sensation and national icon Barbara Ann Scott took to the same ice the Flyers had played on that morning. Every one of the players was there to cheer her on as she competed in the women's figure skating finals. To them Barbara Ann was family. She was like their younger sister. They, like her twenty big brothers. And the feeling was mutual. From Olympic Night back in Ottawa all the way to St. Moritz, Barbara Ann watched the Flyers' games whenever she could, and the boys went to see and support her performances whenever they could. Together they planned to bring home double gold to Canada.

The biggest crowd since the opening ceremonies crammed into the bleachers and flooded onto the snow-covered terraced cliffs overlooking the ice. Fully seven thousand spectators had flocked to the rink to watch the glamour girl of the Winter Olympics take on twenty-four other competitors. Hundreds of newsreel cameramen and reporters cranked up their machines and readied themselves to capture every frame of her dazzling performance at the Olympic Stadium.

Although the ice had been quickly scraped, watered down, and refrozen after the Canada versus Czechoslovakia hockey game, the warm afternoon sun worked its devilish magic and turned areas of the surface into a slushy mess. Barbara Ann walked the entire ice before her performance, taking stock of the softest spots and deepest ruts. She tweaked her routine and planned to use the smoother parts of the ice for the riskiest manoeuvres of her four-minute program.

Decked out in a white, fur-trimmed costume with a matching white Dutch cap, the blonde-haired, blue-eyed ballerina of the ice sported "lucky" number thirteen on her sleeve. Calm and collected, she made her way to one end of the rink and waited for the live band to launch into her medley of music. Over the next four minutes, she skated with precision personified and blew everyone away. The Flyers, wedged in among the crowd, screamed their heads off with excitement.

Canadian Press reporter Jack Sullivan, like everyone else in attendance, was awestruck. "The dimpled World and European champion made spins, spirals and loops look like child's play as thousands of spectators shouted hoarsely 'Barbeli, Barbeli'—[a] pet Swiss name for the 19-year-old Canadian."

Because of the poor ice conditions, Barbara Ann modified her program on the fly and did one double loop off the top instead of three. The choppy ice didn't stop her from wowing the audience with three axels, an axel sit spin, and various dance steps. Later she swapped another combination of double loops for double salchows. The ebullient crowd was absolutely enthralled with her impeccable performance. Whether she was up on the saw-toothed toes of her silver blades or flying flat out at top speed, she presented the epitome of grace and beauty. To the spectators it seemed as if the diminutive ice ballerina was dancing, twirling, or leaping every second of her performance.

As she completed her routine and glided off the ice on one foot, roaring applause reverberated through the Olympic Stadium. No matter what the judges thought, the crowd had been bowled over by the young Canadian beauty queen. Two hundred photographers joined a tidal wave of fans and crushed in with shutters clicking as they swarmed around her. Barbara Ann's mother turned to Ab Renaud and Reg Schroeter, sitting nearby, and called out: "Here, you big boys, put her up on your shoulders and help her through." With enormous toothy smiles, Schroeter and Renaud quickly hoisted her up on their shoulders above the cheering crowd. Reg dug into his air force parka and passed Barbara Ann a piece of a Swiss chocolate bar. Barbara Ann beamed down at them and said, "This must be hard on you, boys." Reg replied, "Don't worry, we like it." She bit into the chocolate bar and smiled to the waving fans. Amid the cheers, the laughs, and the smiles, photographers snapped off a blast of pictures, and the enduring image of her taking a bite of chocolate while perched on the shoulders of her hockey brothers was flashed around the world.

Up above the masses, Barbara Ann watched as her marks were posted on the giant scoreboard. Eight of the nine judges awarded her first place. The young girl decked out in white became the first Canadian ever to win a gold medal in Olympic figure skating. Moments later, in the calm and quiet of her dressing room, she confessed to reporters: "I've never been so tired in my life. I was very careful. This was the chance I've been waiting for all of my life. I didn't want to miss it."

What a day for the boys in blue. That morning they held their own and battled the world champion Czechs to a tie. In doing so, they secured themselves a solid chance at winning not just a medal but perhaps even the gold. Then they watched their "kid sister" make history and capture Canada's first-ever gold in figure skating. Later in the afternoon they hobnobbed rinkside with Hollywood A-listers Burgess Meredith and Paulette Goddard.

Back in their comfy digs at the Stahlbad Hotel, Patsy Guzzo wrote: "Barbara Ann Scott performed flawlessly on wet ice. Eileen Seigh of the U.S, trying to catch up, fell on her fanny three times and had a very wet bottom at the finish."

With the end now in sight, many of the boys were starting to feel a little restless and looking forward to getting out of the small mountain town. The daily grind of week after week of no drinking and early nights was starting to wear thin. The boys were itching to let loose—especially those who continued to ride the bench. Forbes, Brooks, King, Gilpin, and Taylor had come all this way, and it was looking more and more as if they would not be lacing up for the remaining games. At least once the Olympics were over, they would get to mix it up on the ice again in the coming exhibition games across Europe.

That night back at the Stahlbad, Patsy Guzzo received an offer from the Italian hockey team to come and coach them the next year in Milan. He was flattered by the concept, but there was no way he would entertain such a dramatic move without first running things by his wife back in Ottawa.

On Saturday, February 7, the Swiss skies opened up once more and delivered a heavy snowfall that cascaded down onto St. Moritz. Beautiful as the thick, fluffy snowflakes were, they wreaked havoc for the organizers, who were doing their best to finish off the final two days of events. The boys were slated to take on the Austrians in the second round of hockey matches at Suvretta rink. By now they had proven themselves to be worthy adversaries, and many in the media figured the Canadians would have little trouble making short work of the Austrians in the early afternoon game.

Roy Forbes was hoping that Coach Boucher might allow him and a few of the other guys who had been sidelined to finally suit up. Not only could they more than handle the Austrians, but by subbing them in, Boucher would give the boys who had played hard a chance to recharge for the next day's final battle against the high-powered Swiss team. But Frank Boucher stuck to his plan and kept the Canadian lineup unchanged. Night after night, the full weight of who played and who sat rested squarely on his shoulders. Frank later admitted that benching those five talented guys day after day was probably the toughest decision he had to make in his entire life.

As they lined up by the bench in the swirling snowstorm, Frank was adamant that the boys stick to his plan and play a strong defensive game. That being said, if there were any opportunities to maximize their scoring chances, they must capitalize on them to keep up with the high-scoring Czechs. Despite that day's heavy snow, early morning game results were already in. Czechoslovakia had hammered the Swiss team 7–1, handing the hometown squad their first defeat in the Winter Games. In other action, Sweden annihilated Italy 23–0, giving their goal average a healthy boost. And the United States took down Britain 4–3. To remain in contention with the Czechs, Swedes, and Swiss, the Flyers had to not only beat the Austrians but also pile on the goals and keep the puck out of Murray's net.

Barbara Ann Scott squeezed in between the guys rinkside and joined them on their bench as the game began. One minute into the first period Wally Halder opened up the scoring parade. Reg Schroeter, George Mara, Patsy Guzzo, and Ab Renaud followed suit by setting up and unloading a barrage of shots that whizzed past the Austrian goalie. By the end of the first period the Flyers were ahead 5–0. Like their earlier match against Britain, this one was stopped so the players could periodically to shovel off the ice.

For the first time in their dance at the Winter Olympics, the Flyers did not clock a single penalty all game. Although the boys in the powder-blue jerseys dominated control of the puck, both teams played a clean and friendly game. Murray Dowey was spectacular in net. From the bench, Roy Forbes marvelled at the young wizard's talent in between the posts. "He was an absolute standout with that glove hand. He was just magical. The Europeans just didn't know what to make of him."

Partway through the match, U.S. referee Walter Brown could no longer stomach the throbbing pain in his foot. Skating on borrowed blades that were too small for him, Brown had developed a sore and infected toe. He made his way to the Flyers bench, and Sandy promptly got out his medical kit bag and removed Brown's toenail right then and there, much to the delight of the boys.

Shift after shift, the points mounted; the Canadians hated running up the score against the Austrians, but it had to be done. By the end of the second period it was 10–0. Four minutes into the third, 12–0. The Flyers were knocking down their opponents like pins in an alley. As the Canadians bowled over the Austrians and chalked up their sixth win, Murray Dowey logged his fourth shutout.

Two weeks earlier, bookmakers and hockey pundits had written off the Flyers and relegated them to the "also-ran" category. Now, heading into their final day of action, the "misfits" from Canada were sitting at the top of the standings. They were tied for first place with the superpower from Czechoslovakia. Both teams had registered six wins and a tie. The day before, the boys in blue had been cheering on Barbara Ann Scott as she captured Canada's first gold medal at the Games. Could the Flyers make it two? To do that they would need to beat their nemesis, the Swiss—the team that had soundly taken them out at the knees in exhibition play, just days before the opening of the Winter Olympics.

The RCAF Flyers official team photo. Front row (left to right): Murray Dowey, Ted Hibberd, Orval Gravelle, Ab Renaud, Roy Forbes, Pete Leichnitz, Patsy Guzzo, Ross King. Back row (left to right): George McFaul, André Laperrière, Frank Dunster, Louis Lecompte, Reg Schroeter, Hubert Brooks, Andy Gilpin, Wally Halder, George Mara, Irving Taylor, Dr. Sandy Watson, Frank Boucher.

PART FOUR

Per Ardua Ad Astra (Through Adversity to the Stars)

Game 8. Muscling it up with the Swiss in front of Murray Dowey in net.

THE QUEST FOR GOLD

15

Morning broke over St. Moritz with a brilliant winter sunrise. It was shaping up to be yet another picture-postcard day in the mountain playground for the world's rich and famous. This was it, the final day of the Olympics. Afternoon temperatures were forecasted to climb to just over ten degrees Celsius. While some of the spectators sipped their drinks and basked on their open-air balconies, exuberant about the warm sunshine, Sandy Watson, Frank Boucher, and a few of the men of the RCAF Flyers were fighting back serious butterflies. Two key hockey matches still remained in the race for worldwide bragging rights. First up, the Czechs were playing the United States. Later, the Canadians were pitted against the Swiss.

The Flyers game wasn't due to get going until early afternoon. If the baking sun continued to beam its warm rays onto the ice, the players would be stepping out onto a swimming pool for their final match. The mildness of the weather, coupled with the fact that they were squaring off against the last team that cleaned their clocks, played havoc in the minds of a few of the boys.

Up until now, they had kept their emotions in check and had not allowed the pressure to seep into their bones and get the better of them. As the boys were getting dressed and going through their last-minute preparations, George Dudley, secretary-manager of the Canadian Amateur Hockey Association, delivered an emotional pre-game pep talk. He told them, "You boys left Canada under heavy criticism by the newspapers and self-appointed hockey 'experts' and you sailed under a cloud of uneasiness and distress." He and the rest of the nation knew they could pull it off and bring home the gold. But win or lose, Dudley wanted them to know they had represented Canada well, and he was solidly behind them.

In early morning action, the Czechs played their final game against the United States and beat them 4–3. The Czechs were now clearly out ahead in first place. To snatch the gold away from them, the Flyers needed to not only beat the Swiss but to win by at least two goals. The complexity of the round-robin scoring meant that even if the Flyers won, the Czechs could still take the gold medal if the Swiss scored too many goals. The boys in blue needed to win, but they also needed to keep the Swiss from scoring against them.

At 1:00 p.m., thousands of rabid Swiss fans swarmed into the Olympic Stadium to watch their hometown national team once again crush the mighty underdogs from Canada. They packed the wooden bleachers, while thousands more spilled out of the stands, pressing shoulder to shoulder on the cliffs and hills that surrounded the rink. Down at ice level the space along the boards was jammed four-deep with newspaper reporters and photographers. Meanwhile newsreel cameramen were positioned on makeshift platforms behind both nets and at strategic locations around the ice and in the stands. Spectators donned sunglasses to mitigate the glaring sun that continued to roast the arena. Many were in just sweaters with their sleeves rolled up; others were decked out in snazzy light sports jackets.

The atmosphere was electric. The stadium hummed like a hive in anticipation of the puck drop. As the teams were readying to take to the ice to warm up, Patsy Guzzo crossed paths with Swiss hockey icon and national idol Bibi Torriani. Torriani tried an old trick to psych Guzzo out. He told Patsy the Swiss were going to take it easy on the Canadians as they hated the Czechs and wanted the Canadians to win the gold. Had it been Patsy's first day in Switzerland he might have actually fallen for Torriani's ploy, but he saw right through the ruse.

The entire Canadian contingent, along with the Flyers' most vocal cheerleaders, Barbara Ann Scott and Bea Grontved, wedged themselves in among the masses of hometown fans. The Swiss crowd was whooping it up and making quite the ruckus, shaking cowbells and chanting to their Swiss hockey heroes. Murray

Dowey and the men about to take to the ice for the first shift could hardly hear Coach Frank Boucher's soft-spoken final edict. They huddled in close and hung on his every word. "I'm not interested in a lot of goals, as long as Murray can keep them out of the net. If you get an opening, you can go, but you must come back when your play is finished. That is a must! Remember. Defence, defence, defence."

With his trusty cap blocking out the sun, Murray led the boys as they stepped onto the rink for the match of their lives. The instant they crossed the threshold, their blades sunk into two inches of mushy, snowy ice. Afternoon temperatures now pushed thirteen degrees Celsius. Carrying the puck was going to be next to impossible.

Pumped up with adrenaline, both teams went on the offensive right from the start. The Swiss trotted out their nasty stick work, slashing and hooking at will. The Flyers played the body but were conscious of not giving the referees anything to call them on.

Four minutes into the first period, Wally Halder deftly took the puck from the Flyers zone, literally ran over the length of the slushy rink, and teed up a low corner shot at Swiss goalie Hans Banninger. The Swiss netminder kicked out a rebound straight at Halder, which he grabbed and rifled back at the net as three Swiss players descended on him. Banninger booted the puck behind the net, where Reg Schroeter was waiting to pounce. Schroeter snatched the puck away from the Swiss defence and fed it back out to Halder in front of the net. Wally whirled away from the

Swiss defenceman and flicked in a beautiful backhand goal that put the Flyers out ahead 1–0. It was Wally's twenty-first goal of the Olympics.

Moments later Louis Lecompte got hauled off for a two-minute penalty when a Swiss player took a dive after bouncing off the big defenceman. On top of the bad ice, the Flyers were clearly up against terrible refereeing that was pointedly in favour of the hometown Swiss team. Officials Eric De Marcwicz of Britain and Van Reyshoot of Belgium called penalty after penalty against the Canadians. As Bunny Ahearne had predicted way back in London, the European refs turned a blind eye to the chippy slashes, jabs, and spears the Swiss players inflicted on the Canadians, whereas anything the Flyers delivered that looked remotely like a body-check would result in a penalty.

Roy Forbes gritted his teeth in frustration on the bench. There was nothing he could do but watch. With both teams playing all out, he witnessed Wally Halder getting tackled, grabbed, and slashed left, right, and centre by the Swiss during one shift. Forbes was beside himself. He could not fathom the officials' reluctance to call anything against the hometown favourites. When Wally tried to lay an open-ice hit against one of the Swiss, he missed his target and fell flat. The Swiss player promptly took a dive. Amazingly, Van Reyshoot thumbed Wally off the ice with a five-minute major penalty.

Canadian Press reporter Jack Sullivan later wrote: "The ice conditions and the refereeing were so bad that at times the game threatened to develop into a farce." CAHA big shot George

Dudley was stewing behind the Flyers bench. He paced back and forth, chain-smoking. Sandy Watson was on a razor's edge. Frank Boucher remained the calm in the storm. There was nothing they could do about the refs or the ice but play the game to the best of their abilities, and Frank knew what his boys were capable of.

Despite the partisan refereeing, the boys in blue held the line and shouldered the Swiss attacks. Murray rebuffed their repeated shots, and the short-handed Flyers silenced the Swiss gunners and wrapped up the first period with a 1–0 lead.

Three minutes into the second period George Mara and Patsy Guzzo launched another Canadian assault. In a fast break up centre ice, George golfed a sweet pass up to Patsy. Despite the heavy slush, Guzzo was flying at top speed. He raced around his opposing wingman and split the defence. The Swiss goalie came out to try to cut down the angle, but Patsy faked him out and fired a high shot over Banninger's shoulder that neatly tucked itself into the top corner of the net. It was Patsy's prettiest goal of the entire Olympics and his biggest thrill of the Games. Mara and Guzzo celebrated mid-ice with a bear hug as the boys on the bench erupted over the team's second back-breaking goal. They had hit the magic two-goal margin.

On the Swiss bench, Coach Wyn Cook was perplexed. He could not get his guys to penetrate the Flyers' wall of defence even on the power play. Whenever they did manage to press the Canadians and crank out a few decent shots, Murray Dowey continued to stonewall them. The baking afternoon sun was turning the ice into a thick layer of slush. Every ten minutes the action had to stop so the players could shovel and scrape the rink. Swiss fans were becoming more and more agitated as the game progressed.

As the second period came to a close the game was turning into a spectacle, with the Flyers drawing twice as many penalties as the Swiss. Ted Hibberd was cross-checked from behind and slammed heavily face forward onto the ice by Swiss defenceman Heinrich Boller. Remarkably, the refs awarded Hibberd with a penalty along with Boller for the cross-check. But the "no-hope Canadians" kept up the pressure and headed into the third period with a 2–0 lead. If the Flyers could hang on, the gold medal would be theirs.

Midway through the third period, the Swiss were on life support. Reg Schroeter raced in, split the Swiss defencemen, and hammered off a bullet. Reporter Jack Sullivan remarked that Schroeter's shot "skipped like a stone over water, then skipped over the goalie's stick." The Canadian boys on the bench hung over the boards, banged their sticks in euphoria, and cheered. The Flyers were up 3–0. The gold medal was now within arm's reach. On the cliffs and terraced hills above the rink, some among the Swiss crowd began to gather handfuls of snow from the ground.

Standing in net, bent over and watching the play up ice, Murray Dowey was shocked when a snowball whizzed by his head, then another and another. And then one hit him, smack dead in the side of his head. Bewildered, Murray called over to the ref and complained. "What's going on here? You have to stop this." The refs ignored him. They just let the game continue.

They didn't stop play and talk to Wyn Cook or Frank Boucher or any IOC officials. Meanwhile, the irate Swiss fans pelted more snowballs at the Flyers, hitting Patsy Guzzo and a few other Canadian players.

With just minutes left in the game, Heinrich Boller, the same Swiss player who delivered the dirty cross-check to Teddy Hibberd earlier, crowded into Murray's crease. A scramble broke out in front of the net, and Boller slashed Frank Dunster in the head with a two-hand chop. Dunster went down and Boller spun around and punched Murray Dowey in the face. Boller was given only a two-minute penalty. Incensed, Murray quickly checked to confirm he wasn't bleeding and decided to keep his hands down and his mouth shut. The Flyers had put up with a boatload of terrible refereeing. Murray figured if he said anything he would probably get called for talking back to the ref.

The Flyers poured on the pressure. Then the final whistle blew. Bursting with pride, all the boys cleared the bench and rushed the ice in a swirling mass. They leapt onto Murray Dowey and smacked each other in glee. They were oblivious to the jeers of the bitter Swiss fans as they celebrated in the middle of the ice. The final score was 3–0.

Despite all the obstacles—from the snowballs, to their rushed preparations, to their shaky start back in Ottawa, the "misfit" Canadians had achieved the impossible. The RCAF Flyers had taken down the mighty Swiss national team in a decisive victory in front of a hostile hometown crowd, and they had scored enough goals to push the Czechs into second place. After eight Olympic games, the Flyers remained undefeated. They tallied sixty-nine goals against their opponents while allowing just five in their blistering run to the podium. In the process, they followed Barbara Ann Scott's lead and captured Canada's second gold medal at the Games of Renewal.

With beaming smiles and sticks raised jubilantly in the air, Sandy Watson, Frank Boucher, and the rest of the boys lined up on the ice arm in arm and posed for photographers as the new world and Olympic champions. As the reporters snapped pictures, the boys waved over CAHA boss George Dudley and Canadian Olympic Association heavy Sidney Dawes to join them in the euphoric celebrations. Against all odds they had accomplished what no one thought was possible just a couple of months earlier. And they did it in record-setting fashion.

Murray Dowey logged his fifth impressive shutout at the Games. By allowing just five goals over eight games, Murray posted a breathtaking 0.62 goals-against average. His remarkable skill in the cage earned him an Olympic record. To this day, Murray's record stands unbeaten.

Wally Halder scored twenty-one goals and George Mara seventeen. They still hold the number-two and number-three positions for most goals scored in one tournament at the Olympics. The number-one position is held by big Czech gunner Vladimir Zabrodsky, who fired in twenty-seven goals. The Czechs were victims of the round-robin numbers game. They too played fantastic hockey in St. Moritz and finished up with seven wins and one tie. Although they were a powerhouse at scoring, it was the Flyers' stellar goals-for/goals-against quotient that bumped the Czechs down to silver.

As the fifth Winter Olympics drew to a close, the boys in blue lined up two by two and climbed onto the temporary wooden pallets assembled at centre ice for the medal presentation ceremony. Murray Dowey was standing next to George Mara. Amid the cheers and the din of the Swiss and the Czech players sidling up on either side of them, George leaned over and said to Murray what every one of the boys was feeling: "This is the proudest moment of my life." Tough guy Frank Dunster was grinning from ear to ear. Marcel Heninger, chairman of the Swiss Olympic Committee, presented each of them with a gold medal in a burgundy leather case. The Swiss orchestra launched into the Canadian national anthem, and the emotion of the moment overtook many of the hardened warriors, bringing virtually all of the boys to tears.

The Flyers were in a daze. As they scooted for the dressing room at the stadium, members of Canada's other Olympic teams grabbed at them and cheered them on. They blew kisses to the crowd, thrust their arms in the air, gave the thumbs-up, and excitedly yelled to reporters, "We've done it, boys!" Reg Schroeter, André Laperrière, and Frank Dunster chimed in, "We couldn't be happier." Thirty-three-year-old defenceman Louis Lecompte had his arm in a sling, the result of a brutal slash during the hard-fought match. He added, "I never thought an old man would be an Olympic winner." In the melee of bodies Patsy Guzzo had tears running down his face. Red Gravelle kept repeating over and over, "Am I proud! Am I proud!" Sandy Watson called out,

"It's the best team in the world!" When one of the boys called on Frank Boucher to make a speech, the room went dead silent. Frank calmly looked around at each of the guys and said: "Fellows, I am proud of you. I want to thank you all, and that goes for the boys who didn't play. You're a great gang and I knew you'd do it." Later back in Ottawa, Frank would confide to his wife that it was the biggest accomplishment of his life.

A few of the guys in front of their Czech "taxi."

THE LONG ROAD HOME

16

Back at the Stahlbad Hotel, it was time to celebrate. Hundreds of telegrams from Canada and abroad poured in congratulating the Flyers. Prime Minister William Lyon Mackenzie King cabled them, as did external affairs diplomat Lester B. Pearson, along with Air Marshal Wilf Curtis, Defence Minister Brooke Claxton, the chiefs of the naval and army staff, CAHA president Al Pickard, family members, friends, and even female admirers. Members of the British hockey team that had won Olympic gold in 1936 wired them: "Congratulations to the new champions from the Ex." Sandy read a few of the choice messages to the boys as they prepared for the evening's celebrations.

Those same Canadian newspapers that had once blasted the Flyers now jumped on the bandwagon and championed their success. The next morning, the *Ottawa Journal*'s page-one headline read: "Flyers Bring Title Back to Cradle of Game. Rags to Riches Saga Climaxed by Victory."

Back in Ottawa, André Laperrière's proud sister, Renée, was bouncing off the walls. She hollered and cheered along with her parents when they heard the good news. They cabled André a hearty congrats and couldn't wait for their gold-medal champion to come home.

In St. Moritz, the Flyers were the toast of the town. RCAF group captain Robert Cameron was a Winnipeg boy who was now serving as Canada's air attaché in Prague. Cameron pulled some strings in the ritzy mountain town and lined up a huge feast. He held a reception for the team at the Stahlbad, and the liquor flowed like water.

The boys cleaned up real nice for their victory party. They sported grey flannel dress pants, crisp white shirts, pink-and-white-striped ties, and smart blue blazers with a maple leaf on the breast pocket. Members of the Canadian ski and skating teams also joined the festivities. George Mara tapped his father's massive liquor-and-wine importing firm to bolster the free-flowing booze by coughing up a bottle of premium liquor for each of the guys to enjoy. Sandy's restrictions were lifted and the handcuffs were off. The boys could finally blow off some steam and bask in the glory of their triumphant win.

After the speeches and formalities, the party made its way into town. Some of the guys hit the Kurhaus hotel for beer; others spread out and painted the town red. André Laperrière and Andy Gilpin didn't slide back to the hotel until 4:00 a.m. Nearly seventy years later, sitting in his lounge chair in Kelowna, Roy Forbes looked up at the ceiling as he ruminated about that night so long ago. He grinned and shook his head. "God, we had a great night in one of those bars there. I tell ya, it was a great night!"

Bright and early the next morning the celebration continued. A few of the boys were nursing hangovers and some of the others had barely caught a wink's sleep, but no one was going to miss Hubert Brooks's and Bea Grontved's big day. Dressed in their military uniforms, the Flyers escorted Hubert and Bea to a small Roman Catholic chapel that was perched high above St. Moritz and overlooked the Olympic Stadium.

With snowbanks piled high over their heads, they filed into the tiny stone chapel for the ceremony. Bea was wearing a beautiful dress, heels, a light fur coat, and an electric smile. Hubert was dashing and debonair in his military dress. Brooks had asked Sandy Watson to stand in as his best man. Barbara Ann Scott readily agreed to be Bea's maid of honour. The couple asked RCAF group captain Robert Cameron to give the bride away.

When the newlyweds emerged from the chapel, the boys formed an honour guard with their hockey sticks raised in an arch. Newspaper reporters and photographers fired off a barrage of photos. Arm in arm Hubert and Bea walked under the hockey sticks positively aglow. At just twenty-six, the young man from Bluesky, Alberta, had lived quite a life. Inside he was bursting with emotion. He could not think of a better way to culminate his first quarter century than marrying the love of his life in a storybook ceremony in St. Moritz.

As the wedding party congratulated the newlyweds outside the church, members of the press called out for more poses and pictures. They asked Hubert to plant a posed kiss on the maid of honour, Barbara Ann Scott. While the boys and Bea had a hearty laugh, Brooks and Barbara Ann accommodated the photographers. Much to Hubert's and Bea's amusement, it was his kiss with Barbara Ann that made the news cycle the following day.

After a brief celebration party and reception at the Stahlbad, it was time to get back to business. Barbara Ann made tracks to Davos, where she would be trying to defend her world title in two days. Sandy gave Brooks a few days off so he and Bea could enjoy an abbreviated honeymoon in St. Moritz. Meanwhile, the rest of the Flyers packed up for a late-afternoon train to kick off the start of the team's post-Olympic European exhibition game tour.

Already, St. Moritz was a shadow of its former self. The V Olympic Winter Games were over. The Olympic flame had been extinguished. Many of the hotels had already begun shuttering their doors. Gone were the crowds and the excitement. By the time the boys made it to the train station for the first leg of their journey, it seemed like a completely different world than the one they had steamed into just two weeks earlier.

The "honour guard" at Hubert and Bea Brooks' wedding.

The relief and elation of winning the gold medal were quickly replaced by the cold, hard reality that the boys still had nearly two months of exhibition games ahead of them before they could go home. For the next seven weeks they criss-crossed through Europe as ambassadors for Canada, taking on local teams, regional champions, and other national teams, like their old foes the Czechs and the Swedes. The exhibition games weren't lined up just as a gesture of civic goodwill. The Flyers needed a percentage of the gate receipts to pay for their expenses and cover the cost of their return sailing to New York.

For the first week they bounced around Switzerland. Their next stop was Czechoslovakia. Sometimes they travelled by airplane; other times they went by special trains, buses, even sleighs that hauled them and their gear through rough remote passes. After Czechoslovakia, they were on to France, and then to Holland, Sweden, Britain, and Scotland.

In the afterglow of the Olympics the Flyers were treated like champions everywhere they went. They had become the darlings of the European hockey community. It was a far cry from the reception they received prior to the Games. Night after night, in town after town, thousands of fans came out to watch their hometown heroes take on the new Olympic champions. At many of the stops on their tour, the boys were wined and dined at civic receptions and banquets. Hockey-mad European fans and dignitaries showered them with gifts such as scarves embroidered with the word *Canada*, pencils, ashtrays, medals, cut-glass vases, even metal cups engraved with a maple leaf design. Before and after exhibition games they were mobbed by fans who were desperately seeking autographs. Female admirers slipped letters under their hotel room doors, and some even included pictures. One of Murray's fans confided that she was writing him not because he was a "good hockey player, but because he was a good-looking hockey player."

With the pressure of the Olympics behind them, many of the guys seized the opportunity to finally pick up presents for their loved ones back home. Murray Dowey bought his wife some fine blouses and jewellery. He picked up a beautiful silver cigarette case for his dad and some fancy French perfume for his mother-in-law. Other boys bought Swiss watches and Czechoslovakian crystal. Patsy Guzzo picked up some dolls and handkerchiefs for his little girl, Lee; some perfume and a musical clock for his mother-in-law; and some jewellery for his wife.

They played in front of the Dutch royal family in the Hague, and in front of fifteen thousand in Brno. In Paris they beat Le Club Racing de Paris with backup goalie Ross King in net. Ross lost two teeth when he took a puck in the face during that match against the French. Sandy sutured in six stitches and Ross was back in net for the rest of the game. In Sweden the boys feasted on eggs, ham, milk, and a variety of meats before they headed back to Great Britain and the slim pickings of a country still under post-war rations.

By the end of March they had travelled some fifteen thousand miles and played before an estimated 350,000 fans. After playing thirty-five games in seven countries, the gruelling schedule had taken its toll on them all. They had fulfilled their obligations as hockey ambassadors for Canada, and their cut from the exhibition games meant Sandy now had enough money to cover the return trip home. Bruised, battered, and exhausted, they were ready and eager to get back to their families.

On Tuesday, March 30, the Flyers hopped off the bus and dragged their bags into their old digs at the Crofton Hotel in downtown London. The same lady who had checked them in way back on January 15 was again sitting behind the front desk. She was still wearing her fur coat, her warm gloves, and her hat. The boys dropped their gear in their spartan rooms and headed out to the Garden Clover Club, where Bunny Ahearne threw them a going-away bash. While they feasted in the club on some quality food, many of the guys had their first glimpse at the way of the future: television.

By noon the next day they had boarded the *Queen Elizabeth*'s sister ship, the *Queen Mary*, and finally set sail for home. With their spirits high the walking wounded made their way down to their tourist-class cabins. Nearly all the boys had lost weight— some as much as ten pounds. André Laperrière had a juicy gash under his right eye and a puncture wound over it. Louis Lecompte's arm had healed, but now he had a cheekbone fracture. Roy Forbes and Reg Schroeter were both sporting one-inch gashes on their foreheads. Frank Dunster was nursing extensive bruising over both thighs and a cut nose. Patsy Guzzo had pulled groin muscles.

Sandy Watson recognized that his boys looked as if they had been on the losing end of a bar fight. He told reporters who had gathered on the ship, "Five days on board will fix them nicely. They will get home in good shape."

Along with their gold medals and the world championship cup, one of their prized possessions was Murray Dowey's much-loved, much-taped and retaped goal stick. "It is the only survivor of more than three hundred sticks we brought over with us and we wouldn't part with it for one million dollars," said trainer George McFaul. Only five goals snuck past that stick during the team's incredible run to the podium. Some felt the stick belonged in a museum. Newlywed Hubert Brooks, meanwhile, was coming home with two prizes: a gold medal and the love of his life.

the work looked and is a disappointment. I never did see those memorable days in any other home, and it was not a noble medal that we hung on its face.

The homecoming parade in Ottawa.

OLYMPIC CHAMPIONS

17

On April 7, a breath of cool, wintery air lingered across downtown Ottawa. Despite the chilly temperatures the sun was shining and the trees that lined Elgin Street were full of tiny buds, heralding the arrival of spring. For days military bands had been practising drills and songs in preparation for the festive welcome home ceremony for the nation's Olympic-champion RCAF Flyers. Hundreds of people jammed into Ottawa's Union Station eagerly awaiting the team's arrival. Giant banners that read "Canada is proud of you" draped the walls. The full complement of the RCAF Central Band, bolstered by the RCMP's band, waited at the ready with their hands on their instruments. Barricades were set up to contain the gathering crowds.

Outside the station, thousands more lined the parade route that led past the National Defence Headquarters, ending up at the team's old stomping grounds, the Beaver Barracks. At 1:00 p.m. the train steamed into Ottawa's Union Station, and the boys stepped out into a wall of sound. They were greeted by a huge fanfare of fans, family, military officials, and well-wishers. The two bands blasted out "Captains of the Clouds" to the cheers of exuberant fans. Defence Minister Brooke Claxton and old friend Buck Boucher were among the first to grab the boys' hands and congratulate them for a job well done. Tears were flowing; husbands, wives, and sweethearts embraced, and babies were passed over to the fathers, like Reg Schroeter and Patsy Guzzo, who had longed to see them for over three months.

After a few moments for personal greetings, the hockey lords filed into a fleet of Buick convertibles and took to the streets of Ottawa for a formal parade. The city was abuzz with excitement for the underdogs who had surprised the world and brought glory to Canada's armed forces. With a marching band out in front, the cars wound their way past thousands of spectators who lined the streets four to five people deep. Motorcycle outriders cut a swath up both sides of the street to prevent fans from rushing the cars. As the boys waved to the fans, photographers ran in for close-ups and newsreel cameras whirred away. Overhead, three silver Dakotas did a low flyby and dipped their wings in salute.

André Laperrière's little sister, Renée, could not believe her brother was suddenly so famous. She was having the time of her life, watching the spectacle of all these strangers cheering, shouting, and applauding for her big brother. In among the mob of spectators on the parade route, she couldn't contain herself. She kept turning to those around her, pointing and shouting, "That's my brother! That's my brother!"

For Murray Dowey, winning gold and coming home to the warm reception was the highlight of his life in sport. For Patsy Guzzo, it capped a wonderful ending to the saga of the RCAF. What better way to end his playing days than with a gold medal for his country? For Roy Forbes, the experience was bittersweet. He'd made great lifelong friends, played some of the best hockey of his life, and had a damn good time in the process. But to this day, he still burns inside a little. He still wishes Frank had let him play during at least one of those eight crucial Olympic games.

CANADA'S DOUBLE GOLD AT THE 1948 Winter Olympics had a galvanizing effect on the country. Coming out of the war years, the wins by Barbara Ann Scott and the RCAF Flyers helped provide a natural boost to many Canadians still struggling in the aftermath of post-war gloom. But the spotlight for the Flyers quickly faded, whereas the flame for Barbara Ann Scott burned even brighter.

In the ensuing weeks, months, and years the graceful figure skater became hugely popular. Barbara Ann Scott was clearly the biggest story for Canada to come out of the 1948 Winter Olympics. For her welcome home parade, a hundred thousand fans descended on the streets of Ottawa. The media and masses latched onto her wholesome appeal and incredible talent and propelled her to become Canada's sweetheart. Hollywood came calling. Young girls aspired to be her, and Reliable Toys created the Barbara Ann Scott doll, which sold well from 1948 until 1954. She was crowned the unrivalled queen of Canadian figure skating. She was inducted into the Canadian Olympic Hall of Fame in 1948 and Canada's Sports Hall of Fame in 1955, and was made an Officer of the Order of Canada in 1991.

For the men of the Flyers things went a little differently. After the parades, the parties, the celebrations, and the headlines, the boys who won gold quickly dissolved into the background. There were no big endorsement contracts, and none of them chased fame or NHL careers.

Before they officially disbanded on April 11, 1948, the boys got together to divvy up all the wonderful gifts and mementos the team had been given on their post-Olympic tour. They put everything on a table and drew numbers out of a hat to decide who picked first. André Laperrière drew the first straw. One by one they dealt out the vases, pins, flags, cups, trinkets, trophies, and banners. And then, after being together for months, they went off on their separate paths once again.

Every man in the service was given two weeks' leave, then it was back to his regular duties. The guys who were called in off the reserves list reported back to their civvy jobs. The titans of business were back at work. The Flyers' moment of glory was short and sweet. A blip in time and then they faded into history.

Over the years the guys got together for the odd game of golf or the occasional anniversary reunion. Although they were spread out across the country, some of the pairings and cliques carried on. Whenever Murray Dowey found himself in Montreal or André Laperrière made it to Toronto, the old roomies would meet for dinner. Wally Halder and George Mara remained life-long friends and eventually worked together with the Olympic Trust of Canada. Roy Forbes and fellow warrior Frank Dunster remained close friends until the bitter end. Patsy Guzzo's small sports store in Ottawa became a regular meeting place for the boys to pop in for a quick chinwag and a catch-up.

As the years passed by, Reg Schroeter was the glue that kept all the Flyers together. He took it upon himself to be the team's historian and archivist. In the aftermath of the Olympics, Reg returned to his job in Ottawa and worked in government until his retirement in 1980. He continued playing senior hockey and passed on a chance to play with the Boston Bruins in the NHL, as that would have meant leaving his family for long periods and giving up his government job. He continued playing hockey until 1992, while also refereeing at the amateur level. As the team's "unofficial volunteer" historian and archivist, Reg kept tabs on everyone and maintained a detailed scrapbook of newspaper clippings that he shared with all the guys and their families up until his death from stomach cancer in September 2002.

Roy Forbes went back to Trenton and finished up his meteorological courses. He transferred out of the RCAF and moved over to the army in 1952, when he was invited by the brigadier general to play for the army hockey team at the upcoming 1952 Olympics in Oslo. It took Roy about ten seconds to make the decision to leave the air force and join the army for a second crack at playing hockey on the Olympic stage. But the Korean War broke out, and Forbes once again had to answer the call to serve his country. He served as a platoon commander in Korea and worked his way up the army ranks until he retired after more than forty years of service. A fighter forever, Roy outlived his beloved wife, Jeannie, and many of his friends. When I last saw Roy he was ninety-four. He no longer had the balance to lace up and take to the ice, but he still enjoyed watching hockey in his trailer outside Kelowna. Roy passed away on April 12, 2017, six days after he celebrated his ninety-fifth birthday.

Hubert Brooks launched himself right back into his military world. Earmarked for a career in the intelligence field, Brooks followed a path in the air force that led him to the rank of wing commander. His postings and intelligence experiences continued to take him around the globe. As Canadian military intelligence officer responsible for the Middle East, Brooks was on the ground immediately after the Israeli Six-Day War to represent Canada and have a look at the captured Russian arms. When the October Crisis lit up in Quebec in 1970, the federal government tapped Brooks to assess the situation on the ground, as he was one of the few people they had who truly understood guerrilla warfare. After his retirement from the military in 1971, Brooks became the director of housing at the University of Ottawa, where he was instrumental in creating new affordable housing for students. He also carried on his volunteer work with the Royal Air Forces Escaping Society. On February 1, 1984, he passed away of a sudden heart attack while working at his desk at the University of Ottawa. The university named a student residence in his honour.

Frank Dunster never returned to the Ottawa Fire Department. He stayed with the RCAF for another twenty years and piloted everything he could get his hands on. Well into his thirties he was in the cockpit piloting CF-100s, earning himself the new nickname "Old Guy" from the younger upstarts. Frank nearly made it back to the Olympics in 1956, when the team he was coaching almost won the Allan Cup. One of his greatest moments came in late 1987, when he was invited to carry the Olympic torch partway through Ottawa as it made its way towards Calgary for the 1988 Winter Olympics. A diehard smoker who never was into running, Dunster blazed a trail down Bank Street with a huge smile on his face. His kids were in awe that their dad actually found the lungs to run with that torch. Frank's light went out on April 9, 1995, when he passed away from cancer.

Murray Dowey headed straight back to his job as a clerk at the Toronto Transit Commission and stayed there until he retired at sixty as the superintendent of administration. He never played serious hockey again. Fast Hands could have had a professional baseball or hockey career, but he opted to raise a family, have a life closer to home, play in the senior leagues, and stay at the TTC. After the Olympics Murray became friends with Czech goalie Bohumil Modry and often sent him packages of goods overseas to help him out. Murray still has the ball cap that George McFaul got him to block out the sun, as well as his skates and blocker. Like Frank Dunster, Murray got a chance to get close to the Olympic flame once again. In 2010, he was asked to carry the torch through Toronto on its route towards Vancouver's Winter Olympics. Originally the plan was to have Murray hold the torch out the window of a streetcar in a public relations stunt with a nod to his long connection with the service. Murray told the organizers, "Not a chance. That flame will whip inside and light up my hair. I'll jog with it." At ninety-one he still has his "fast hands" and is solid on his feet.

André Laperrière returned to the University of Montreal to continue his studies. He turned down offers to play with the New York Rangers year after year. While playing for his university team he won the Canadian Intercollegiate Hockey Union championship and graduated with his degree in graphic design. A pull to join the public service inspired Laperrière to serve on the Outremont city council from 1970 to 1982. He continued to skate, ski, and play golf and tennis well into his late eighties. His body gave out and he succumbed to bone cancer at ninety, on March 8, 2015.

George Mara returned to take the helm of his father's business empire. Not long after Mara's return from Switzerland, Frank Selke came calling to see if George would lace up for the Montreal Royals and then play with the Montreal Canadiens in the Stanley Cup playoffs. George scored a bunch of goals for the Royals but got plowed in his sixth game and separated his shoulder. That put an end to his playing career. George spent the rest of his life immersed in his two passions, business and hockey. He served as an executive on the board of Maple Leaf Gardens for more than a decade. In the late 1960s he helped establish and then chaired the Olympic Trust of Canada for two decades. Known for his philanthropic efforts, Mara helped to raise millions of dollars to support Canadian Olympic athletes. George passed away in August 2006, just a few months shy of his eighty-fifth birthday.

Wally Halder slid back into the world of business and advertising. But he didn't stray far from amateur sport. Although he retired from serious active play, he still carried a deep passion for hockey. He coached the University of Toronto's Trinity College team for a few years and instilled in his kids a love of the sport on the backyard rink. During a friendly tennis match with his lifelong pal George Mara, Wally decided to leave the advertising world and join George as president of the Olympic Trust of Canada. He was an incredible fundraiser and public speaker and stayed in that position until 1988. Wally loved amateur sport and the Olympic spirit—it was a celebration of the youth of the world coming together to compete. He never missed an Olympics. When Wally took ill and was in hospital, George came to visit every day with a McDonald's milkshake. Arguably the best amateur hockey player in the world in 1948, Wally succumbed to cancer in October 1994.

Patsy Guzzo continued to lace up for the RCAF for a few more years. He also kept up his impressive pitching game well into his late fifties. When he wrapped up his career in the air force, Patsy opened up a small Ottawa sporting goods store that became the stomping ground for many of the boys. Kind and generous to the core, Patsy would give away hockey gear to kids who couldn't afford it. The '48 Olympics remained one of the highlights of Guzzo's exceptional amateur sports career. He picked up a few nicknames on the road to St. Moritz and back. Press in Switzerland called him "Oiseau," or "the Bird," because of his speed and finesse. In Czechoslovakia they called him "the Dancer" because of his smooth play and agility. He was dubbed "the Angel" in Paris. The poetic, religious family man died in Ottawa on January 19, 1993.

Ab Renaud carried on with his job in government and continued to lace up for the RCAF after the Olympics. Later, he took to the ice for the army. The speedy, solid winger played competitively for another decade as a player–coach in the New York–Ontario league. At eighty, Ab married his longtime family friend Lorraine. He passed away just before Christmas in December 2012.

Louis Lecompte returned to the RCAF's photographic unit and eventually made his way to Kenya, where he worked for Canadian External Affairs doing aerial survey work. His passion for hockey never waned. He brought his beloved hockey skates with him to Africa on the off chance he could find some artificial ice there. When he passed away in 1970, Louis was buried with his Olympic ring. His skates and sweater were donated to Canada's Sports Hall of Fame.

Orval "Red" Gravelle continued to work as a machinist in the RCAF. He was offered a chance to go professional and play with the New York Rangers, but the fiery forward turned them down. Red opted instead for the stability of a life in the air force. But the scrappy winger didn't turn his back on hockey. He laced up for years and played in amateur leagues, senior leagues, and industrial leagues as well as refereeing and coaching. Tragically, Red passed away in January 1997 when he was struck by a train near his home outside Trenton while attempting to retrieve his pet dog near the double tracks.

Ted Hibberd went back to his job at the Metropolitan Life Insurance Company in Ottawa. He continued to play hockey with the RCAF Flyers for a few more years and raised a family of three girls and two boys. Although Ted's memory banks are not quite what they used to be, he is one of the last Flyers still with us.

Pete Leichnitz returned to his job with the government and then pursued a lengthy career with Canadian General Electric. The speedy centre and best buddy of Ted Hibberd passed away in December 2011.

Andy Gilpin carried on with his career in the air force for just under thirty-five years. Hockey also continued to be a passion of Andy's throughout the decades. He was a regular spokesman for the team, often regaling kids with stories about his time in the air force and in hockey. He also never tired of lacing up the skates. Andy retired to Trenton and played on a line with old pal Red Gravelle. Active his entire life, Andy skated weekly up until his death at age ninety-three in March 2014.

Irving Taylor resumed his work in the air force until his retirement in 1965. He was an ardent supporter and founding father of minor hockey and amateur sport in the Ottawa area. Irving passed away in December 1991.

Ross King returned to Whitehorse and played for the air force team in the Yukon. During the 1953–1954 hockey season, Ross was called up by the Chicago Black Hawks and played in the NHL for a couple of games. He retired to the prairies and was one of the early Flyers to make the long walk home. Ross passed away in 1972, when he was fifty-three years old.

Dr. Sandy Watson continued his career with the RCAF and was promoted to wing commander in 1949. Never one to sit still, he studied ophthalmology at Harvard University and officially retired from the RCAF in 1959. He taught and became head of ophthalmology at the University of Ottawa and was also eye doctor to a long list of prime ministers and their families. Sandy was instrumental in raising money for and creating the Ottawa Eye Institute, widely recognized as the finest eye hospital and research centre in Canada. In 1987, Watson received the Order of Canada for his lifetime achievements. A scrapper until the end, he died of cancer on December 28, 2003.

Frank Boucher was posted to London after the Olympics, and hockey, as with all the Bouchers, remained a huge part of his life. He stayed in London an additional four years as the managing player for the Wembley Lions. In 1952 Frank led the Lions to the English national title. Back in Canada, he kept on the skates as the playing coach for various RCAF teams up until 1968, when he retired from the RCAF. He settled into retirement on his farm outside Ottawa, where he passed away from throat cancer on December 12, 2003—just two weeks before his good friend Sandy Watson.

George McFaul continued to train many of Ottawa's championship-calibre hockey and football teams. He also spent countless hours on the ice as a referee and was highly regarded as an exceptionally resourceful and skilled trainer and equipment manager. George stayed in the RCAF until his retirement in 1967. He went on to a second career in construction and renovations. George passed away in November 2008.

In 1988 the RCAF Flyers were honoured at the Calgary Olympics. In 2008 they were inducted into Canada's Sports Hall of Fame.

While these men may not have been the best individual hockey players in Canada, they were certainly the best team to represent our nation. Whether they were called to duty to fight or to play, the men who pulled on the powder-blue jerseys never hesitated. Rather, they jumped in with both feet and displayed qualities of courage, determination, and humility in the face of what must have seemed like insurmountable odds. Their story is one of inspiration, admiration, and the incredible Canadian drive to reach down and pull off the unthinkable.

"In the end what matters is that when everybody said it couldn't be done, the RCAF Flyers went ahead and did it."

—Hubert Brooks

ACKNOWLEDGEMENTS

I'll never forget the day Dugald Maudsley of Infield Fly Productions first told me about the saga of the RCAF Flyers. Todd Kealey from Canadian Forces Morale and Welfare Services had brought it to Dugald's attention, and Dugald wanted to know if I was interested in coming on board to write and direct a documentary about the hockey team. I knew nothing of their story, but I was instantly captivated and eager to be involved in the project.

For the better part of a year I worked closely with Dugald and the amazing team at Infield Fly Productions to help bring the tale of these amazing men to a television audience. The documentary, *Against All Odds: The RCAF Flyers*, would never have gotten off the ground without the incredibly thorough and impeccable research and organizational skills of Marion Gruner. Marion's research and initial interviews with the remaining Flyers and their family members formed the bedrock of the documentary. Upon that foundation, Elspeth Domville's stunning visual research wizardry and Eric Wiegand's deft photo-restoration work helped shed light on the wealth of pictures, newsreels, and visual materials squirrelled away in basements and stock footage houses from here to Europe.

With a television project there is a limited amount of information, backstory, and character development that one can impart in between the many commercial breaks. There was so much more to the incredible lives of these national heroes who had been long forgotten.

I am so happy the stars aligned and a chance conversation with Brad Wilson at HarperCollins breathed new life into the story in book form. Brad's curiosity about the personal details behind the men on the team and his encouragement for me to expand on the documentary inspired me to tackle a more detailed telling of the lives of these hockey heroes. I am grateful to Brad and to editor Meg Masters for their focused guidance and expert hand in the editing of the manuscript. Their brilliant insights, in combination with the clever work of the diligent team of professionals at HarperCollins, have elevated this project.

The heart and soul of this book owes itself to a number of key people who have selflessly shared so much with me. Surviving members of the team Murray Dowey and Roy Forbes graciously spent hours and days captivating me with their life stories over the months. They welcomed me into their homes and were able to provide exquisite details of their childhoods, adolescence, and adult years. My conversations and time spent with André Laperrière also filled me with inspiration and awe. Without them, there would be no book.

I cannot begin to express my thanks and gratitude to Ralf Brooks, Tom Schroeter, and Mary Rose Guzzo, custodians of their fathers' stories. By getting access to the unbelievable wealth of research material, diaries, pictures, and family history that they have collected, I felt as if I were meeting with and interviewing their beloved dads myself. The information they gave me has been indispensable in the writing of this book.

I am deeply indebted to the generosity of the family and friends of the boys in blue, many of whom made available their private collections of photographs and recollections from stories their fathers passed on to them. I could not have weaved the tales of these men together and filled in some of the gaps without their selfless sharing and perspectives. Many thanks to Joyce Balharrie, Diane Boyce, Diana Brooks, Kevin Dowey, Brian Dunster, Dennis Dunster, Neil Dunster, Wayne Dunster, Gary and Julie Forbes, Andy Gilpin, Greg Halder, Matt Halder, Ted and Anna Hibberd, Nancy Hibberd, June Horvath, Phyllis Gravelle, George Mara Jr., Janet Nancarrow, Lori Speigelberg, Renée Thomson, and Dr. John Watson.

Again, I want to thank Todd Kealey of Canadian Forces Morale and Welfare Services for bringing this tale to my attention.

Last but not least, I want to thank the two beautiful, brilliant women in my life, Sari and Zahara. Your patience, your understanding, your inspiration, and your love have been instrumental in helping me write this first book. When I doubted myself, you kept me going. When I needed a lift, you were always there to help guide, support, and inspire me. I could not have accomplished this without you both. I am so fortunate to be sharing this journey with you.

NOTES

The lion's share of information I gathered for this book came from interviews I conducted over the course of two years with key surviving members of the team and their family members.

Details of Hubert Brooks's amazing life story as well as quotes that appear from him throughout the book are used with the permission of his son, Ralf Brooks. Ralf has painstakingly assembled a treasure trove of information, diary entries, official documents, and family history of the Brooks clan and presented it on his website, hubertbrooks.com. Aside from spending many hours speaking with me, Ralf generously gave me access to the materials he has gathered at hubertbrooks.com in order to help me bring his father's story to life in this book.

I turned to Mary Rose Guzzo's wonderful reproduction of her father Patsy Guzzo's heartfelt diary, *My Trip . . . Journey of an Olympic Gold Win* (Ottawa: Baico Publishing, 2009), for quotes I have attributed to Patsy Guzzo. Patsy's diary also served as another layer of first-hand information and impressions to help support the research I conducted in my interviews.

At various points throughout this book I also relied on some of Pat MacAdam's candid interviews and thorough research, which can be found in his book *Gold Medal "Misfits": How the Unwanted Canadian Hockey Team Scored Olympic Glory* (Ancaster: Manor House Publishing, 2007), to back up my own research.

Reg Schroeter, the team's unofficial records keeper, amassed every newspaper clipping he could get his hands on that related to the RCAF Flyers' 1948 Olympic adventure. Reg's son Tom Schroeter generously gave me access to the scrapbooks that he now maintains in his dad's memory. The scrapbooks included a wealth of newspaper clippings from the *Ottawa Citizen* and the *Ottawa Journal* as well as brochures, telegrams, photographs, service records, and even articles from foreign papers that related to the boys' hockey games in exhibition overseas.

Chapter 1: Ottawa

For descriptions of weather conditions, I tended to lean on a few different sources. Sometimes my interviews with the men involved in the story yielded all the necessary information and details. At other times, I pulled from daily news sources, including local newspapers such as the *Ottawa Citizen* and the *Ottawa Journal*. I also used diary entries from Patsy Guzzo or Hubert Brooks to help give a picture of the climate and environment on many occasions. References to specific temperatures and meteorological conditions were also gleaned from Environment Canada's historical data files, recorded at various weather stations across the country.

My descriptions of Buck Boucher's appearance and dress were derived from photographs taken of the Flyers during the early days of tryouts in Ottawa. Information about Tommy Gorman's Ottawa Auditorium came from Pat MacAdam's *Gold Medal "Misfits"* as well as Jim McAuley's *The Ottawa Sports Book* (Burnstown: General Store Publishing House, 1987).

Ottawa Citizen journalists Frank Swanson, Tommy Shields, and Jack Koffman extensively covered the Flyers from the get-go, as did Canadian Press sports editor and reporter Jack Sullivan. I primarily relied on the paper and scanned photocopies of their stories that I had access to from Tom Schroeter and Ralf Brooks. Many of the complete news stories relating to the team can also be found online through a Google news documents search.

There were a lot of Canadian citizens with opinions and information about the Canadian Amateur Hockey Association's response to the new amateur rules from the International Olympic Committee in the summer of 1947. Many of my interviewees supplied me with information about it. I based my account of this issue on their perspectives, in combination with numerous articles that appeared that summer and into the fall in the pages of the *Ottawa Citizen*, the *Ottawa Journal*, the *Montreal Gazette*, and the *Winnipeg Tribune*.

I leaned on Marion Gruner's excellent research and interviews with Professor Jonathan Vance for detailed information about Canadian airmen and their contributions to and losses in World War II. Marion's facts were derived from her talks with Professor Vance and from writings found in his many books: *A History of Canadian Culture* (Don Mills: Oxford University Press, 2009), *High Flight: Aviation and the Canadian Imagination* (Toronto:

Penguin Canada, 2002), and *Maple Leaf Empire: Canada, Britain and Two World Wars* (Don Mills: Oxford University Press, 2012).

Biographical information about Dr. Sandy Watson and Frank Boucher came from talks with Sandy's son, Dr. John Watson, and Frank's daughter, Diane Boyce. I also drew on information found in Pat MacAdam's book *Gold Medal "Misfits."*

Chapter 2: The Games

Background material regarding the early days in the formation of the team was primarily drawn from my interviews with family members and the remaining players. Again, I drew from newspaper articles written by Jack Koffman and George Forster that appeared in the *Ottawa Citizen* over the first couple of weeks of October 1947.

Details about the Games of Renewal and the preparations that were under way in St. Moritz were pulled from a variety of sources. A great deal of information can be found by trolling through the International Olympic Committee's official website, olympic.org. The site contains a wealth of information about specific Olympic events and participants, as well as pictures.

Ralf Brooks has also pulled together a mass of information about the V Olympic Winter Games and presented it on his website, hubertbrooks.com. The official *Rapport Général sur les Ves Jeux Olympiques d'Hiver, St. Moritz 1948* can be found there. The hubertbrooks.com website also contains pictures, postcards, and official paraphernalia that Hubert collected when he was playing overseas.

Details about the British team that won gold at the 1936 Olympics in Garmisch-Partenkirchen came from interviews I conducted. Pat MacAdam's *Gold Medal "Misfits"* was also referenced for information.

Ottawa Citizen reporter Frank Swanson was another journalist who wrote extensively about the early formation of the team and its tryouts. Buck Boucher's and Brooke Claxton's comments about the team in the making, as well as various discussion points about the calibre of players available through the RCAF ranks, were drawn from details presented in Mr. Swanson's many articles. Those articles appeared in the newspaper on October 18, 20, 21, and 22.

Information about Buck's practice sessions came from my discussions with the players. Again, Reg Schroeter's extensive collection of Ottawa-area newspaper clippings throughout the month of October also helped me paint a picture of the tryouts and gather additional details about the number of men coming and going through the revolving door at the Ottawa Auditorium.

Biographical details of Hubert Brooks's early days and family history were given to me by Ralf Brooks in interviews and through information he provided via his excellent website, hubertbrooks.com.

Chapter 3: The Boys in Blue

The lion's share of information relating to each player's early life came from interviews conducted with family members, such as Patsy Guzzo's daughter Mary Rose and Orval Gravelle's wife, Phyllis.

Details about the games played in late October and early November were gleaned from interviews with players like Roy Forbes and from newspaper articles that appeared in the various Ottawa papers.

Roy Forbes relayed much of the information about his early life to me over our many discussions. I also picked up extra bits of information from my talks with his two sons, Gary and Brian.

Buck Boucher's announcement regarding the team's selection appeared in the *Ottawa Citizen* on November 20. It is also mentioned in the *Montreal Gazette* on November 21.

Chapter 4: Olympic Night

Weather details were pulled from newspaper reports for the day and from information available through Environment Canada's historical data files, recorded at local weather stations.

Olympic Night was extensively covered in the Ottawa-area newspapers in the run-up to and the days following the big event. Tommy Shields, Jack Koffman, and Bob Abra filed numerous articles in the *Ottawa Citizen* from December 10 through December 16, 1947. Roy Forbes also provided me with first-hand impressions and details of the event. In addition, Roy still had a weathered hard copy of the official program and some of newspaper clippings relating to the big night.

For those interested in seeing some of the brochures and advertisements, as well as the official program, Ralf Brooks has some of the material available on hubertbrooks.com. Interviewees like Tom Schroeter also contributed fantastic insights into the extravaganza.

Details concerning the army-versus-Flyers match were pulled from interviews with Roy Forbes and various family members. I also leaned on the extensive coverage provided by reporters and columnists that appeared in the *Ottawa Citizen*, the *Ottawa Journal*, and the *Montreal Gazette* on December 15, 16, and 17.

Facts about the new men brought in from the New Edinburgh Burghs and background on Louis Lecompte and Andy Gilpin were largely derived from interviews with family members. Tommy Shields's column in the *Ottawa Citizen*, combined with articles that appeared in the newspaper on December 17, 18, and 19, also provided additional details and perspective.

Biographical details about Frank Dunster, aka the Blue Line Masher, were provided to me through interviews with his sons as well as his official RCAF records.

Chapter 5: Calling in the Big Guns

Interviews with family members like Diane Boyce, Tom Schroeter, and Ralf Brooks provided perspective on the call out to the big guns to bring in some top new amateur talent. This was also well covered in the Ottawa newspapers over the last week of December.

Many of the details of Wally Halder's and George Mara's inclusion on the Flyers were derived from interviews with their family members. In his book *Gold Medal "Misfits,"* Pat MacAdam also relates elements of both Wally's and George's early days in hockey and in the war. Diary entries from Hubert Brooks as well as interviews with other family members helped give me a picture of the three newcomers' acceptance onto the team.

Interviews with André Laperrière and his sister, Renée, Thomson supplied me with all the details regarding André's early upbringing and inclusion on the team.

Sandy's typed list of supplies that the men were to pack for their trip overseas was provided to me by Ralf Brooks and Tom Schroeter.

I turned to Jack Koffman's and Tommy Shields's newspaper articles and columns in the *Ottawa Citizen* on December 31 for some of the specifics regarding Dick Ball's sudden departure from the roster. My interviews with Murray Dowey provided me with details regarding his relationship with Sandy Watson and that bizarre late-night phone call where Sandy told him about Dick's condition and invited Murray to join the Flyers.

Hubert Brooks's diary entries, in combination with interviews with family members, were my principal source of information relating to the team's send-off. My descriptions of the men's appearance were derived from photographs. Again, this team event was well covered by Tommy Shields and Jack Koffman in the pages of the *Ottawa Citizen* on January 8, 1948, and also in the *Montreal Gazette*. Reporter Norm Altstedter also wrote about the Flyers' trip overseas in the *Ottawa Citizen* on January 9, 1948.

The biographical material on Murray Dowey was drawn from my interviews and conversations with Murray. Biographical material concerning Frank Dunster was courtesy of my interviews with his sons.

Chapter 6: Europe Bound

Many of the details of the train ride from Ottawa and the team's arrival in New York were from Patsy Guzzo's diary, *My Trip . . . Journey of an Olympic Gold Win,* and from Murray Dowey's recollections.

My interviews with Roy Forbes and André Laperrière in concert with Hubert Brooks's writings provided many of the details about their time in New York and their experiences on the *Queen Elizabeth.* Interviews with family members and Patsy Guzzo's wonderful, candid diary entries helped fill in some of the gaps and provide additional colourful anecdotes.

Many of the guys remembered that bus crash with the tram just after they arrived in the U.K. The Canadian Press carried a brief description of the event on January 15. I also leaned on Reg Schroeter's personal photographs of the scene to help describe the damage.

Chapter 7: Into the Fire

Much of the details, emotions, feelings, and actions of Hubert Brooks were pulled from his writings, which can be found on the website hubertbrooks.com. I acquired additional information through my interviews with his son, Ralf Brooks. Hubert also authored a few wonderful magazine articles that chronicled his exploits. The articles were published in *Weekend Magazine,* volume 7, number 40 (October 5, 1957), and in volume 7, number 41 (October 12, 1957).

Ralf generously gave me access to his father's operational records books, telegrams that were sent home to his family,

Hubert's POW identification cards, and personal correspondence and letters within the Brooks family's possession relating to Hubert's ordeal.

Descriptions and Hubert's impressions of Stalag VIII-B and the Lamsdorf prison camp were derived from his own writings, as previously noted. The websites stalag-viiib.com and lamsdorf.com also served as gateways to numerous sources of maps, documents, photos, and information pertaining to the POW camps.

The particulars of Hubert's multiple escape attempts were pulled from his many writings, which Ralf made available to me.

Chapter 8: Freedom Fighters

Details of Hubert Brooks's and John Duncan's time with the Polish Underground movement and the Armia Krajowa were drawn primarily from Hubert's account, found on hubertbrooks.com. As mentioned earlier, Hubert also published some information covering this chapter of his life in an article he wrote for *Weekend Magazine*, volume 7, number 41 (October 12, 1957).

Details about the Wilk unit and the AK were largely drawn from Hubert's recollections, available on his website. Interviews with Ralf Brooks also helped provide perspective. Some of the materials gathered by Ralf Brooks at hubertbrooks.com include wonderful pictures from the estate of Jozef Weglarz as well as material from the memoirs of Jozef Weglarz. There are also photos from the Instytut Pamięci Narodowej and the Institute of National Remembrance Archive in Krakow, Poland,

and materials from Dr. Jerzy Krzewicki, son of Major Julian Krzewicki. I leaned on some of these materials in my descriptions of the battles Hubert engaged in.

Chapter 9: Ramping Up in Exhibition

Patsy Guzzo's diary, *My Trip . . . Journey of an Olympic Gold Win*, provided me with much of the wonderful colour about the Crofton Hotel. Interviews with the players as well as Hubert Brooks's writings fleshed out many of the details of their lodgings and the exhibition matches the boys played in.

Background information on Bunny Ahearne came to me through interviews with family members. Additional facts pertaining to Bunny's background were drawn from Pat MacAdam's *Gold Medal "Misfits."*

I pulled many of the details of the exhibition games from my talks with Murray Dowey, Roy Forbes, and André Laperrière and the diary writings of Hubert Brooks and Patsy Guzzo. Additional facts were drawn from numerous Canadian Press newspaper articles that appeared in the *Ottawa Citizen* between January 16 and January 23, 1948.

My discussion of sport in the military is based on research Marion Gruner obtained from former Hamilton Warplane Museum archivist David Pridham's graduate paper, "'A Natural Resource': Watching, Using and Playing Sports in the British Commonwealth Air Training Plan during World War II." Interviews with historian Dr. Jonathan Vance also provided information on the topic.

Descriptions of the lavish Wembley Arena and the boys' flight to Paris were drawn from interviews with the players and from the diaries of Patsy Guzzo and Hubert Brooks. Information and details relating to the game against Le Club Racing de Paris were also pulled from interviews and from Canadian Press newspaper coverage that appeared in the *Ottawa Citizen* and the *Montreal Gazette* on January 22, 1948.

Chapter 10: On the Run

Roy Forbes's operational records, in concert with interviews I conducted with Roy, provided much of the material relating to his fall from the sky and his time on the run in France. I also consulted Roy's official evasion report. Secondary interviews with his two sons, Brian and Gary, provided additional details and perspective.

Chapter 11: Tuning Up in Europe

I leaned on Patsy Guzzo's diary, *My Trip . . . Journey of an Olympic Gold Win*, combined with interviews with the players as well as Hubert Brooks's writings, to describe the boys' flight from France to Switzerland.

Roy Forbes, Murray Dowey, and André Laperrière had vivid memories and recollections of their time on the road together in Europe and those exhibition games in Switzerland. I gleaned additional details about the games and the weather conditions from the Canadian Press news coverage that appeared in the *Montreal Gazette* and the *Ottawa Citizen* between January 23 and January 26, 1948.

Interviews with family members and the diaries of Patsy Guzzo and Hubert Brooks were consulted to help me set the scene in St. Moritz.

Pat MacAdam's *Gold Medal "Misfits"* was a resource I looked to regarding Frank Boucher's final team selection. Interviews with his family members and players also provided me with perspective on Frank's decisions.

Personal photographs from the collections of Hubert Brooks and Reg Schroeter helped me gain a picture of the heady, beautiful atmospheres on display in the mountain towns.

Interviews that Marion Gruner conducted with Professor Jonathan Vance provided clarity regarding survival rates in Bomber Command as well as details relating to the RCAF and the air war. Frank Dunster's biographical information and specifics concerning his wartime experiences were relayed to me in interviews with his family members. Additionally, I consulted Frank Dunster's service records, his operational airman's records sheets, his recommendations for honours and awards, and detail sheets of sorties carried out. I also looked to Spencer Dunmore's excellent *Above and Beyond: The Canadians' War in the Air, 1939-45* (Toronto: McClelland and Stewart, 2006) for information about Bomber Command and the attacks on Nuremberg.

Chapter 12: Let the Games Begin

The furor over the two competing American teams was well covered in the press. I consulted articles touching on the controversy that appeared in the *Ottawa Citizen, Winnipeg Tribune,* and

Montreal Gazette between September 4, 1947, and February 7, 1948. Articles by sports editor Jack Ellis in the *Stars and Stripes*, volume 2, number 55 (Thursday, January 29, 1948), also provided helpful details. Interviews with players Murray Dowey, André Laperrière, and Roy Forbes in combination with reflections found in the diaries of Patsy Guzzo and Hubert Brooks offered additional perspective and details on how things played out regarding the two American teams in St. Moritz.

My description of the opening parade of ceremonies was based largely on the diary reflections of Patsy Guzzo and Hubert Brooks in combination with personal photos as well as official Olympic photos of the procession of athletes. Canadian Press newspaper descriptions of the event along with information presented on the official IOC website, olympic.org, were also consulted. My descriptions of the two American teams' marching attire in the parade was derived from period photos, Patsy's diary reflections, and information found in Pat MacAdam's *Gold Medal "Misfits."*

I relied on a number of sources to pull together my account of the first game against Sweden. Interviews with Murray Dowey, André Laperrière, and Roy Forbes provided the backbone. Patsy Guzzo's and Hubert Brooks's journal reflections supplied me with further details, as did interviews with family members like Renée Thomson, Diane Boyce, and Tom Schroeter. I also leaned on CP reporter Jack Sullivan's article in the *Ottawa Citizen* along with Tommy Shields's commentary in his column Round and About.

My descriptions of the cafes and atmosphere the boys waded into in St. Moritz were derived from interviews with the players in combination with the diary writings of Patsy Guzzo and Hubert Brooks. I also drew from personal photos that Tom Schroeter and Ralf Brooks made available to me.

For my account of the Flyers' second match against Britain, I relied on many of the same sources. Interviews with family members and players in combination with the diaries of Patsy Guzzo and Hubert Brooks provided the foundation. I gleaned additional details from Jack Sullivan's February 1, 1948, article "Flyers Blank Britain in Storm," which appeared in the *Ottawa Citizen*.

Chapter 13: In the Thick of It

My descriptions of the weather in St. Moritz were derived from Patsy Guzzo's diary account and backed up by data provided in the "Bulletin Meteorologique" section of the official *Rapport Général sur les Ves Jeux Olympiques D'Hiver, St. Moritz 1948*.

Interviews with the players and with family members as well as reflections gleaned from Hubert Brooks's writings provided much of the information for my account of the match against Poland. Jack Sullivan's article on February 2, 1948, for the Canadian Press ("RCAF Team Plasters Poles with 15–0 Count") was referenced for additional details. *Ottawa Citizen* correspondent Basil Dean's article on February 9, 1948 ("Flyers Don't Like Piling Up Scores on Weak Teams"), was also consulted.

Frank Boucher's daughter, Diane Boyce, helped provide me with much insight into her father's mindset during the Olympics.

My interviews with Roy Forbes and Murray Dowey also provided me with perspective on Frank's inner struggle regarding who to play and who to keep on the bench. I also looked to Pat MacAdam's interview material with Frank that appears in *Gold Medal "Misfits."*

Details about the Flyers' match against Italy were gleaned from multiple sources. I looked to Jack Sullivan's Canadian Press articles ("RCAF Winners Routing Italy 21–1" and "RCAF Tied with Czechs for First Place"), which appeared in both the *Ottawa Citizen* and the *Montreal Gazette* on February 4, 1948. First-hand accounts from Roy Forbes, Murray Dowey, and André Laperrière were my principal sources. Patsy Guzzo's diary and Hubert Brooks's account also provided details and reflections. I referenced personal photographs of the boys before and during the match to help with my descriptions.

My account of the much-anticipated and heated match against the AHA American squad is derived largely from interviews with players Murray Dowey, Roy Forbes, and André Laperrière. Hubert Brooks's writings on the game also contained a great deal of information regarding the temperature, ice conditions, and atmosphere. I looked to archival footage of the American team in action as well as official IOC photos for my descriptions of the pre-game chant. Many of the Flyers also commented on this in my interviews with them. Further details and specifics of the game and action were pulled from the excellent Canadian Press articles "Canada–US Hockey Match Postponed" (February 4, 1948) and "Whip U.S. Pile Up 12–3 Victory" (February 5, 1948).

Chapter 14: The Mighty Czechs

I have drawn mostly from my interviews with Murray Dowey, André Laperrière, and Roy Forbes as well the diaries of Hubert Brooks and Patsy Guzzo to recount the Flyers' match against the Czechs. I also pulled from interviews with other players' family members and an interview Marion Gruner conducted with Czech player Oldrich Zabrodsky, Vladimir's brother. Further game details were gleaned from the February 6, 1948, Canadian Press news article "Flyers and Czechs Battle to Scoreless Tie: RCAF Team Has Good Chance for St. Moritz Title" and Jack Sullivan's article on the game in the *Ottawa Citizen*, "Canadians and Czechs in 0–0 Tie: Another Terrific Match for Murray Dowey."

Barbara Ann Scott's remarkable gold medal performance was well covered in the press. All the boys were there to witness her performance and remembered it well. Many of the Flyers, including Reg Schroeter, Patsy Guzzo, and Hubert Brooks, snapped photographs of the action and the aftermath, which I looked to for reference. There are also videos of her performance available for screening on YouTube and pictures on the IOC website, olympic.org.

Montreal Gazette articles posted by Jack Sullivan on February 7, 1948, such as "Dazzling Display Gives Barbara Ann Long Cherished Dream of Olympic Title," provided me with additional details of her performance and the judges' reactions. I also referenced the United Press reporter's article "Home, Hubby and Baby Ambition of Barbara Ann, Spurning Movies," which appeared in the *Montreal Gazette*.

My sources for the Flyers' game against the Austrians included interviews with the players and their family members as well as Hubert Brooks's recollections found on hubertbrooks.com. Game action was also well chronicled in articles found in the morning and evening editions of the *Ottawa Citizen* on February 7, 1948: "Canada Defeats Austria 12–0 at Olympics—Flyers Now Tied with Czechs; Play Swiss Sunday" and "Canadians Swamp Austria as Czechs Win: Deciding Games Sunday."

Chapter 15: The Quest for Gold

My account of the final game against Switzerland is based to a large extent on the interviews I conducted with Murray Dowey, Roy Forbes, and André Laperrière. Patsy Guzzo's excellent diary, *My Trip . . . Journey of an Olympic Gold Win*, and Hubert Brooks's recollections found on hubertbrooks.com were also consulted for details.

I looked to archival photos and newsreel footage of the match that can be found through the IOC/Olympic Museum Collections and on the website olympic.org to help with my descriptions of some of the plays.

Actions and events of that big day were also chronicled in the many newspaper articles written by CP reporter Jack Sullivan. Major sources include "Unbeaten Flyers Annex Olympic Puck Title: Partisan Officials, Crowd Mar 3–0 Victory Over Swiss," "Canada's RCAF Team Wins Olympic Hockey Crown," and "I Knew You'd Do It: Boucher Tells Champions" (*Ottawa Citizen*, February 9, 1948).

I pulled additional information from "Flyers Overcome Swiss 3–0 to Capture Olympic Title: Surmount Handicaps of Slushy Ice and Partisan Refereeing to Triumph" (*Montreal Gazette*, February 9, 1948). Also Pat MacAdam's fine book *Gold Medal "Misfits"* was consulted.

Statistics and data relating to Murray Dowey's, George Mara's, and Wally Halder's impressive records can be found in the Olympic Hockey Record Book section on the website NHL.com. Andrew Podnieks's book *Canada's Olympic Hockey Teams: The Complete History, 1920-1998* (Toronto: Doubleday, 1997) provides further context. I consulted sports-reference.com as another source for statistics data. Additional details relating to the games can be found in the official *Rapport Général sur les Ves Jeux Olympiques D'Hiver, St. Moritz 1948*.

Chapter 16: The Long Road Home

Again, interviews with the surviving players in concert with the writings of Hubert Brooks and Patsy Guzzo were my principal sources of information regarding the parties and events following the winning game. I also leaned on personal and promotional photographs for some of my descriptions. Tom Schroeter and Ralf Brooks provided me access to copies of a number of the telegrams and correspondence the team received.

Canadian Press newspaper articles extensively covered the events in St. Moritz in the days after the big game. I looked to "Flyers Stage Great Victory Celebration," "Hundreds of Cables Sent to Winners of Olympic Crown," and "Victorious Canucks

Deluged with Cables," which appeared in the *Ottawa Citizen* on February 9, 1948, among others, for information.

Interviews with Ralf Brooks along with the writings of Hubert Brooks were the principal sources of information relating to the wedding of Hubert and Bea. CP reporter Jack Sullivan's article, "Wartime Romance Has Happy Ending," on February 9, 1948, along with Brooks's personal photos of the wedding were also sources I leaned on to help with my description of the event.

Details and specifics relating to the Flyers' post-Olympic exhibition tour, which spanned February 10 to March 30, 1948, were derived from Reg Schroeter's and Ralf Brooks's thorough compilation of newspaper articles. I also leaned on the diaries of Patsy Guzzo and Hubert Brooks as well as interviews with other family members. Personal photographs that were made available to me by the families helped colour my description of the post-Olympic tour. All the guys had clear memories of the punishing tour. Additional details concerning the injuries sustained during the tour were pulled from the CP article "Bruised Flyers, Hockey Champs, Sail for Home," March 31, 1948.

Chapter 17: Olympic Champions

There were many articles in the *Ottawa Citizen*, the *Ottawa Journal*, and the *Montreal Gazette* on April 6, 7, 8, and 9, 1948, that chronicled the team's triumphant homecoming and celebrations. I referenced "Reception Set for Olympians," "Thousands Greet RCAF Olympic Champs at Ottawa," "Olympic Hockey Champions on Way Home," "City Welcomes Olympic Champions Home:

Aircraft Streak Across Skies as Triumphant Players Paraded Through Downtown Streets," and "Olympic Cup Where It Belongs, Governor General Tells Flyers."

I also looked to official letters that family members received from the RCAF with details and directions about the homecoming parade and celebrations. I leaned on newsreel footage of the parade ceremony and reception in conjunction with photographs to help describe the crowds, banners, and fanfare that was on display. Interviews with the players as well as family members like Renée Thomson, Dennis Dunster, and Tom Schroeter, in addition to recollections that Hubert Brooks penned on his website were also used as my primary sources of information.

I turned to Pat MacAdam's *Gold Medal "Misfits"* for information concerning Barbara Ann Scott's storied career and meteoric rise after the Olympics. Additional information about her doll was found through the Canadian Museum of History.

Details regarding the boys' subsequent lives were largely derived from interviews with many family members and from a series of obituaries. Pat MacAdam's *Gold Medal "Misfits"* was also referenced for additional biographical information concerning a number of the men who are now gone.

The Hubert Brooks epigraph is from his previously cited recollections, which are found at the phenomenal website hubertbrooks.com.